PRAISES FOR *ENVIRON*

"*Environmental Crisis* focuses on the ways of knowing that are at the very roots of unsustainability, "the crisis of crises" that threatens to end human civilization as we know it. Dr. Bryant as editor and lead author along with the other 8 chapter authors have thought critically and creatively about the dominant methods Western societies use in developing knowledge. These dominant epistemologies and their implementation have had positive impacts but also continue to have negative impacts that are increasingly exploiting and devastating the natural environment including people who are part of racial minorities and or economically poor. Readers will deepen their understanding of this aspect of the status quo in our culture and learn about urgently needed potential changes in our ways of knowing."

—**James E. Crowfoot**, PhD., Professor Emeritus of Natural Resources and Urban and Regional Planning and Dean Emeritus, School of Natural Resources & Environment, University of Michigan and former President of Antioch College.

"*Environmental Crisis* covers a wide range of issues related to the environmental crisis, ethics and the role of knowledge. The central question raised is whether the environmental crisis is related to how we know the world or how we often exploit knowledge for the benefit of man at the expense of nature. For teachers, students, and members of the general public, who have a keen interest in the environment, *Environmental Crisis* is essential reading. As the authors pointed out, there are many questions and not enough answers, but *Environmental Crisis* will certainly provide the reader with enough information to come away with the tools to look at the environment and knowledge in a different and sustainable way."

—**Professor Percy Bates**, Professor of Education, University of Michigan. Served as Deputy Assistant Secretary of Special Education in the U.S. Department of Education, and served as the Assistant Dean at the University of Michigan School of Education.

"Dr. Bunyan Bryant—once again—has provided readers with a penetrating book which includes thoughtful analyses of seven distinct subject areas related to contemporary issues in environmental justice. *Environmental Crisis* is an ambitious undertaking that contextualizes and illuminates major barriers to applying and achieving appropriate scientific thinking and knowledge to environmental justice concerns, especially in the local, state and regional areas as well as on a national level. *Environmental Crisis* will be of special interest to environmental justice advocates, lawyers, academicians, public officials as well as those who are new to the ongoing debate pertaining to environmental justice. Given the excellent information provided in this volume, it is truly a must read.

—**Kwame A. Mark Freeman**, PhD, Adjunct Professor, University of Massachusetts." Formerly Program Manager and Executive office for Environmental Affairs, Commonwealth of Massachusetts.

"*Environmental Crisis: Working for Sustainable Knowledge and Environmental Justice*" is a major achievement. For nearly four decades, Bunyan Bryant has helped to expand the frontiers of environmental advocacy and environmental justice. Building on this work, he has assembled here a compelling array of critical and forward-looking voices which, through careful and considered arguments, illuminate the idea and practice of sustainable knowledge. In so doing, they make the case that we must look critically and creatively at how knowledge is created distributed, and used. This is essential, they show us, if we are to fully understand and—most importantly, respond to—the environmental crisis which today confronts us with ever grater urgency.

—**Stephen Ward**, Assistant Professor, Center for Afro-American and African Studies and Residential College, University of Michigan.

ENVIRONMENTAL CRISIS OR CRISIS OF EPISTEMOLOGY?

Working for Sustainable Knowledge and Environmental Justice

Edited by

BUNYAN BRYANT

NEW YORK

ENVIRONMENTAL CRISIS OR CRISIS OF EPISTEMOLOGY?

Working for Sustainable Knowledge and Environmental Justice

Edited by Bunyan Bryant

ISBN 978-1-60037-840-9 (paperback)

Library of Congress Control Number: 2010933337

Published by:

Morgan James Publishing
1225 Franklin Ave. Ste 325
Garden City, NY 11530-1693
Toll Free 800-485-4943
www.MorganJamesPublishing.com

For this book I want to thank my wife Jean who has always been here in times of need. I appreciate her encouragement as I worked to complete this book. I also want to thank Mark Chesler who provided helpful insights and words of wisdom in the editing of this book. Also I would like to thank Shana Milkie and Laurie Sutch for their ongoing support during this project.

TABLE OF CONTENTS

INTRODUCTION

ENVIRONMENTAL CRISIS OR CRISIS OF EPISTEMOLOGY: WORKING FOR SUSTAINABLE KNOWLEDGE

Bunyan Bryant, Ph.D*.

Environmental justice refers to those cultural norms and values, rules, regulations, behaviors, policies, and decisions to support sustainable communities where people can interact with confidence that their environment is safe, nurturing, and productive. Environmental Justice is served when people can realize their highest potential without experiencing discrimination based on race, class, ethnicity or national origin. Environmental justice is supported by decent paying and safe jobs; quality schools and recreation; decent housing and adequate health care; democratic decision-making and personal empowerment; and communities free of violence, drugs, and poverty. These are communities where both cultural and biological diversity are respected and highly revered and where distributive justice prevails.

This book was hard for me to edit because it goes against the grain of my intellectual training since the start of graduate school. In graduate school, scientific methodology and quantitative analysis were supreme and therefore not to be questioned. If one wanted to get ahead in academia, one had to develop proficiency in statistics and research design. In the days

* Although Bunyan Bryant's major faculty appointment is in the University of Michigan School of Natural Resources and Environment, he also has an adjunct position with the University's Center of Afro-American and African Studies (CAAS). Professor Bryant is a Thurnau professor and also a member of the faculty in urban planning at the University of Michigan. He and Professor Paul Mohai have edited a book entitled Race and the Incidence of Environmental Hazards: A Time for Discourse (1992). He is also co-principal investigator of the University of Michigan 1990 Detroit Area Study on Race and Toxic Waste. He was the co-facilitator of the Symposium on Health Research and Needs to Ensure Environmental Justice, 1994 and served on EPA's National Environmental Justice Advisory Council.

before the advent of the personal computer, I spent countless hours in class and in the library memorizing formulas and completing problem sets—all of which was for me like learning a foreign language. Although qualitative analysis was available, it was seldom held in high esteem because the information obtained from such analysis failed to meet the rigorous standards of linear quantitative analysis. But as time went by, I began to feel that many of the research outcomes of the university were not being used effectively to help Michigan's urban communities such as Detroit, Flint, Benton Harbor, and Grand Rapids, as well as other large metropolitan areas across the country. Major universities have been involved in Detroit for years, and I cannot see any detectable differences from their involvement.

But this phenomenon is not unique to Michigan cities because cities all over the world are suffering. Why do people suffer in Kashmir, Kabul, the West Bank, Calcutta, Johannesburg, Moscow, Baghdad, and other cities even when universities and their research efforts are involved? Poverty is not confined by geopolitical boundaries of cities: it is found in the hinterland throughout the world. Questions have been raised as to whether research reduces poverty (Growing Affinities, 1999), particularly in light of the growing plight of massive numbers of disempowered poor people throughout the world. Development specialists around the world are asking why poverty continues to reign in so many places despite the huge social, economic, and technological advances in science occurring at the end of the last century and the beginning of this one. Is there an inverse relationship between the amount of money spent on research and the increase in world poverty and environmental degradation? Why has our environment progressively declined and world poverty increased since the 1992 UN Conference on Environment and Development in Rio de Janeiro, even in the face of corporate globalization?

Knowledge generation or its use has often failed to make a significant difference in environmental protection and in the plight of the poor, and in many cases the situation for these groups will continue to worsen in the foreseeable future. People of color and the poor in both developed and developing countries experience over-exposure to toxins because of their physical proximity to polluting industries and hazardous waste disposal facilities. Something is fundamentally wrong when such wide-scale suffering exists. Although advancement in science has been linked to civilizations of the past and here more recently to the research paradigm of the West, this paradigm has been historically associated with progress and the general improvement of the masses. Today, science and its by-products have a different face made real by the birth of the atomic bomb and by the writings of Rachel Carson (Silent Spring, 1962) who warned us of poisoning the earth and its inhabitants on a scale unimaginable.

As the metaphor goes: the fox is very smart and knows many little things, but the hedgehog knows one big thing really well and that is that everything is connected (Hales, 2002). In spite of the many small contributions of the fox, such as databases of genomes and genes, molecular genetics, and other scientific marvels, the hedgehog knows that human beings and the natural world are on a collision course. To date, we are affecting the global ecosystem in terms of pollution of the oceans, global climate change, and the introduction of synthetic chemicals. The human environmental footprint is larger and poses a worse threat than those of all other species on the planet. We need to downsize our footprint or it could threaten our very existence here on earth.

People overburdened by environmental insults often look to science for hope, certainty, relief, and solution. They seek relief from the stress and anxiety that come from not knowing or not being able to predict with any degree of certainty their future health status or that of their loved ones. When scientists or policymakers are slow to respond or fail to respond to the immediate demand for answers, the result is often irrational behavior and the loss of confidence in policymaking and the scientific communities. Often a solution for one problem becomes yet another existential problem in a different area (Commoner, 1976; Colborn, Myers, and Dumanoski, 1996). Solutions to technically-caused problems can lead to further unpleasant and unanticipated surprises in that those thought to be the safest chemicals or technological solutions often prove to be the most dangerous. It became clear to me that positivism[1] was not the only problem-solving approach. In fact, it is often the least effective approach in many instances when dealing with the environmental injustice problems we face today. Colborn, Myers, and Dumanoski (1996) state:

> Ultimately, the risks that confront us stem from this gap between our technological prowess and our understanding of the systems that support life. We design new technologies at a dizzying pace and deploy them on an unprecedented scale around the world long before we can begin to fathom their possible impact on the global system or ourselves. We have plunged boldly ahead, never acknowledging the dangerous ignorance at the heart of the enterprise. [The] dilemma is like that of a plane hurtling through the fog without a map or instruments.

---

1 Positivism is a research paradigm of which quantitative method is a subset. Some researchers of the qualitative method use both methods in their research.

Producing new problems in order to solve old problems will keep us on the unending scientific treadmill. Is it ethical to create new problems in order to solve old ones? Is it ethical when people affected by scientific decisions or policies are not involved in the decision as to whether new or potential solutions should replace old ones? Should they be involved in deciding which present or future problems would present greater risk? A failure to bring socially responsible ethics to science may allow scientists to continue bringing more powerful and uncontrollable means of destruction into existence.

Brief History and Controversy

In April of 2002, a national conference entitled "Environmental Crisis or Crisis of Epistemology: Working for Sustainable Knowledge" was held at the University of Michigan School of Natural Resources and Environment. This conference was not the first one held at the U-M School of Natural Resources and Environment that addressed important environmental issues. In 1990, Professor Paul Mohai and I organized a retrieval/dissemination conference entitled "Race and the Incidence of Environmental Hazards: A Time for Discourse." Two outcomes resulted from this 1990 conference: 1) a book of readings named after the conference, and 2) a series of meetings with Environmental Protection Agency (EPA) Administrator William K. Reilly and later EPA Administrator Carol Browner. Along with the help and input of other scholars and community groups, this conference had a major impact on getting the United States Environmental Protection Agency to craft environmental justice policies. In fact, there were several events that took place in the 1990s that addressed environmental justice at the federal level.

In 1991, the first National People of Color Environmental Leadership Summit was held. More than 500 people of color gathered in Washington, D.C. to tell their stories of the poisoning of their communities. The assembled group crafted 17 Principles of Environmental Justice, principles that were taken back home and used in organizing efforts. Soon after this summit, the EPA created the Office of Environmental Justice under President George H.W. Bush's administration and the National Environmental Justice Advisory Council under President Bill Clinton's administration. In 1994, the Health and Research Needs to Ensure Environmental Justice Conference, sponsored by several government agencies, community groups, and professors, was held in Crystal City, Virginia, just outside of Washington, D.C. More than 1,500 people attended and shouted that they didn't need more research—they knew what the problems and solutions were—but needed instead the resources to solve the problems. While the conference was in session, President Clinton signed the Environmental Justice Executive Order 12898 in the Oval Office.

Meanwhile, people across the country in high-impact communities were desperately struggling against environmental injustices in their communities, and in the process they played a major role in the legitimization of community-based research. Today a number of quantitative studies chronicle the fact that low-income communities and communities of color are disproportionately impacted by environmental hazards. Race more than income is a greater explanatory variable in the spatial location of these environment insults (Asch, 1978; Berry, 1977; Bryant, 1995; Bryant and Mohai, 1992; Bullard, 1994a, 1994b; Burke, 1993; Gianessi, Peskin, and Wolff, 1979). Regardless of the scope of the study (local, regional, or national), its design, or the background of the researcher (professional or nonprofessional), race was a greater predictor for the location of hazardous waste disposal sites than was income. But more importantly, people who live in these polluted areas are more likely to suffer from toxic-induced and aggravated disease (Campbell and Tobias, 2000; Chakraborty, 2001; Fox, 2002; Keeler et al., 2002; Mennis, 2002; Montgomery and Carter-Pokras, 1993).

As a scholar who stands outside the field of philosophy and who is deeply embedded in the environmental justice community, I am concerned about the high and disproportionate rates of morbidity and mortality of low-income groups and people of color. Often knowledge produced is not sustainable or it may be socially and environmentally destructive; sometimes the peer-review process or the human subject review committees are not robust enough to predict future outcomes of new knowledge or its use. As an environmental justice scholar-activist, I must push for different methods and knowledge firmly rooted in a different philosophy and/or experience than ones that come from Europe. I must push for a way of knowing that takes us beyond the traditional scientific paradigm of disembodiment, decontextualization, atomization, fragmentation, and isolation. I seek a method of knowing that is both participatory and interdisciplinary to give more meaning and strength to our problem-solving capabilities. We need a scientific methodology that will address temporal relations of the long-term and complex rhythmic cycles of the earth and pollutants beyond our senses. But why haven't more such scholars been spun from the soil of America, scholars who will forcefully challenge the epistemological approach to linear thinking that was developed in Europe? We have been too preoccupied with the accumulation of knowledge, wealth, and their benefits without attending to their dire consequences.

To help facilitate a deeper understanding of the environmental justice crisis, two political scientists, two cultural anthropologists, one urban and regional planner, and six philosophers from across the country were contracted to write and present scholarly papers at a three-day retrieval/dissemination conference entitled *Environmental Crisis or Crisis of Epistemology: Working for Sustainable Knowledge* held at the University of Michigan in 2002. In addition, sixteen participant observers from a variety of disciplines were invited to the conference including philosophers and/or graduate students from Michigan and around the country. The thirteen presenters included one Native American, three of African descent, seven whites, one Asian, and one Latino. Out of the thirteen, four were females. The racial and gender makeup of the sixteen participant observers reflected that of the presenters. To this group, and particularly to the philosophers attending the conference, I posed two questions: "What is sustainable knowledge?" and "Are we experiencing an environmental crisis or a crisis of epistemology?" I thought it would be useful to ask the latter question since 17th Century Eurocentric philosophical thinking has shaped the way in which we know the world as well as our academic disciplines.

I also thought it would be fitting to bring together a racially-mixed group of scholars, men and women, from different disciplines to observe the extent to which their experiences, knowledge, or worldviews differed from one another and to see if their values and knowledge differed from the prevailing knowledge and values of 17th Century Eurocentric thinking. Throughout the conference, there were moments of passion as conferees presented and debated the issues. Some participants were hit on the very skull of their values as they were challenged to go beyond the traditional canons of knowledge-seeking. Several 90-minute small group discussions were held throughout the three-day conference—at least one per day—to allow participant observers and presenters to engage with each other in more intensive dialogue. What is compiled in this book are ideas from the perspectives of the presenters. While the issue of sustainable knowledge was thought to be too vague by some, others attempted to challenge its meaning.

For the past 36 years, I have been involved in environmental justice work (formerly known as environmental advocacy), and I decided to take stock of where we stand today in solving many of the current social and environmental problems. When we observe the vulnerabilities of low-income people and people of color, we find they are often a group of ill people as compared with their more affluent white counterparts. They are more apt to suffer from heart ailments, diabetes, and stress-related or toxic-induced and toxic-aggravated disease. Although all health problems cannot be blamed on the environment, a considerable amount of sickness is related to toxic-induced and toxic-aggravated disease. Millions of people in this country and throughout the world suffer from asthma, skin rashes, burning eyes, irritated throats, cancer, birth deformities, and sterility. While most studies have focused on the physical health of people, few studies have concentrated upon the psychological ill-health and the stress that come from living in proximity to polluting facilities or industries. To be healthy and affluent in this society often means ill-health for the less affluent, because wherever one finds extreme wealth, one will also find extreme poverty, environmental degradation, and disproportionate amounts of morbidity and mortality among the poor.

Poverty may be a greater causal agent of disease than any one microbe or chemical. When people are affluent, they are usually better-educated and healthier. In societies where wealth is more evenly distributed, the health status of people is generally better (Ashby Sharpe, Chapter Two, p. 67). But while most of our attention has been on poverty, wealth—not poverty—may be the problem, because the social and environmental degradation and the hazards we face today are integrally linked to the scale and intensity of our actions in the pursuit of wealth. In our relentless pursuit of wealth, we often discount the future because extreme wealth and its by-products take away opportunities for future generations. If we can solve the problems of wealth then perhaps we can solve the problems of poverty and environmental degradation. This leads me to believe that perhaps we have been asking the wrong questions. Is wealth the problem more so than poverty? Are we faced with a crisis of wealth and extravagance? Are we faced with an environmental crisis? To what extent are we faced with a crisis of epistemology? To what extent are we producing sustainable knowledge? To what extent are our problems related to the political economy of scientific inquiry? Who benefits from knowledge generation? Who benefits the most? If we focus on these questions, we will stand a better chance of getting at the fundamental or root cause of many of the problems we face today.

In this chapter I use the concept of epistemology quite broadly in terms of how we know, what we know, and what we do with what we know. Perhaps we are experiencing a crisis not only of what we know, but a crisis of how we know what we know and what we choose to do with what we know. Some of the conference participants, on the other hand, thought that it was not a crisis of epistemology, but rather a crisis of values. Yet epistemology is a value-laden social construction for viewing the world as we have come to know it. The values and social construction of epistemology informs our pedagogy, our scientific inquiry, and our truth. With respect to the question above regarding sustainable knowledge: how do we define sustainable knowledge? Although sustainable knowledge is difficult to define, the challenge is for us to do so or we will perish. When people speak to the issue of sustainable development, this is to suggest there is development that is unsustainable. By the same token, when we place the adjective "sustainable" before the word knowledge, it suggests there is knowledge that is unsustainable. Perhaps we can define sustainable knowledge by defining knowledge that is unsustainable, particularly when knowledge or its outcome results in global climate change, endocrine disruptors, acid rain, depletion of the ozone layer, nuclear waste, infertility and sterility, depletion of energy sources, over-population, world hunger, destruction of the global ecosystem, science serving aggressive military ends, and the destruction of indigenous knowledge systems. We must not only define sustainable knowledge, but we must take corrective action because our very existence here on the planet is at stake. Also, for this book, knowledge in very general terms not only includes the science of all disciplines, but it includes holistic and indigenous knowledge of various epistemic communities throughout the world. Because knowledge is diverse, we should celebrate and respect its pluralistic character; it should not be privatized, but made accessible to the community as a whole.

Again, the issue of sustainable knowledge was found by some to be too vague and yet others challenged the notion that such knowledge should be more than just sustainable. Therefore, we did not reach consensus on its definition. For the purpose of this book I am defining sustainable knowledge as that knowledge that sustains us beyond Maslow's basic needs in his hierarchy of needs (Maslow and Psychological Films, Inc., 1968). Some people think that sustainable knowledge carries with it the idea of just barely surviving upon the planet. Sustainable knowledge is more than that. It is knowledge that sustains us far beyond the basic need for food and shelter, and freedom from thirst, want, and need. It is knowledge that sustains and moves us toward Maslow's self-actualization[2] and well beyond materialism and our need to over-exploit our resources and degrade our environment. Sustainable knowledge is also knowledge processes or embodiments that are consistent with the earth's life cycle as reflected in its biodegradable time-space capacity.

Some make the distinction between the creation of knowledge and its use. Science cannot be divorced from its use nor should scientists be divorced from their responsibilities or from social and ethical considerations because to do so

---

2 This hierarchy is usually depicted as a pyramid with five levels ranging from the most basic needs at the bottom to the most complex and sophisticated at the top. From bottom to top, the levels are biological needs (food, water, shelter); safety; belongingness and love; the need to be esteemed by others; and self-actualization, the need to realize one's full potential. According to Maslow, the needs at each level must be met before one can progress to the next level. Maslow considered less than one percent of the population to be self-actualized individuals. However, he believed that all human beings possess an innate (even if unmet) need to reach this state. http://web.utk.edu/~gwynne/maslow.htm.

would be a reflection of the reductionist training that separates the parts from the whole (Viederman, 1997). To make the distinction between the creation of knowledge and its use puts it in the realm of the mind/body dualism of Descartes and his colleagues, perhaps the basis of many of our social and environmental problems. The inventors of knowledge should be held responsible for its use as should the users of knowledge, particularly if it results in environmental harm or morbidity or mortality. The creators of knowledge should be held accountable because knowledge is no longer retrievable once it is made public. It can be used for constructive or destructive purposes, by terrorists or non-terrorists alike. For example, the knowledge of uranium enrichment can be used by terrorists to inflict wounds and cause unprecedented deaths for millions of people. Once information is out, there is no retrieving it; there is no "cancel" button once knowledge is disseminated. It is important that we ask the right questions and use appropriate methods of problem-solving before it is too late.

I hope this book will invite substantive discussions regarding knowledge generation and its role and use in society. We recognize that Western science has contributed to the betterment of humankind. Western science has helped us eradicate or dramatically reduce polio, smallpox, yellow fever, typhoid fever, and many other communicable diseases. Western science has extended life expectancy and has improved the quality of life for people as evidenced by better working conditions, better homes, better schools, and better neighborhoods. We continue to be fascinated by science and by our discoveries in DNA cloning and sequencing, population genotyping, and other marvels that attempt to put us beyond the control of nature. But while science has benefited the few, the masses of people in the world go untouched by much of it and in some instances their conditions have been made worse. Science for the few does not come without social and environmental costs for the majority of the people of the world. In this book we are not dispassionate observers, but rather we are passionate human beings who care about our teaching and scholarship and how this impacts the world at large. If you detect anger or pain as you read this book, it comes from the very depths of our experience. We ask you to sidestep the anger or the pain and listen to what we have to say and join us in a discourse to help bring meaning and understanding to our collective work and to the scientific community at large. Because we do not pretend to have answers to epistemological or political questions raised in this book, we hope to stimulate meaningful dialogue. At this point I want to address four concerns that I have about knowledge and its generation. I am deeply concerned about: 1) the political economy of scientific inquiry and the commercialization of knowledge; 2) the issues of certainty and the role of positivism in our understanding of the world; 3) the role of experts and their potential for usurping democracy by making decisions that belong in the village square, and 4) epistemology and how it relates to the environment, nature, and culture.

The Political Economy of Scientific Inquiry (PESI) and the Commercialization of Knowledge

To understand the crisis of the environmental justice community, one has to understand how research is done in the academy and how research results are distributed. Although the academy embraces the notion of value neutrality in its research enterprise of billions of dollars, it is anything but value neutral. Even though universities enjoyed a considerable amount of autonomy in the past, that is no longer the case in that most research projects carried out in universities are sponsored research projects funded by powerful outside interest groups. Although research has always been done within a political and economic context, that is more true today than in the past. I refer to this crisis as the political economy of scientific inquiry because it is the forging of a partnership between private and public sectors that led to the commercialization of science and the corruption of scientific ideals (Ho, Novotny, Webber, and Daniels, 2002). Because the commercialization of science is associated with many modern technological developments including nuclear, chemical and biological weapons and because these projects are often political and detrimental to humans and the complex web of life, both government and private support of these projects threatens the neutrality of science. Universities and other scientific institutions have succumbed to the whims of powerful interest groups that often dictate through their funding priorities the research agenda of the academy (Ho, Novotny, Webber, and Daniels, 2002). It is the failure of science to deliver or provide satisfactory answers or outcomes to be distributed equitably. Why do orphan diseases go begging for funding? Why did it take so long for AIDS research money to be forthcoming? In order for AIDS research to be funded by the government, concerned people had to take to the streets in protest against government and scientific inaction.

When knowledge is generated, it is often communicated in such a way that it cannot be democratized for people in the village square (although the Internet might be changing that). Knowledge is often generated for the use of professional or corporate elite groups or for faculty and students who use knowledge to write books and articles for their degrees, promotions, tenure, and a variety of other reasons and not for laypeople to make informed decisions. Our brothers and sisters from Africa and India have expressed deep concern about PESI; they are concerned about knowledge, its generation, and its use. To them, certain kinds of knowledge or scientific paradigms have led to the development of technology that has been destructive and dehumanizing and which ultimately led to or legitimized totalitarian regimes and social inequities.[3] They view science as a system of knowledge that works in the interests of the dominant class of society and serves as the role of legitimizer and normalizer (Mpanya, Chapter Five, p. 136).

This form of inquiry not only resulted in the commercialization of science, but in the undermining of the public trust in science and scientists in that independent scientists working for the public good have become a thing of the past (Ho, Novotny, Webber, and Daniels, 2002). Governments at various levels often failed to put people before profits. Research institutions have become big businesses in their own right, seeking to commercialize their discoveries rather than preserve their independent scholarly status. Often our public monies are diverted to support research that benefits corporate or powerful interest groups, while too few dollars are allocated to promising approaches that support the public good. I have often said that if welfare mothers were given $100 million and told to spend that money on research interests at a university of their choosing, their research choices would likely be radically different than research choices made, for example, by Dow Chemical, General Motors, or the U.S. government and its agencies.

The commercialization of knowledge by universities and the corporate sectors will undoubtedly play a major role in globalization. Universities themselves are not only looking to their faculty for products to market or the commercialization of knowledge, but they also look to their faculty to provide consultation at every level of globalization. Presidents, deans, and faculty sit on the boards of many prestigious companies. Many business schools in particular support the World Trade Organization (WTO) and international trade agreements, even though it means that nations the world over have to concede much of their flexibility to protect their citizens because they can no longer advance their health and safety independently (Wallach and Sforza, 1999). When governments approved these WTO agreements they became a part of an institutionalized and political structure that holds them hostage to an unaccountable system of transnational governance designed to increase corporate profits, often with disregard to

3 When President George W. Bush failed to appear at the United Nation's World Summit on Sustainable Development in 2002, he missed a unique opportunity to address both national and international security. Many of the world's problems and terrorist attacks are related to impoverished conditions and people unable to meet their needs. Making a commitment to help rid the world of poverty would have gone a long way in stemming the tide of terrorism and enhancing national and international security.

social and ecological protection (Wallach and Sforza, 1999). Corporations draw strength from the knowledge of universities or from knowledge of their own making to help them to exploit human and non-human resources more efficiently. While we abhor the abuse, the barbarism, and the inhumanity of people and the destruction of the land by Columbus and the conquistadors who came after him and their greed and vicious search for wealth, these incidents are not isolated in the past. Today the modern conquistadors are corporate barons of national and international corporations (Lopez, 1990). In many developing countries as well as some of the developed ones, scientific or accumulated knowledge is used to pillage the land for resources and exploit workers, particularly women and children, by paying them starvation wages, forcing them to live in unsanitary housing, and making them endure unsafe working conditions. Because the accumulation of scientific knowledge has benefitted the few leaving the vast majority of people of the world poor and landless, this has contributed to world disequilibrium of crisis proportions. Globalization, undergirded by PESI and technology, will pave the way for a new nation-state of citizenship based upon corporate membership that will extend across geopolitical boundaries (Barnet and Miller, 1974).

Yet corporate barons believe they can use their commercialized knowledge more efficiently to foster change in the world if nation states are out of the way. Many of these corporate barons believe that nation states as we know them today are obsolete and stand in the way of progress (Barnet and Miller, 1974). While the mantra of the corporate sector is the globalization of the market as the solution to world problems, it has already realized many of the goals through the World Trade Organization. Under this governance system, the majority of the world's people will come under its control in order to enhance the power and wealth of the world's largest corporations and financial institutions rather than the economic, health, and social well-being of people around the globe (Wallach and Sforza, 1999). Sitting behind closed doors in Switzerland, these non-elected bureaucrats will shift the decision-making away from local and national governments, making cross-boundary trading among corporations easier and moving one step closer to developing a new corporate nation-state. The WTO and trade agreements will have devastating consequences on the livelihood of the poorest countries of the world. In their quest for global economic and political dominance, they have usurped democratic processes by impinging upon nations to control commercial activity with democratically enacted laws. In this scheme of things, there is no democratic participation or any foundation for citizen struggles for just and fair distribution of wealth, health care, human rights, environmental justice (Wallach and Sforza, 1999), and the equitable distribution of knowledge. In other instances, the privatization of knowledge made possible by a new trade-related intellectual property's regime in industrialized nations may encourage bio-piracy and/or the exploitation of indigenous knowledge on a global scale such as the world has never seen. Without the commercialization of knowledge supported by government, these corporations would not be able to exploit human and natural resources in ways that oppress, marginalize, and keep billions of people dependent and poor.

But what does all this have to do with environmental justice? There can be no globalization without the accumulation and creation of knowledge. Often knowledge-driven globalization promises more growth and development for nations of the world, but it is not without a price. Wherever there is extreme economic growth and development there is also extreme poverty, which includes extreme environmental degradation and environmental injustice. The history of national or multi-national corporations and economic development has been uneven. While a small percentage of people profit from economic growth and development, the majority of the people fail to advance economically or their economic condition may worsen. Globalization may promise more of the same as global corporations use new and accumulated commercial knowledge to pillage the earth for highly cherished resources. The masses of people may become even more vulnerable to environmental injustice as world resources become scarce, making it hard for people to eke out a living to sustain themselves. Undoubtedly globalization will take place. But the question is: who should control the process? Who should control how knowledge should be used or disseminated? If the process of knowledge distribution is controlled by multi-national corporations, then we can expect uneven economic development and all the problems of environmental injustice. If the process of knowledge distribution is controlled from the bottom up or if the community control of the distribution of knowledge is accessible in non-jargon terms, then perhaps we have a chance of controlling the rate and direction of economic growth, development, and justice. In any event, the task will not be easy.

Issues of Scientific Certainty

While the political economy of scientific inquiry and its research outcomes may contribute to world disequilibrium of crisis proportions, there is another crisis underway that is even more fundamental, and this is perhaps the crisis of epistemological certainty. How do we know, and how do we know what is valid and reliable information? While uncertainty, particularly uncertainty we associate with science no matter the discipline, and the richness of scientific uncertainty has often been unappreciated or misunderstood by the general public (Pollack, 2003), it is the mother's milk of science that drives scientists in their quest for knowledge. Although uncertainty abounds in the world of science, it is also an everyday fact of life. In our daily lives we have learned to live with a certain degree of uncertainty (Pollack, 2003). Just about every time-space-distant relation or future event that we plan is fraught with uncertainty. We plan to help increase the odds that our efforts will come out in our favor. Even when we cross the street we may wait for the traffic light increasing the probability of certainty that we will get safely to the other side.

The job of science is to bring certainty to the uncertain and to point to new uncertainties. But in doing so we often create a greater uncertainty than that posed by the original problem or we often create uncertainties yet to be discovered, some of which could have catastrophic effects. Much of science finds probable certainty through mathematics, tests of significance, and various models that approximate reality. We build models and import ideas that are inappropriate and have no real meaning in the world. Language of mathematics predisposes us to think in a certain way and thus view the world in a certain way—a way that is incompatible to the world at large. To find certainty we often find ourselves entangled in words, pictures, models, and ideas of the world that are both confusing and paradoxical (Peat, 2002). To know the world through abstract symbols of mathematics and statistical averages has no material base in reality, but exists only as ideas (Berry, 2000). When we talk in terms of percentages, averages, and beta weights, we are not talking about reality; we are talking about an abstract language that approximately represents reality. Berry states, "[T]he abstract, objective, impersonal and dispassionate language of science can help us know some things with certainty" (Berry, 2000). The chance of being certain about phenomena is often related to short-span temporal and space relations or short latency periods. Often laypeople cannot speak the more complex mathematical language of science or certainty, but they can speak to their pain, their fears, and their sickness. Scientists often make the assumption that people from the community are too irrational or too ill-informed to understand the complexity or deeper meaning of science and scientific certainty. To win credibility with community groups, it behooves scientists to assume that people are smart and capable of learning complex information and that they speak in a language that is less abstract and more grounded in understandable certainty.

Throughout the ages, people have had to deal with uncertainty; it is a part of life. Humans have had to in some instances creatively adapt to uncertainty because uncertainty always obscured our understanding of past or future events. To make decisions in the absence of certainty is the challenge that we must always face. But dealing with uncertainty is problematic particularly when scientists fail to give clear answers to questions posed by community people. Community groups ask questions such as: "Will my kids succumb to cancer within the next ten years?" Scientists often fail to directly answer such questions posed by the environmental justice community and instead respond with statistics such as how many parts per million of a given pollutant from the local incinerator are most likely to cause cancer. With respect to life and death issues, the environmental justice community becomes suspicious of scientists and policymakers when their demands for certainty and immediate solutions are not forthcoming. When scientists fail to give immediate answers and solutions to life and death concerns, they become suspect and often lose their credibility, which contributes to a sense of a deepening crisis. They stand to lose even more credibility if they work for companies that have a stake in the environmental injustice outcome. Laypeople are suspicious of government agencies whose inaction on policies or demands seemingly protects industry or the status quo.

The issue of certainty becomes more important during the production and use of multiple chemicals and technologies thought to make life easier. As human life evolved, so did our consciousness and our notions of space, time, and causality. Problems we face today are more complex than the problems faced by our ancestors. Who do we turn to for our answers? From where do we obtain unbiased information? Uncertainty is the price we pay every time we modify nature or the universe or produce synthetic products (Peat, 2002). In many cases, the price we are asked to pay for uncertainty is too high. People of color and low-income groups are often asked to pay a higher price for uncertainty when their communities host polluting facilities or when they find themselves overburdened by environmental insults. Is it fair for these people to pay a higher price for uncertainty than more affluent citizens do? Is it fair for them to pay the price of uncertainty when a large percentage of them are too poverty-stricken to buy insurance to protect themselves against uncertain environmental harm? People living in proximity to polluting facilities are the people most in need of protection, but the least likely to be insured. The preoccupation with their health status and that of their families often contributes to a sense of an ongoing and unresolved crisis. While people of color and low-income groups may not understand science, they understand the political context in which scientific decisions are often times made.

Positivism: Certainty and It's Shortcomings

Understanding much of the environmental crisis we experience today requires understanding 17th Century Eurocentric thinking. We must understand the thinking of Newton, Locke, Descartes, Bacon, and others who created and/

or built upon the concept of positivism. Positivism makes the assumption that in order to be positive about phenomena, it must be quantified. Positivism also is based on the assumption that not only can nature be understood, but it can be controlled and dominated by humans through science, mathematics, and the quantification of phenomena. To meet the standard of worthwhile knowledge and objectivity, the researcher must stand aloof and observe from the outside the phenomena being studied. Immateriality such as values, love, and dreams cannot be easily quantified or tested according to scientific methodology of positivism and therefore cannot be legitimate knowledge or elevated to legitimate means of scientific inquiry. Positivism assumes that worthwhile knowledge comes from disembodiment, decontextualization, atomization, fragmentation, and isolation of subclasses of subjects randomly selected for observation and quantification. It is through this process that worthwhile knowledge can be used to prove, extend, or disprove theoretical constructs. It is also through calculation, measurement, and quantification of phenomena that linear causality can be established (Adam, 1998). Over the years, positivism has been valorized and held in high esteem because it offered a promise of solutions and control of nature that fed our anthropocentric needs and fantasies of living above and beyond the laws of nature. Science not only gives us the impression that we can live beyond nature, but that it can fix things that have gone wrong; it can reverse "bad" decisions or outcomes. Scientists assume that mistakes can be corrected through increased knowledge and better technology. We are led to believe that through further research we can reverse any damage done to the planet. Living beyond the control of nature will be at what cost to nature, at what cost to the poor, and at what cost to us all? Who would benefit and who would benefit the most? These are questions that we must continue to ask ourselves.

What are the shortcomings of positivism? How might positivism contribute to our misunderstandings of nature? How does this epistemological approach relate to our current environmental crisis? There are several critiques, which are as follows: 1) While the Western intellectual tradition of worthwhile knowledge has been limited to the quantification of observation and while this method or approach has tended to restrict the focus of scientists to short-term and isolated events, these research results often yield a limited range of meanings, creating the over-simplification of complex phenomena (Smulyan, 1983); 2) A considerable amount of scientific knowledge has been turned into an abstraction where the particular is absorbed or obscured by the general and where information about the individual creature is lost somewhere between the species and the specimen or where the individual creature is lost somewhere in scientific classification (Berry, 2000); 3). Berry goes on to state that the synthesis is less than the thing explained because the scientist is ordering and only making sense out of as much as he or she knows, which is less than the phenomenon itself; 4) Even in laboratory science, rhythmic interdependencies are negated and the contextual and time-temporal distortions of living beings become irrelevant. To control, program, and manipulate, the subclass of subjects must be abstracted from their interdependencies, and thus context and valuable information may be lost in the process (Adam, 1998: 5) The crisis of our epistemology may be reflected not only in our inability to solve the long-term harmful effects of single toxins or chemicals, but we also may not able to find solutions to the synergistic effects of these chemicals or chemicals that may be innocuous individually but become toxins when mixed together; and 6) Certain circumstances may be a confounding influence when the latency period is too long between symptom and exposure because risks may be unbounded with reference to time and space, making it difficult for scientists to establish causality, blame, or liability, or for one to be compensated or insured against environmental harm (Adam, 1998). In spite of these shortcomings, positivism still proves to be useful and in fact indispensable to a considerable number of scientists. To know the parts of a thing, how they are joined together, what things do and do not have in common, and the laws and principles that govern objects can yield important and useful information. Such inquiries are native to human thought and work, but we must recognize the tools we have at our disposal are limited.

To me, global climate change is the epitome of an environmental crisis where science and technology have gone wrong; it is the epitome of scientific forces that may propel us into oblivion. The forces responsible for global warming must be challenged because global warming will affect every living creature on the planet. It may turn out to be the greatest environmental injustice of all as poor people and people of color the world over experience the differential impacts of climate change. In mass, the poor and people of color will be forced to migrate in search of food and jobs because of flooding or droughts. Movements across geopolitical boundaries will exacerbate regional conflicts as people compete for too few resources. The poor and people of color will spend a higher proportion of their income than their more affluent white counterparts on medical health care as tropical diseases move north and as they experience the effects of climate change. They will have fewer resources at their disposal with which to protect themselves against a changing climate. Hurricane Katrina will look like a picnic compared to things to come.

Another example of a crisis of science and technology that has gone wrong is found in the chemical industry. While the results of our experiments may serve us well in the short-run, we have failed to calculate their long-term effects. Each year science produces thousands of new drugs that find their way into the marketplace. Countless numbers of synthetic chemicals and materials are manufactured, many of which are based upon the fossil fuel economy. This fossil fuel economy, mediated by science, is not only responsible for most of the greenhouse gases, but also for many of our synthetic chemicals that may become endocrine disruptors or that are suspected to cause a variety of cancers and sterility, thus threatening our very existence here on the planet earth. In addition, human-produced chemicals such as PCBs, DDT, chlordane, lindane, aldrin, dieldrin, endrin, toxaphene, heptachlor, and dioxin (the latter of which is produced as a by-product of many chemical processes and during the burning of fossil fuels and trash) move through the food chain on particles of fat or vanish into vapors that ride the winds to distant lands (Colborn et al., 1996). These hormone-disrupting chemicals are found not only in animals living on the highest mountains, but they are found in animals living at the depths of the oceans. They are found in the Inuit people living their traditional life in the Arctic; they are found in poor people on the streets of Delhi. These chemicals are pervasive in our bodies, and we cannot escape their impact because there is no place here on earth that is safe from them (Colborn et al., 1996). Our earth is like a ship set adrift without a rudder, heading for a crisis of unimaginable proportions. Each new commodity or chemical that enters the market is a potentially grave experiment with outcomes that will not be known for years to come. It is people of color, indigenous populations, and the poor who are least able to protect themselves against environmental "wrongs".

Still yet another example of a crisis of science and technology that has gone wrong is the development of DDT. DDT is an organochlorine insecticide used to control mosquitoes and other insects. In Borneo in the 1950s, the World Health Organization's (WHO) solution for the malaria-stricken people of Dayak was to use DDT. At the beginning, the spraying of DDT seemed to work because mosquitoes died and malaria declined. But then an expanding web of side effects began to take place. Because the DDT had killed tiny parasitic wasps that had previously controlled thatch-eating caterpillars, the roofs of people's houses began to collapse. Although the colonial government issued sheet-metal replacements for roofs, the people could not sleep when tropical rains turned the tin roofs into pounding drums. At the same time, DDT-poisoned bugs were eaten by geckoes and they in turn were eaten by cats. When the DDT began to build up in the food chain, the cats died. Without the cats, the population of rats exploded. When WHO was threatened by outbreaks of typhus and sylvatic plague, rat-borne diseases, it was obliged to parachute 14,000 live cats into Borneo. This became known as "Operation Cat Drop," one of the most unusual missions of the British Royal Air Force (forwarded from Hawken, Lovins, and Lovins, 1999). This is only one example of how solving one problem can create a series of other problems. There are others to be sure.

Years ago when we began polluting the earth, we polluted small spaces, and the earth took a short time to heal itself. Today, when we pollute the earth, we pollute large spaces, and it takes a much longer time for the earth to heal. Our acceleration of growth and development over time and space has outstripped our ability to understand its dire consequences. Perhaps we are facing an environmental crisis that is not graspable within our present conceptual tools[4], although what is not graspable today may be tomorrow. Can we grasp the nature and extent of the problem before it's too late? As mentioned before, we do not have the power to detect the synergistic effects of chemicals or their harmful yet undetected impacts or their long-term effects. The crisis of epistemology is real because the world of simple linear causality, of proportional relations between action and effect, and of human time-scales for political planning is no longer possible (Adam, 1998). As time goes on and we find the world is more complex, we may not be able to depend upon scientifically derived certainty or our ability to accurately predict the future. Often times these problems cannot be identified through the mediating loop of science, because much of the phenomena we create takes place outside the everyday experiences of our senses (Adam, 1998). World famous physicist Albert Einstein once said: "We cannot solve the problems that we have created with the same thinking that created them" (forwarded from Viederman, 1997), yet we continue to try to do so. To date, we have been extremely lucky that we have not created a crisis of extensive and irreversible proportions that threaten life on the planet as we know it today. But the threat of global climate change looms heavy in the future.

---

4 The problem with science or technology is that many of their by-products are nonreversible. The process cannot be reversed when energy goes from an usable state to an unusable state. When people die, they cannot be brought back to life. No matter what we do, the process cannot be reversed. If we cannot reverse certain phenomena or processes, then we should be extremely careful of our use, treatment, and production practices. This has not been without cost although the marvels of science and technology have created substitutes. As Barry Commoner once said: "There is no such thing as a free lunch." A new chemical or product often creates a problem in another area. Thus we often keep solving problems and in the process we create other problems, and the treadmill of science continues creating more work for scientists. While some arguably say that science solves problems in the long run, the question becomes how many people have to suffer or die before the problems are solved and before new problems are created? I view this state of affairs as a crisis of epistemology because scientific methodology is not robust enough to provide us with answers—at least not in the short time. Meanwhile, people continue to suffer or even die.

While positivism may have served us well in a world of fewer chemicals and products, it is now being scrutinized because often we can no longer use it to find workable and meaningful solutions for both the short- and long-term. Positivism under certain conditions can be useful for counting and comparing things bounded in time and space. But we still must exercise caution when dealing with chemicals or toxins because what may seem to be bounded in time and space may not be and could have long-term catastrophic results. Science today, perhaps more so than in the past, is fraught with uncertainty and indeterminacy (Adam, 1998). Because of long latency periods, it is difficult for scientists to establish a direct connection between symptoms and exposure. The time-space distance between symptom and exposure not only affects this generation, but the effects of such exposures may only show up in future generations.[5] What we have is a scientific revolution that gives us a picture of a fragmented world and a world of statistical models unable to deal with nature's complexity. To reverse this perilous trend we must question epistemological approaches more vigorously in order to understand the world. We need a new research paradigm that will be more environmentally benign and socially responsible, and one that takes into consideration the time-space environmental effects (Adam, 1998). We need a research paradigm that produces sustainable or environmentally benign knowledge. To continue business as usual, to fail to assess where we are, and to determine where we want to be could result in a missed opportunity. If we fail to take stock of our situation and make appropriate plans, we will blunder into the future with all its dire consequences. Although I advocate for a new epistemological approach to knowledge, this does not mean that we jettison the Newtonian linear model. It just means we must recognize its limitations and be willing to challenge more vigorously its possible outcomes. It can be done because nothing is permanent and neither is the social construction of science. In fact, the only thing that is permanent is change itself. We must become diligent in our resolve to manage change and to find new and effective ways of producing sustainable knowledge and ways of protecting ourselves from environmental harm. We must move beyond post-modernity to produce a new scientific reality. This is the challenge of the 21st Century.

Positivism: Issues of Democracy and Participatory Research

The outcomes of positivism have been a threat not only to the biophysical environment, but they have been a threat to democracy. The concentration of

4 The Six Nations Iroquois Confederacy recognizes the importance of future generations. The idea is that each decision made today should be considered in light of its impact on the seventh generation from now. The concept of the seventh generation encourages us to undertake conservative thinking and careful deliberation.

knowledge in the hands of experts who decide what is best for the masses may pose a crisis for democracy. Both the process and outcome of a considerable amount of research are so abstract and specialized that dialogue can take place only among professionals. The more specialized or abstract we make knowledge, the more we take the decision-making from the village square. The more specialized or abstract the knowledge, the greater the justification of professionals to exclude the community from participatory decision-making, because professionals claim that by virtue of their specialized knowledge and training, they know best. Professionals and the knowledge they create may be a greater crisis for democracy than any outside or invading force. Therefore, it is of utmost importance that we find ways to include the environmental justice community in the decision-making process and to be more respectful of its knowledge. We must find or use a more liberating and democratic epistemology in our pursuit of knowledge. In some instances, we must look to indigenous knowledge or other forms of existing knowledge for answers to many of our environmental and social problems. Although indigenous knowledge may not have all the answers to our contemporary problems, perhaps some of it can be used to make significant contributions because much of that knowledge has been tried and tested throughout the centuries. We must also train a new cadre of professionals who can humble themselves to work effectively and democratically with community groups and indigenous populations in order to solve community problems. The University of Michigan School of Public Health has made community-based research a major thrust of its research and teaching portfolio. And although other institutions of higher learning embrace community-based research, they are small in number. A considerable amount of work needs to be done in order to augment research endeavors that integrally involve the community in the decision-making process. We must bring democracy and knowledge generation and testing back to the village square.

Although positivism is perhaps the most traditionally prevalent research paradigm found on most university campuses, other research paradigms do exist namely: action research, participatory research, community-based research, qualitative research, and ethnographic research. Often in research that is action-oriented, participatory, or community-based, people affected by the problem are integrally involved in the problem definition, questionnaire construction, data gathering, and analysis. This methodological approach is consistent with the democratic principles that we hold in high-esteem. People feel good about participatory research because this research paradigm brings the decision-making back to the community. Perhaps some form of participatory research best serves the community when it focuses on using the precautionary principle because this sidesteps the arguments of causality and errs on the side of caution. What do we do when we cannot wait until all the information is in before making an important decision? Participatory research may help us make the best possible decision given the science, intuition, wisdom, and information we have at a given time. Failing to act could mean irreversible outcomes. To protect environmental justice communities from environmental harm, the precautionary principle must become, if not the first, an important line of defense. It is simple and points directly to an uncomplicated solution, although that solution in many instances may not be precise and may be expensive.

Yet positivists in their critique of other epistemic communities focus on issues of validity and reliability. How do these research paradigms of the non-positivistic tradition demonstrate reliable and valid information? How can they be useful when their methodology fails to pass the traditional scientific test of rigor? How can the information be trusted when the researcher is intricately involved with subjects under study rather than being a detached observer? How can the results of these research paradigms be certain of phenomena under investigation? Although researchers of this persuasion stake their claim to meaning and understanding and what seems to work, this has not stopped the criticism of positivists. Researchers of the qualitative or non-traditional quantitative persuasion have made tremendous contributions to the advancement of knowledge and have helped us understand complex phenomena and will continue to do so in the foreseeable future. In many cases they have returned decision-making to the people by making research participatory and by involving local people affected by the problem. But let me hasten to add that none of the episteme communities have the answers or the research methodology to solve many of our social and environmental problems. Although those involved in participatory or community-based research may not have the solutions to problems, they often feel empowered and have a sense that their citizenship is not compromised. The crises that we may face today or tomorrow will extend well beyond the capability of any one episteme community. But we must try and try harder. If we fail to heed the problems that result from global environmental change or long latency periods or ungraspable threats to humankind, then the academic critique of episteme communities may become terminal because we will no longer exist. We must be vigilant in our resolve to work for a new social construction of science that will deal effectively with 21st Century global environmental problems, particularly problems with long latency periods.

Crisis of Epistemology in the Environmental Justice Communities and Science, Culture, and Nature

Thus far we have discussed the issues of certainty and positivism and the dilemmas they pose particularly in the 21st Century as we produce more toxins and become more aware of the limits of our methods and tools for understanding long-term environmental effects. Although we view ourselves as being in a state of environmental crisis, that crisis is perhaps more of a crisis of epistemology of how we know and what we choose to do with what we know. This crisis will only deepen if we fail to understand the temporal complexity of environmental toxins—toxins that resist to be known by our senses and our theoretical constructs and methodologies of traditional science. This crisis will deepen if we fail to understand the long latency periods and the long rhythmic cycles of planet earth. This crisis will deepen if we fail to understand the invisible nature of the threats or where these threats escape our senses (Adam, 1998). This crisis will deepen if we fail to understand the synergistic effects of chemicals or the multiple long-term effects of a single chemical. Much of the science from our epistemology approach has led us down the road to greater crises because technological intervention into the culture may have an impact unrestricted in time and space. Thus, culture "produces and legitimizes hazards that are beyond the control of institutions, science, politics and the market" (Beck, forwarded from Adam, 1996:36).

Perhaps the crisis of epistemology, of what we know and what we do with what we know, undergirds our science and technology, culture and nature. Epistemology, science, culture, and even nature to a great extent are social constructions all integrally related. We cannot speak of culture without speaking of the effects of epistemology as reflected in science and technology and their by-products. Epistemology is not only the backbone of our science and technology, but it plays an important role in our culture. If we have an unsustainable epistemology we will potentially have a crisis of culture or one that is unsustainable or maladaptive.

Culture embodies epistemology and extends its influence to nature. Although we have the tendency to view nature as distinct and separate from culture, this is not the case. Nature has been manipulated and exploited to the extent that boundaries between nature and culture have become blurred. When we design and manage national parks and wilderness areas, they reflect our culture more than they reflect nature. It does not mean that nature fails to have free standing, but whenever we modify nature, we impose culture (Cronon, 1995). Any modification of nature, such as the extraction and use of resources and their attending pollutants, is more culture than nature because contemporary environmental degradation is inescapably tied to human activity. More specifically, this loss of distinction between nature and culture is reflected in the depletion of the ozone layer; global warming; acidification of the soil, water and plants; depletion of fish stocks, biodiversity, and rainforests; and general environmental degradation. The impact of culture upon nature is a crisis that runs deep in our psyche, so deep that we often are oblivious of its workings. In order to understand this crisis more thoroughly, we must understand our culture and its impact upon our attitudes, behaviors, and nature as a whole.

Culture may be conceived of as a number of social constructions that determine our worldview no matter who we are. Culture is rapidly changing, much of it mediated by science and technology. Speed and efficiency mediated by technology allow us to exploit more of the earth's energy resources and contribute more to the world's pollution. From the beginning of time, culture has played an adaptive function allowing people to live in the most harsh conditions. Has our culture taken us beyond adaptation to a culture of convenience, of quick buying and selling, planned obsolescence, and throw-away cities, communities, neighborhoods, and people? People of color and low-income groups are often disproportionately impacted by our cultural misfortunes. Rappaport (1986) once said that culture is man's greatest invention because it allows humans to adapt to any place on the face of the earth. It allows information to be extended down through the ages in order to benefit each succeeding generation. As we strive to understand the role of epistemology, science, and technology that undergirds our culture and as we try to understand the social and environmental impacts of culture, we must ask ourselves the question: Is culture still adaptive or has culture become maladaptive? If it has become maladaptive, then we must make some meaningful mid-course corrections.

In Search of an Epistemology for Sustainable Knowledge

In our search for sustainable and just k nowledge, we must not give up hope. To give up hope only makes room for despair. I am sure that we can solve the problems of today and the potential problems of the future. I remain hopeful because in this country we have some of the best minds and people of good will in the world who can make a difference and prevent large scale problems of crisis proportions. Perhaps a part of our epistemological crisis stems from the fact that scientists and laypeople alike have been confident that science can control and put humans beyond the laws of nature. Although traditional epistemological approaches are appropriate for problems bounded in time and space, they are not enough. Until we develop an epistemological approach to better deal with the synergistic effects and problems of long latency periods or dangerous environmental effects that are beyond our senses, then we should implement an epistemological approach based on a sustainable attitude (Anderson, 1998). Robert (1991) took a sustainable attitude to knowledge generation when he came up with a set of now familiar questions (listed below) to guide our research and production practices. If we apply his questions to the production of nuclear power plants, they point us in the direction of saying "no" to nuclear power plants. For example: 1) "Is the chemical, material or resulting byproduct(s) naturally found in nature?" Plutonium, some of which has a half life of 24,000 years, is not naturally found in nature, and therefore it should not be produced; 2) "How persistent is it?" Because plutonium will be around for a long time, perhaps we should not produce it; 3) "Does it bio-accumulate?" Yes, we know that fission products will bio-accumulate in plants and animals (more research is needed on their extent and impact); and 4) "Is it possible to predict the tolerance limits of such a stable, unnatural substance?" No, since the complexity of the ecosystem is essentially limitless. Almost any amount of plutonium 239 would pose a threat to humans and/ or the ecosystem.[6] Plutonium is one of the most toxic substances known to humans, and this is perhaps the most compelling reason why we should not produce it.[7] The persistent and toxic level makes this toxin inconsistent with the earth's life cycle. We must use these questions as guides to help us develop an epistemological approach based upon a sustainable attitude in order to build sustainable and just communities. We must not only use Robert's guidelines to help us build both an epistemological approach to alter our cities and production systems, but we must implement an epistemological approach to help us build cities to mimic nature. In nature there is virtually no waste since the waste from one life-form becomes the food for another life-form. If we build cities to mimic nature then perhaps there will never be a need to extract

6 The questions Robert raises above tread on the notion of academic freedom because we should be able to produce knowledge for the sake of knowledge. Should one be able to produce knowledge without any constraints? Should one be able to produce knowledge regardless of its consequences? These questions are most likely to cause much debate.

7 In the 1980s the University of Michigan Senate Assembly, the governing body of faculty, passed the end-use clause. The end-use clause basically stated that no faculty member should engage in research with the end-use of killing or maiming people. Although the end-use clause was soundly defeated by the Board of Regents, I think we were on the right track in that knowledge must not be used for military purposes or destructive ends. Although the goals of military research are blatant, are there other more insidious forms of research that are ultimately destructive or have the potential for being so? We call upon universities throughout the nation to take stock of their knowledge production and the interests served by it. We call on universities to take a more active role in producing knowledge that is safe, sustainable, and just.

coal and oil from the ground (Anderson, 1998) so that people can live in clean, healthy, and productive communities regardless of race, color, or creed.

Using science to help build a sustainable and just society requires sacrifice on the part of each of us. We must use science to build systems that will respect people and nature and to allow for energy conservation. We must use science to build systems that allow us to become non-materially based and that support Maslow's self-actualization where growth and development focuses upon shaping and expanding our inner selves rather than on the use and destruction of our highly cherished natural resources.

Sustainable knowledge must contribute to the greater good and not to powerful interest groups to be used for dominance and the wanton destruction and exploitation of the planet. We need an epistemology for teaching, learning, creativity, and healing the planet. We need an epistemology that will define our world and our relationship to it; we need an epistemology that offers hope to move us beyond the social and environmental crisis we face today. Perhaps we need an epistemology that will help us know *in* nature rather than know *of* nature. To know of nature is to continue "the business as usual" of attempting to subvert the laws of nature, while to know in nature requires us to respect and have reverence for nature and its laws. To know in nature and to reflect a sustainable attitude in our quest for survival will require us to divorce ourselves from the fossil fuel economy. But taking such a bold step does not mean that we will rid the world of toxins because some toxins are naturally found in nature. We must not, however, add to the toxins already out there. If we attempt to live beyond the laws of nature, we may encounter problems that could threaten every human being on the face of the earth.

In Chapter One, Tesh discusses how science is integrally related and influenced by culture. She points out that changes in the culture and the culture of environmentalism have begun to affect the work of environmental epidemiologists which, in turn, has led to new environmental findings. We are in a period of cultural change when an increasing number of people agree with environmentalists that nature is fragile, interconnected, organic, whole, and vulnerable to harm from non-natural things. This cultural change has allowed a new generation of epidemiologists to be less reductionist than traditional epidemiologists and to design innovative studies to show the relationship between environmental toxins and public health.

In Chapter Two, Sharpe posits that cause and effect have played a major role in setting the terms of the environmental justice debate. One part of that debate is whether racial and economic minorities in and outside the U.S. bear a greater risk of harmful biophysical effect from toxic exposure than do their more affluent white counterparts and others. The other part of that debate centers on whether these differential risks are the result of discrimination. Ashby helps us understand equality through the ideas of Aristotle. Although she supports the precautionary principle in the short run, she feels the issue is much broader and more complex. The social determinants of health indicate that it is not the wealthiest countries that have the healthier people, but it is the countries that have the smallest income differences between rich and poor. She calls for a redistribution of income and other advantages including social and environmental benefits to the least well-off or society will not flourish. She appeals to John Rawls' theory of social justice.

In Chapter Three, Callewaert gives an overview of environmental justice starting with the 1976 Black Lake conference in Michigan entitled: *Working for Environmental and Economic Justice and Jobs*. Following this, he recognizes the Warren County, North Carolina struggle and its environmental justice contribution. He makes us aware that the public health initiatives by Hull House in Chicago were perhaps the precursors to the environmental justice movement. This is followed by an environmental ethics overview. He speaks about the divergence and complementarity of both the environmental ethics and environmental justice movements. With his discourse, Callewaert states there is an imprecise definition of justice and equity in the literature. In his chapter, Callewaert considers three environmental justice case studies and appeals to John Rawls' theory of social justice as a way out of the environmental injustice dilemma.

Ranco's Chapter Four clearly outlines the cultural conflict between the Penobscot Nation, the Lincoln Paper and Pulp Mill, and the Environmental Protection Agency (EPA). The Penobscots believed the EPA did not fulfill its Trust Responsibility to them because although the calculated risk of dioxin in fish consumption may have fallen within the boundaries of "acceptable risk" for the general population as authorized under the Clean Water Act, the EPA took into consideration only the risk of cancer from eating fish. Therefore, this was not acceptable to the Penobscot nation because the "acceptable risk" did not include risks associated with foraging for medicines and food along the river, swimming in the river, and using reeds along the river for the production of housewares. The Penobscots were looking for a wider range of meaning and threats posed by dioxin—not just cancer.

In Chapter Five, Mpanya critiques Western knowledge by comparing it with other episteme communities. He finds scientific knowledge to be partial, limited, and subject to unintended or unanticipated consequences. He feels the reductionist nature of this knowledge takes into account only limited variables and focuses on a single outcome. Because of this, it is difficult to predict the behavior of complex systems. Other issues faced by environmental justice groups in their struggle to protect their communities are that: 1) People are often unable to sense the danger of environmental pollutants because they are colorless and odorless; 2) Community groups receive conflicting scientific information; and 3) Knowledge is sometimes withheld from the community because of the fear of lawsuits or other kinds of community reprisals. Mpanya calls for support in a variety of ways to help the community to protect itself against environmental harm. He ends by saying that "(t)he problem of environmental justice therefore will remain intractable because of these social and epistemological limitations and cannot be dealt with except by implementing more democratic and participatory processes that would bring together a multiplicity of perspectives to decision-making."

In Chapter Six, Chatterji and Shapiro report that the academy in the United States and elsewhere has been instrumental in ethical knowledge production and has made significant contributions to social change. But they also expose the academy as the primary site that continues to sanction unjust processes of knowledge production that legitimize radical inequities based upon race, class, gender, sexuality, age, ability, nationality, religion, and ecology. To expose these problematic forces or to demystify, challenge, recreate, or deconstruct the truth requires critical knowledge. The authors report that we must shift to build alliances with communities in order to define research, scholarship, teaching, and curricula and extra-curricular activities and to create a public intelligentsia in the service of social change and justice. The authors give examples of their land reform work and participatory democracy and their work in the Asia Forest Network. The participatory or emancipatory research they carry out with the forest community is interwoven with their definition of sustainable knowledge.

Jamieson's Chapter Seven chronicles the history of climate change cases and illustrates that these natural occurrences depend on social, economic and political conditions that are functions of human agency. He then speaks about the rise of climate change in the science and policy area and the events leading up to and beyond the Kyoto Protocol. Along the way, science became a substitute for meaningful action which was politically effective. In the face of tough political questions, it was easier for Americans who are fascinated with science to call for more and better science. But while more and better science answers questions, it also creates new questions and provides ammunition for the skeptics. In addition, being generous with funds for scientific research is one way of muffling the voices within the scientific community that have been the most effective advocates of climate change action. Jamieson says, "Although dressed in the language of science, the debate is not really epistemological: it is a way of evading the demands of justice." He suggests a type of Marshall Plan and mitigation rather than adaptation as potential solutions.

In this book we do not have all the answers, but hopefully will raise some provocative issues for debate. We feel such a debate is important because it might suggest we make mid-course corrections in how we know the world and how knowledge, the fruits of that knowledge, and technology should be distributed. As mentioned before, the difference between the hedgehog and the fox is that the fox is really smart and knows many things. The hedgehog knows only one thing very well, and that is that everything is connected. I think that while we certainly need foxes, we also need many more hedgehogs to survive the 21st Century.

References

Adam, B. (1998). *Timescapes of Modernity: The Environment and Invisible Hazards*. New York: Routledge.

Anderson, R. C. (1998). *Mid-Course Correction: Toward a Sustainable Enterprise: The Interface Model*. Atlanta, GA: Peregrinzilla Press.

Asch, P. (1978). Some Evidence on the Distribution of Air Quality. *Land Economics*, 54(3), 278-297.

Barnet, R. J. and Miller, R. E. (1974). *Global Reach: The Power of the Multinational Corporations*. New York: Simon and Schuster.

Beck, U. (1996) Risk Society and the Provident State. In B. Szerszynski, S. Lash, and B. Wynne, (Eds.), *Risk, Environment and Modernity: Towards a New Ecology*. London: Sage.

Berry, B. J. L. (1977). *The Social Burdens of Environmental Pollution: A Comparative Metropolitan Data Source*. Cambridge, MA: Ballinger Publishing Company.

Berry, W. (2000). *Life Is a Miracle: An Essay Against Modern Superstition*. Washington, DC: Counterpoint.

Bryant, B. (1995). Issues and Potential Policies and Solutions for Environmental Justice: An Overview. In B. Bryant (Ed.), *Environmental Justice: Issues, Policies, and Solutions*. Washington, DC: Island Press.

Bryant, B. and Mohai, P. (1992). *Race and the Incidence of Environmental Hazards: A Time for Discourse*. Boulder, CO: Westview Press.

Bullard, R. D. (1994a). *Dumping in Dixie: Race, Class, and Environmental Quality* (2nd ed.). Boulder, CO: Westview Press.

Bullard, R. D. (1994b). *Unequal Protection: Environmental Justice and Communities of Color*. San Francisco: Sierra Club Books.

Burke, L. M. (1993). Race and Environmental Equity: A Geographic Analysis in Los Angeles. *Geo Info Systems*, 9, 46-47.

Campbell, M. J., and Tobias, A. (2000). Causality and Temporality in the Study of Short-Term Effects of Air Pollution on Health. *International Journal of Epidemiology*, 29, 271-273.

Carson, R. (1962). *Silent Spring*. Greenwich, CT: Fawcett Publications.

Chakraborty, J. (2001). Acute Exposure to Extremely Hazardous Substances: An Analysis of Environmental Equity. *Risk Analysis*, 21(5), 883-895.

Colborn, T., Myers, J. P., and Dumanoski, D. (1996). *Our Stolen Future: Are We Threatening Our Fertility, Intelligence, and Survival? A Scientific Detective Story*. New York: Dutton.

Commoner, B. (1976). *The Poverty of Power: Energy and the Economic Crisis* (1st ed.). New York: Knopf, distributed by Random House.

Cronon, W. (1995). *Uncommon Ground: Reinventing Nature*. New York: W.W. Norton and Company.

Fox, M. A. (2002). Evaluating Cumulative Risk Assessment for Environmental Justice: A Community Case Study. *Environmental Health Perspectives*, 110 Suppl 2, 203-209.

Gianessi, L., Peskin, H. M., and Wolff, E. (1979). The Distributional Effects of Uniform Air Pollution Policy. *U.S. Quarterly Journal of Economics*, (May), 281-301.

Growing Affinities. (1999). December ISSN0122-8048. 1, 7-11.

Hales, D. (2002). Commencement Speech at the University of Michigan School of Natural Resources and Environment. Ann Arbor, Michigan.

Hawken, P., Lovins, A. B., and Lovins, L. H. (1999). *Natural Capitalism: Creating the Next Industrial Revolution*. (1st ed.). Boston: Little Brown and Co.

Ho, M. W., Novotny, E., Webber, P., and Daniels, E., (2002). *Towards a Convention on Knowledge. Draft* 7, from http://www.twnside.org.sg/title/jb23.doc

Keeler, G. J., Dvonch, J. T., Yip, F. Y., Parker, E. A., Israel, B. A., Marsik, F. J. (2002). Assessment of Personal and Community-level Exposures to Particulate Matter Among Children with Asthma in Detroit, Michigan as Part of Community Action Against Asthma (CAAA). *Environmental Health Perspectives*, 110, 173-183.

Lopez, B. H. (1990). *The Rediscovery of North America*. Lexington, KY: University Press of Kentucky.

Maslow, A. H., and Psychological Films, Inc. (1968). *Maslow and Self-actualization*. Santa Ana, CA: Psychological Films.

Mennis, J. (2002). Using Geographic Information Systems to Create and

Analyze Statistical Surfaces of Population and Risk for Environmental Justice Analysis. *Social Science Quarterly*, 83(1), 281-297.

Montgomery, L. E. and Carter-Pokras, O. (1993). Health Status by Social Class and/or Minority Status: Implications for Environmental Equity Research. *Toxicol Ind Health*, 9(5), 729-773.

Peat, F. D. (2002). *From Certainty to Uncertainty: The Story of Science and Ideas in the Twentieth Century*. Washington, DC: Joseph Henry Press.

Pollack, H. (2003). *Uncertain Science—Uncertain World*. New York: Cambridge University Press.

Robert, K. H. (1991). Educating a Nation: The Natural Step. *In Context*, No. 28(Spring), 10-15.

Rappaport, R. (1986). Lecture on Culture. Ann Arbor, Michigan. University of Michigan School of Natural Resources and Environment.

Smulyan, L. (1983). *Action Research on Change in Schools: A Collaborative Project*. Paper presented at the Annual Meeting of the American Education Research Association. Montreal, Canada.

Viederman, S. (1997). *Knowledge for What? Scientists and Conservation.* An unpublished speech. Peking University.

Wallach, L., and Sforza, M. (1999). *The WTO: Five Years of Reasons to Resist Corporate Globalization*. New York: Seven Stories Press.

1

ENVIRONMENT, SCIENCE, AND CULTURE [1]

Sylvia Tesh, Ph.D.*

If environmentalism is beginning to weigh on science, this would not be the first time that culture had an effect on the world of research. Indeed, as many analysts have shown, the culture within which scientists work has an impact on what they do. It tells them what questions are worth asking, what methodologies are most appropriate, and what interpretations are reasonable (Feyerabend, 1975; Kuhn, 1962; Latour, 1990; Longino, 1990). Scholars in this field describe the influence of racism on science (Krieger and Fee, 1994), of concepts of hierarchy and linearity (Gould, 1981), and of sexism (Keller, 1987; Martin, 1991).

Introduction

In this essay I use the term environment in two senses. In the first sense "environment" is the object of scientific study – the earth's soil, air and water, and its plants, animals and ecosystems. In the second sense "environment" is the cultural space within which scientific studies are produced. My aim is to show that the cultural space influences the scientific studies.

This is hardly a new idea. Philosophers of science and social constructionists have argued for nearly half a century that culture influences science. Most of the people making that argument, however, either take no position about the goodness or badness of the cultural influences (e.g. Kuhn, 1962) or they concentrate on cultural influences they consider to be bad like racism and sexism (Gould, 1981; Harding, 1986; Krieger and Fee, 1994). In contrast,

1 Portions of this paper appeared previously in Tesh, 2000 (see reference section).

* Sylvia Tesh is a lecturer in Latin American Studies at the University of Arizona. She formerly taught in the Department of Political Science at Yale University and in the School of Public Health at the University of Michigan. Her Ph.D. is in political science from the University of Hawaii. She is the author of Hidden Arguments: Political Ideology and Disease Prevention Policy (Rutgers University 1988) and Uncertain Hazards: Environmental Activism and Scientific Proof (Cornell University 2000) as well as many articles.

I examine what I think to be a good cultural influence, environmentalism. I show that environmentalism's ideas about nature have begun to affect the work of environmental epidemiologists and prompt new scientific findings that support the enactment of stronger environmental laws and regulations. Thus, I suggest that the interrelation between scientific knowledge and cultural norms, far from simply being either deplorable or inevitable, can also be a factor in progressive social change.

Environmental Epidemiology

The impetus for this study is the long list of communities exposed to industrial toxins whose claim that their health is endangered is not corroborated by science. Although many of these communities now consider themselves part of the environmental justice movement, organizing to oppose industrial pollution began long before the environmental justice concept was born. The prototype is Love Canal. Between the summers of 1978 and 1980, Love Canal residents, terrified to learn that they were living on top of 21,000 tons of buried chemical waste, used every strategy they could to get the government to evacuate them (Gibbs, 1982; Levine, 1982). Thanks to their work, Love Canal now symbolizes the health problems that can result from exposure to industrial pollution. Even though the people at Love Canal suffered from a variety of cancers, skin ailments, and reproductive disorders, epidemiological studies have not been able to demonstrate there was an excess of these health problems, nor have they been able to link these health problems with exposure to the chemicals (Tesh, 2000). Love Canal is not alone. Nearly every community that has mobilized against industrial pollution has done so without firm science to back them up (Brown and Mikkelsen, 1990; Erickson, 1994; Goldsteen and Schorr, 1991; Gough, 1986; Krimsky and Plough, 1988; Zavestoski, 2002). Those few communities that have won suits against polluters or managed to get more protective public policies can thank political factors, not scientific knowledge.

Why has it been so difficult for scientists to show a causal link between a community's health problems and exposure to industrial waste? To most people in the neighborhood the relationship seems so obvious. They see that many adults have cancer or children have been born with birth defects or miscarriages are common or breathing problems and skin rashes are everywhere. At the same time they know there is a huge, humming electric transformer across the street or the well water is contaminated with pesticide runoff or the air carries smoke from a hazardous waste incinerator. The relation between these health problems and the environmental pollutants seems obvious to many environmental epidemiologists. Yet when they set out to investigate it, they usually follow a standard risk assessment protocol that makes the likelihood of showing a relationship quite small. The central problem is most of the data these scientists need is unavailable. Thus they have to use proxy information. They substitute laboratory experiments for human experience, short time periods represent long ones, small communities symbolize large ones, and proximity to hazardous substances substitute for actual exposures (Proctor, 1995; Rosenbaum, 1995). These difficulties help explain why environmental epidemiologists seldomly can corroborate the claims of grassroots environmental groups.

The risk assessment protocol is a four-step process developed by the National Research Council in 1983 and subsequently adopted by the federal agencies that investigate exposures to hazardous substances. Risk assessments for environmental exposures have traditionally focused on cancer. The problem with the very first step constitutes a warning about the other steps: it's basically impossible to do. It calls on investigators to identify the chemicals to which people in the community have been exposed and to determine whether they are dangerous. The main dilemma is that nearly all of the data on chemical hazards come from tests on laboratory animals, and the tests don't reveal anything directly about the effects of exposure on humans. In fact, each test only shows how one species of animals reacts to exposure to one chemical. It says very little about other animals. A chemical that causes tumors in rats is not necessarily harmful to mice; one that makes mice sick may not affect guinea pigs; and something that gives stomach cancer to guinea pigs might produce esophageal cancer in rats. Moreover, there is frequently variation between the sexes (Epstein, 1978; National Research Council, 1983; Proctor, 1995). With all this uncertainty about animals, extrapolating from them to humans is basically guesswork.

In the second step of risk assessment, investigators are supposed to determine how much exposure would affect people's health. Here again, animal studies are poor guides. In the lab, animals are exposed to extremely high doses of the suspect chemical over a relatively short period of time. The tests do not say what the effect is of exposure to low doses over a relatively long period of time — the usual experience of humans. Human beings could be more sensitive to low doses than animals or they could be less sensitive. The available data show both kind of responses, depending on the chemical.[2]

One might think the way to get around these problems in risk assessment would be to study exposed human populations directly. In fact, that is what the third step directs scientists to do. It tells them to identify the people who have come in contact with the contaminated water, air, or soil, identify the route of exposure (are people most likely to breath, touch, drink, or eat the contaminant?), and figure out the length of time of exposure. The goal is to correlate this information with disease in the community. But the task simply cannot be done accurately. People who live next door to a hazardous waste incinerator, for example, may be less exposed than those who live at a distance, but are downwind or those who are often outdoors. People whose wells are contaminated with agricultural runoff could ingest a great deal or very little of the contaminate depending on how much time they spend at home and how much water they drink. Investigators must depend on self-reports for much of this information, and self-reporting is notoriously unreliable. It is especially unreliable when people know that they may have been exposed to a potent industrial toxin (National Research Council, 1991, 1996).

The reporting problems extend to gathering health data. Even in the best of times most of us do not remember exactly when it was that we or members of our family were sick or exactly what the illnesses were (Harlow and Linet, 1989). Medical records are not much help. They tend to be incomplete, inconsistent, and hard to access. Most importantly, cancers — the main focus of risk assessment – usually have long latency periods. Twenty to forty years may go by between exposure to a carcinogen and the development of a tumor. A health survey done in the interim will indicate that exposure is safe.

Even when the data do show a high level of cancer in a community, investigators have to rule out a host of confounding factors before they are willing to say the cancers may have been caused by exposure to industrial pollution. The cancers might also correlate with things like smoking patterns, diet, occupational exposures, or genetic predisposition. Investigators must show that the cancer profile in an exposed community is different from the profile in

---

2 The few cases where data exist about different responses to low doses do not reveal a pattern. Dioxin, for example, causes liver cancer in female rats when they are exposed to ten nanograms per kilogram of body weight per day (a nanogram is one billionth of a gram), but all the current information on humans suggests that humans can be exposed to considerably higher amounts of dioxin without effects. In contrast, thalidomide, which can induce birth defects in humans at a dosage of half a milligram per kilogram of body weight per day, has no effect on female dogs unless they get over 100 milligrams per kilogram of body weight per day.

a similar, but unexposed community. Most critically, they must show that the level of cancer is higher than expected. Cancer is a fairly common disease. It is responsible for about a quarter of all deaths in the United States annually. But it is not evenly distributed every year. A community might have quite a few cancers during one period of time, none later on, and a medium number of cases later on yet. A cluster of cancers in a neighborhood with a toxic waste dump, however obvious the causal relation may seem, could reflect only the expected uneven distribution of the disease (National Research Council, 1991).

The final step in risk assessment is to combine the information from the first three steps and produce a number, or a range of numbers, indicating the likelihood that exposure to the environmental contaminate will harm people's health. This would seem to be the classic situation where hard data rests precariously atop soft data. Even more problematic, the hard data often appears unreliable because researchers have not been able to show that their information is statistically significant. This is because the rule for statistical significance is exceedingly strict. Investigators must be 95 percent confident (according to a standard mathematical formula) that the sample they have studied represents the real world. This high standard prevents epidemiologists from claiming they have found an excess of disease. Yet in relatively small populations, like those usually exposed to environmental toxins, the rule can also prevent investigators from detecting health risks even when they exist (Rothman, 1990).

These difficulties in gathering and analyzing data go a long way toward explaining why environmental epidemiologists so seldom can say unequivocally that industrial pollution has caused a community's diseases. It is instructive, however, to consider another kind of explanation. The problem may not simply be the inherent difficulty of drawing firm conclusions when you cannot get clear information. The problem may also be that the risk assessment protocol is based on pre-environmentalist assumptions about nature.

Environmentalism and Pre-Environmentalism

Environmentalism is relatively new. The other main social movements today — those for peace and for social equality — began in the 19th Century.[3] Up until the mid-20th Century, environmentalism did not exist.[4] People

---

3 See Environmental Protection Agency, 1994; Epstein, 1978; National Research Council; 1983.

4 I am agreeing here with Samuel P. Hays (1987) who argues that concern for nature was reflected earlier than the mid-1960s in the conservation movement, but that this was a different kind of social movement from environmentalism. I am disagreeing with Robert Gottlieb (1993) who argues that environmentalism began around the turn of the century with the concern for public health. In my view, that earlier movement, important though it was, drew on different political, ecological, and ethical principles.

valued nature simply for the uses to which it could be put, and people were valued for their ability to wrest control over it. That utilitarian view of nature is embedded in the Judeo-Christian heritage and in science itself. It appears first in the book of Genesis, where God tells Adam and Eve to leave the Garden of Eden and "have dominion over the fish of the sea and over the birds of the air and over every living thing that moves upon the earth."[5] More importantly, perhaps, the idea that humans are separate from and superior to nature permeates Cartesian dualism -- the 17th Century concept that made science possible by conceptually reducing the empirical world into distinct, machine-like parts. The effects of this religious and scientific heritage are displayed in the history of Western civilization, a history easily construed as a narrative of increasing control over nature by human beings. What was once frightening and dangerous gradually becomes tame. There is no record that Western people thought of nature itself as endangered or worried the ways they used it could be harmful to human health.[6]

Consider the United States. Before the mid-1960s, projects that dammed rivers, drained marshes, and turned farmlands into subdivisions were hailed as progress. Water pollution was thought to be something one encountered only in undeveloped countries. Air pollution was an accepted part of industrialization. Without giving it much thought people assumed they could throw their garbage "out." Several public schools were built on industrial waste sites without objection from students or parents (Mazur, 1998). A nuclear reactor could have a partial meltdown without causing public protest (Gamson and Modigliani, 1989). Glass producers could boast to potential customers that their bottles were not returnable; a plywood company could run an ad declaring "200-Year Old Redwood Forests Prove the Durability of Malarky Redwood Plywood" (Rauber, 1998). Newspapers and newsmagazines had no environmental beat; legislators had no environmental staff. A common slogan among engineers was, "The solution to pollution is dilution."

This lack of concern about the environment began to change in the 1960s with the publication of a remarkable series of books warning that industrialization was endangering nature. The books included Rachel Carson's *Silent Spring* (1962), Murray Bookchin's *Our Synthetic Environment* (1962), Barry Commoner's *Science and Survival* (1966), Rene Dubos' *Man Adapting* (1965), and Aldo Leopold's *A Sand County Almanac* (1966). The authors built on two earlier ideas. One was the biological concept of ecology (the

5 For a discussion see White, 1967.

6 On concepts of disease causality see Tesh, 1988, Chapter One.

term was coined in 1866) which proposed that nature is not like a machine, as the dominant Cartesian ideology had it, but rather like a living organism. In the ecologists' view, nature cannot be reduced to its parts. In order to understand nature, one must think in holistic terms. The other idea, expressed most eloquently by Henry Thoreau and John Muir, was more religious than scientific. It held that nature is sacred and that human beings have an obligation to revere and preserve it.

Each of these ideas had, at first, a fairly circumscribed application. Ecology was mainly the concern of resource managers and farmers; the idea of cherishing nature applied primarily to specific preserves or parks (Dryzek, 1997; Hays, 1987; Nash, 1989). The new books added a political component to earlier scientific and ethical principles. They warned that the world faced an environmental crisis, and they called for preventive action. As a result they founded a social movement. They constituted what Thomas Rochon calls, in his study of social movements, a "critical community", a network of people "who think intensively about a particular problem and who develop over time a shared understanding of how to view that problem" (Rochon, 1998:24-25). Carson and the other members of this community wrote about the terrible things that would happen because of our failure to understand nature. The core of their argument was that everything natural is by definition perfect, but they cautioned that natural things and processes are fragile, not tough and resilient as people thought. We threaten nature's balance and harmony, they said, when we introduce artificial substances and industrial processes. As Barry Commoner put it, through the eons of time nature has perfected itself. The best already exists. Any new "major man-made change in a natural system is likely to be *detrimental* to that system" (Commoner, 1972:37; emphasis in original).

These new ideas about nature spread amazingly quickly, given how deeply rooted the pre-environmentalist ideas were. They also became more complex. The social movement based on them developed left and right wings (Brulle, 2000; Gottlieb, 1993). Yet the central notions were so powerful that before the end of even one generation, most Americans — indeed most people around the world — had embraced them. In 1990, a majority of Americans told pollsters that they thought the government was not spending enough money on environmental protection, that protecting the environment is so important that standards cannot be too high, and that they considered themselves to be environmentalists (Dunlap, 1991). Even earlier, large majorities agreed with statements like "Humans must live in harmony with nature in order to survive" and " Mankind is severely destroying the environment." (Milbrath, 1984). Public opinion polls in the developing world show that even poor people in developing countries have attitudes similar to Americans (Brechin and Kempton, 1994; Dunlap, Gallup, and Gallup,1992).

No large poll of scientists' attitudes toward environmentalism has been published so we cannot know for sure whether most scientists embrace the new environmentalist ideas. It is clear, however, that scientists today work in a different cultural climate from the one they, or their predecessors, worked in before the 1970s. More specifically, environmental epidemiologists operate in a world where nature is now generally assumed to be fragile and exquisitely vulnerable to harm, where images abound of the interrelatedness of nature and of its harmony and balance, and where people assume that human interference in nature is likely to be detrimental. To be sure, even some committed environmentalists question the certainty of these ideas. Daniel Botkin and other scholars argue that nature was never in balance (Botkin, 1990), and scholars like William Cronon say that "nature" is a social construction and cannot objectively be distinguished from non-nature (Cronon, 1995). Nevertheless there is good reason to describe today's culture as "environmentalist" — a culture wherein the new ideas about nature introduced a generation ago have now become part of the dominant, taken-for-granted ideology. There is also reason to argue that environmentalist ideas have begun to influence the work of scientists.

Science and Culture

If environmentalism is beginning to weigh on science, this would not be the first time that culture has had an effect on the world of research. Indeed, as many analysts have shown, the culture within which scientists work has an impact on what they do. It tells them what questions are worth asking, what methodologies are most appropriate, and what interpretations are reasonable (Feyerabend, 1975; Kuhn, 1962; Latour, 1993; Longino, 1990). Scholars in this field describe the influence of racism on science (Krieger and Fee, 1994), of concepts of hierarchy and linearity (Gould, 1981), and of sexism (Keller, 1987; Martin, 1991).

As an example consider Donna Haraway's critique of an influential study of monkey behavior that sought to understand how social order is created and maintained. The investigator of that study began with the unexamined assumption that societies are like single organisms in that they only have one head. So she identified a dominant male in several groups of monkeys. Then she removed that monkey from each group and observed that the monkeys competed until a new male asserted control, and harmony was restored. The investigation, says Haraway, inaccurately presumed that social order depends on dominance and that competition is the precondition of cooperation. She argues that a study of the same monkeys, focusing on the females instead of the males, would have seen their society as "long-term social cooperation rather than short-term spectacular aggression, flexible process rather than strict structure, and so on" (Haraway, 1987:218).

Or consider Emily Martin's description of reproductive biology's gender bias. She shows that for a long time medical textbooks and peer-reviewed journals published articles describing the fertilization process in terms that assign traditional female and male social roles to the egg and sperm: the egg sits around passively waiting for the industrious sperm to swim up to it and give its existence meaning. Investigators eventually found that sperm are weak swimmers and that rather than invading an egg, they hitch themselves onto its surface and are gradually sucked in. Yet despite this finding, so powerful are gender stereotypes that even "the researchers who made the discovery continued to write papers and abstracts as if the sperm were the active party who attacks, binds, penetrates, and enters the egg" (Martin, 1991:493).

To uncover the ways environmentalism influences scientific research, it is helpful to start with the environmentalist critique of risk assessment. Since the mid-1980s, when risk assessment was adopted by federal government agencies, environmentalists have lodged at least five complaints against it. First, they say, risk assessment concentrates on cancer instead of focusing on the whole range of diseases that can result from exposure to pollution. Second, it presupposes that people are alike in susceptibility instead of attending to their biological and social diversity. Third, it takes clinical illness as the expression of harm instead of noting that harm manifests itself in many other ways. Fourth, it presumes that chemicals behave independently instead of taking into consideration synergistic interactions among them. And fifth, it demands an extremely high standard of proof before it will conclude that exposure to pollution is harmful (O'Brien, 2000; Silbergeld, 1993; Tal, 1997).

In sum, the critics charge that risk assessment reflects a pre-environmentalist view of nature. Despite the fact that the risk assessment protocol was developed in response to worries that synthetic chemicals are health hazards, the protocol carries with it the very reductionism that environmentalism opposes. Its concentration on a single disease, compression of all of humanity into a single person, narrow view of illness, and atomistic concept of chemicals all contrast sharply with the wholism environmentalists promote. Furthermore, risk assessment's high standard of proof clashes with the environmentalist principle that human interference in natural processes is probably dangerous. What the critics tacitly call for is an environmentalist epidemiology, one that sees the world in terms of a broad network of intricate interconnections and recognizes that the air, water, and soil are in many parts of the U.S. — let alone in the rest of the world — probably dangerously polluted. Such a science, they imply, would be more in keeping with reality and therefore a better instrument for discovering health problems caused by exposure to toxic substances.

This is not the first time someone has called for a new kind of epidemiology. The field of study has experienced several internal reformations since it became a science in the early 19th Century - each reformation consistent with a new theory of disease causality, each one fought over by competing groups of scientists, and each one reflecting larger social changes (Greenland, 1987; Tesh, 1988). Whether epidemiology will change again in response to environmentalism cannot be known today when environmentalist ideas are still so new to industrial society. But it is possible to discern new preoccupations among epidemiologists that may signal the beginning of a shift to an environmentalist study of disease, one more likely to demonstrate that exposure to synthetic chemicals endangers public health.

Signs of Change in Environmental Epidemiology

One sign of change is the gathering interest in outcomes of exposure other than cancer. As I noted above, risk assessment usually concentrates on cancer. The focus fits well with early environmentalism. In *Silent Spring*, Rachel Carson barely mentioned other diseases; the whole book seemed to say that synthetic chemicals cause only cancer. Even to this day, "toxic chemical" is in both popular and scientific imagination largely synonymous with "carcinogen." But the coupling has big drawbacks for environmentalism. It means that when suspect chemicals are not found to cause cancer, the rationale for them to be called toxic is shaken. It also means that investigators are less likely to look for, and thus less likely to find, links between exposure to pollution and other health problems.

In recent years, however, some scientists have been looking for, and finding, a connection between environmental pollution and other outcomes. Those receiving the most attention are impaired sexual development (such as decreased sperm counts and undescended testicles), reproductive problems (such as infertility, birth defects, and endometriosis), and cognitive dysfunctions (such as low IQ scores, learning disabilities, and behavioral immaturity). The research on these maladies gained coherence when the chemicals linked to them were grouped together under a new term: endocrine disruptors. Suddenly there was a new category of ailments related to environmental pollution.

Instead of just cancers plus an unwieldy assortment of other possible results of exposure, there are now two firm classifications: cancers and hormone-related conditions. Each kind of malady is dreadful, but hormone-related conditions are especially frightening because they concern an entire, highly complex, physiological system. In the words of one environmentalist, they affect "the very characteristics that make us human" (Cortese, 1996).

By the end of 1997, nearly 300 peer-reviewed studies on endocrine disruptors had been published. Fifty-one endocrine-disrupting substances had been identified — including DDT, kepone, lindane, some PCB cogeners, several dioxins, cadmium, lead, mercury, alkyl phenols, and diethylstilbestrol (DES). And the Environmental Protection Agency (EPA) had put endocrine disruptors among its top five research issues. By 1999, the EPA was in the process of validating methods to screen 87,000 chemicals for hormonal effects (Schmidt, 2001b).

The scientist most acclaimed for identifying this new category of disease is Theo Colborn, principal author of *Our Stolen Future*. The book, which several reviewers called the sequel to *Silent Spring*, contains a detailed discussion of endocrine disruptors as well as a strong indictment of what the authors call the cancer paradigm:

> If this book contains a single prescriptive message, it is this: we must move beyond the cancer paradigm…This is not simply an argument for broadening our horizons to recognize additional risks. We need to bring new concepts to our consideration of toxic chemicals. The assumptions about toxicity and disease that have framed our thinking for the past three decades are inappropriate and act as obstacles to understanding a different kind of damage (Colborn et al, 1997:203).

One obstacle to understanding different kinds of damage, they argue, is the assumption that dose and response are always positively correlated. Relying on the cancer paradigm, environmental toxicologists and epidemiologists assume that high doses are more dangerous than low doses. But endocrine disruptors do not act like carcinogens. The physiological response to them may increase with the dose for a while and then start to diminish (Colborn et al., 1997). So if scientists used endocrine disruptors instead of carcinogens as a model for predicting the human health effects of exposure to a polluted site, they might come up with quite different risk assessments. People exposed to low doses could be at a greater risk than people exposed to high doses. One result of this new model could be more persistent epidemiologists. They would have reason to suspect that a community exposed to low levels of environmental pollution had been harmed and thus might become more dogged in their attempts to find evidence of it.

Another obstacle created by the cancer paradigm is the assumption that individuals directly exposed to pollution are the most appropriate focus of study. The research on cancer leads investigators to think of environmental pollutants as poisons and to assume that pollutants kill cells or attack DNA. But endocrine disruptors do not resemble poisons. Instead, they can be compared to CIA operatives. "They jam signals. They scramble messages. They sow disinformation" (Colborn et al, 1997: 203). And because the messages they scramble are hormone messages, these pollutants may affect not only the individuals directly exposed to them but also the next generation. Colborn and her colleagues suggest that after the 1976 chemical explosion in Seveso, Italy, epidemiologists may have investigated the wrong population or the right population at the wrong time. Epidemiologists asked whether cancer rates had gone up among the people living near the explosion and whether there were obvious health problems. Finding none, they announced that the explosion had not harmed people. But investigators using endocrine disruptors as a model would have looked for delayed effects on the endocrine system, the immune system, or the nervous system. New investigations may or may not find such effects, but these are the kinds of questions the model prompts researchers to pursue.

A second sign of change toward a less reductionist and more environmentalist science is the new attention to distinctive population groups. Until very recently, risk assessment operated under what Robert Verchick (1996) calls a "one size fits all" theory. The average person was taken to be a white, middle class adult, and environmental health studies with this narrow focus were assumed to reveal everything science needed to know about the public's vulnerability to environmental toxins. Now, however, two sub-groups have been carved out of the population and identified as distinctive. One is children; the other is racial minorities and poor people. Both groups are held to be especially susceptible to pollution — children because of their biological characteristics, racial minorities and poor people because of their position at the bottom of the social hierarchy. As a result of recognizing these differences, any community's claim that pollution has affected their health may become easier to demonstrate.

The first big rush of publicity singling out children as especially vulnerable to environmental toxins came in February 1989 when *60 Minutes* ran an emotional story about pesticide residues on apples. The story, reporting on a study by scientists at the Natural Resources Defense Council (NRDC), said that because children ingest more food in relation to their body weight than adults, they get relatively more pesticide exposure (Natural Resources Defense Council, 1989). Four years later the National Research Council finished its own, more complete investigation of children and pesticides. It corroborated the NRDC's findings, added information on the disproportionate exposure children get to toxic chemicals because they play close to the ground, and echoed NRDC's call for stricter controls on pesticides as well as more research (National Research Council, 1993). Joining the campaign, the National Institute for Environmental Health Studies (NIEHS) has made children's environmental health a major focus. In 1997, following several scientific conferences on the topic, the peer-reviewed journal, *Environmental Health Perspectives*, ran an editorial specifically encouraging new research on children's environmental health (Goehl, 1997), and since July 1999, the journal has had a special section on children's environmental health in every issue. Marking the new attention to children's environmental health, the Children's Health Act of 2000 contains a section authorizing the most extensive epidemiological study ever conducted on the health effects of environmental exposures on children. The study, which started in 2004, will follow 100,000 children for 20 to 30 years (Schmidt, 2001a).

The idea that children are more susceptible to environmental threats than are adults has some immediate implications for scientists doing risk assessments. For example, the first step of risk assessment, hazard identification, draws on animal bioassays and epidemiological studies. Yet these data, because they pay little attention to the differences between children and adults, may fail to identify chemicals that are particularly dangerous to children. The exposure assessment step raises similar cautions. Children usually engage in more physical activity than adults; they spend more time close to the ground; they stick more things in their mouths; and they breathe more air per unit of body weight. In addition, the received dose of an environmental toxin (as opposed to the administered dose) can be greater for children. Compared to adults, the rate of absorption is often more rapid in children's bodies because some of their internal membranes are more porous (Buffler and Kyle, 1999). All this suggests that scientists need to use different kinds of assumptions in risk assessment when they study communities where children are exposed to environmental toxins, and these studies will be more likely to discover links between exposure and disease.

A similar phenomena has occurred by defining minorities and poor people as especially vulnerable to environmental pollution. This story began not with scientists, but with a group of ordinary people in Warren County, North Carolina, most of them African American, who tried to prevent PCB-laden soil from being dumped in their neighborhood. During a public demonstration, the police arrested a U.S. Congressman. When the enraged Congressman returned to Washington, he asked the U.S. General Accounting Office to investigate the link between race and the location of hazardous waste dumps. The resulting document (published in 1983) showed that three out of four landfills in the Southeast were in poor and African American neighborhoods. Four years later, the United Church of Christ's Commission on Racial Justice released the results of a larger investigation. This one looked at all 415 operating commercial waste landfills in the United States, as well as at all 18,164 closed or abandoned hazardous waste sites. It concluded that in the nation as a whole, communities with the largest number of hazardous waste facilities have a disproportionate percentage of racial and ethnic minorities and that race is a more significant indicator of the location of these hazardous waste facilities than is socioeconomic status (United Church of Christ, 1987). Since then, many other studies have come to similar conclusions, although some focus on class rather than race.

These studies have come under a certain amount of attack, especially by scholars who criticize the methodology used in them (e.g. Been, 1994; Szasz and Meuser, 1997). Nevertheless, all federal agencies are now required to make environmental justice part of their mission. The EPA, for example, may not issue a permit to a polluting industry until it takes into consideration the ways that cultural, occupational, historical, and economic factors could intensify the pollution's effect on the community. In essence, the EPA must adopt environmentalism's complex view of the world, recognizing interlinkages and multiple causations (Haynes, 1997).

The requirement proposes a significant change in the way epidemiologists study the relationship between public health and environmental pollution. They are now prompted to consider the possibility that the same toxic chemical could have worse effects in poor communities than in wealthy ones. This was the case made in 1997 by residents of a low-income community near Detroit. They prevented a local waste incinerator from burning contaminated demolition wood by arguing that they had already been dumped on by so many other nearby sources of pollution that their bodies could not handle any more toxins (NAACP-Flint vs. John Engler). Epidemiologists have only begun to publish studies using similar analyses. The most common focus is on exposure to polluted lakes and streams. Investigations have shown that while both middle class and poor people live near polluted bodies of water and spend time fishing in them, poor people more frequently use the (contaminated) fish as part of their diets. Thus, they are more at risk than better off people living in the same neighborhood (Haynes, 1997).

A third sign of change toward a more environmentalist epidemiology is the gathering interest in chemical mixtures. Risk assessment assumes that each chemical in the environment has its own inherent properties. Some chemicals are very toxic; some are mildly toxic; some are benign. Thus, even if people are exposed to a great many chemicals at once — a "toxic soup" in popular imagery — if each individual component of the soup is benign, no one's health is at risk.

This reductionist assumption is challenged by research showing that certain individually innocuous chemicals, when mixed, become toxic (Krewski and Thomas, 1992; National Research Council, 1996). The research has obvious implications for environmental epidemiology. If investigators assume that chemicals are only additive when in fact they are synergistic, risks at some sites could be seriously underestimated. Thinking that residents' health problems simply could not be due to environmental exposures, epidemiologists could erroneously attribute any excess morbidity or mortality to other causes or to chance.

Research on mixtures received an apparently big boost in 1996 when a group of investigators at Tulane University experimenting on yeast cells found that combinations of some estrogen-disrupting chemicals are a thousand times more toxic than any of the chemicals alone (Arnold et al, 1996). Unfortunately for environmentalists, the research was "withdrawn" a year later when investigators at other universities were unable to duplicate the findings. But many environmental health scientists are still intensely interested in synergistic chemical reactions. The editors of *Environmental Health Perspectives* urge readers not to let the problems with the Tulane yeast studies distract them "from the larger issues." Although effective research strategies still need to be designed, they say, it is clear from earlier work "with PCBs and several pesticide formulations that synergy and antagonism may occur in circumstances of multiple chemical exposures" (Hook and Lucier, 1997:784). The same journal also ran an editorial by an EPA scientist discussing some of the problems in understanding the effects of chemical mixtures. His conclusion calls out not just for more research, but for new theorization about chemicals:

> There clearly is need to expand our thinking about this problem area... Although many/most of these chemicals may function as imperfect hormones with relatively low potencies, we have not begun to understand what the potential adverse effects are of being exposed continuously to complex mixtures of chemicals with varying abilities to affect multiple signaling pathways both singly and interactively (McKinney, 1997:898).

Other scientists apply the concept of mixtures more broadly. Kriebel and his colleagues, bemoaning the "atomized worldview" of many environmental epidemiologists, say, "In reality, complex biological systems such as ecosystems, human populations, or individual physiology are composed of feedback loops and other interactions which make cause-effect relationships far from direct or linear." They continue: "Interactions are difficult to study, but this should be seen as a challenge to develop more sensitive and complex methods..." (Kriebel et al., 2001). They argue that understanding the effects of environmental pollutants on human health requires the cooperative work of people from many fields using a wide variety of research methods. Such interdisciplinary teams "will be more likely to find new ways to frame hypotheses that lead to insights not possible from narrow disciplinary viewpoints" (Kriebel, 2001:874).

A fourth sign of change is the expanding definition of disease. Interestingly, this change can be seen both as a reinforcement of reductionist thinking and as a step forward for environmentalism. Environmental disease is usually construed (as is all disease) as clinical illness. In recent years, however, certain investigators have defined environmental disease as the minute physiological abnormalities that are sometimes discovered in people who live with pollution. These abnormalities are called biomarkers. Found in samples of blood, adipose tissue, breast milk, or other substances, they can be understood as the first symptom of disease. From this perspective, disease becomes a slow sequence of events over time instead of a fixed clinical illness so it is possible to identify environmental illness early. In the words of the National Research Council, biomarker research is a "fuller method" compared with the "current method" of estimating risks by relating exposure to clinical disease (morbidity and mortality). As a result, health events are less likely to be viewed as binary phenomena (presence or absence of disease) than they are to be seen as a series of changes on a continuum — through homeostatic adaptation, dysfunction, to disease and death" (National Research Council, 1991:220-221).

Biomarker research offers great advantages to investigators making health assessments at hazardous waste sites. First, they do not have to wait until residents get sick. With sophisticated biomarker research methods, they can identify cardiopulmonary disorders or tumors or reproductive health problems in the initial stages. Second, when investigators compare health problems in exposed and unexposed groups of people, they do not have to rely on guesses based on mathematical modeling or on extrapolations from soil, water, or air samples or on questionnaires to know who goes in which group. They are less likely to weaken the power of their studies by mistakenly including large numbers of unexposed people in a group of presumably exposed. Thus, investigators will be more likely to show where pollution has had a health effect(Griffith et al., 1990; Perera, 1987).

Research on the health effects of exposure to lead provides a good example. Until the 1950s, scientists had no convincing way to reject the lead industry's claims that lead in the environment occurred naturally, that the average levels in blood were safe, and that the only serious problems were rare, accidental acute poisonings. But as biomarker technology was developed, a group of clinicians and epidemiologists began examining blood samples from children in Boston and New York City. They were eventually able to correlate high blood-lead levels with learning disabilities, hyperactivity, school failure, and mental retardation. They were also able to correlate high blood-lead levels with exposure to automobile exhaust and paint (Berney, 1993). So clear is this correlation that today when researchers do health studies of children exposed to lead they do not have to show that the children have any clinical illness or observable learning problems, only that they have high levels of lead in their blood. This condition itself is considered a disease called lead poisoning. And because environmental lead can be relatively easily linked with blood abnormalities, and the blood abnormalities with mental and physical illness, the EPA's usual critics (with the exception of the lead industry) rarely include lead in their list of unnecessary regulations.

Biomarker research can also work for certain synthetic chemicals, and there is now a huge interest in it among scientists. It does have certain drawbacks for environmentalists, however. Not all environmental exposures leave markers in the body, and such markers can be caused by other things beside environmental toxins. In addition, biomarker research is excessively reductionistic. It easily leads to a concentration on high-risk individuals instead of on high-risk environments (Vainio and Husgafvel-Pursianen, 1995). Nevertheless, a focus on minute bodily reactions to environmental toxins expands the definition of disease beyond clinical illness. It can thereby rescue environmental epidemiologist from having to show that people they study have health problems in the traditional meaning of the term. Epidemiologists only have to show that people's bodies have started reacting to exposure — that the long disease process has begun.

A fifth sign toward a more environmentalist science is the disquiet some scientists express about epidemiology's validity rules. The demand that investigators be 95 percent certain of their findings obviously biases epidemiology toward the status quo. It is change that must be justified, not a continuation of current exposures. As I noted earlier, such certainty is usually hard to demonstrate in studies of communities exposed to industrial toxins. The textbook explanation for the difficulty is that the communities are typically so small and cancer is such a common disease that a few extra cases cannot be distinguished from the expected variation from one year to the next.

Faced with this situation, some scientists and philosophers of science argue that statistical significance should not be confused with public health significance. They say that what is good for science is not necessarily good for regulation (Cuoto, 1986; Kriebel et al., 2001; Ozonoff and Boden, 1987). It is important to be 95 percent certain of your results if your aim is to add to scientific knowledge about the link between a suspect substance and disease, a kind of knowledge that Carl Cranor (1990) calls "science for its own sake." But, these scholars argue, if your aim is to protect public health and a high standard of mathematical certainty both robs you of a scientific rationale for doing so and justifies those who would expose the public to potentially harmful substances, the standard is unethical. In the words of a biologist who gathered data at Love Canal:

> Before Love Canal I also needed to have 95 percent certainty before I was convinced of a result. But seeing this rigorously applied in a situation where the consequences of error meant that pregnancies were resulting in miscarriages, stillbirths, and children with medical problems, I realized I was making a value judgement. In other issues of public health and safety — bomb threats, possible epidemics, etc.— we do not insist on 95 percent probability of harmful consequences before action is taken. Why is that the criterion in environmental health? (Paigen, 1982:32)

A high standard of statistical significance creates a relatively large number of false negatives —studies erroneously concluding that a substance is safe. False negatives provide no scientific justification for protecting the public's health even though the public may face risks. In contrast, a low standard of statistical significance creates a relatively large number of false positives — studies erroneously concluding that a substance is dangerous. False positives provide a scientific rationale for requiring industries to change their waste disposal practices though the change may not be necessary (Van Doren, 1996). In other words, there is no way to be neutral about mathematical criteria when they are used to evaluate studies of the health effects of industrial pollution. If you demand a high standard of proof before calling a study valid, you automatically side with the industry that produces the substance. If you accept a lower standard of proof, you side with the community exposed to it. The new attention to this reality has given at least some investigators reason to work on environmental health studies even when they expect the results to be deemed scientifically weak.

Conclusion

If science reflects the culture in which scientists live, then as cultures change so should science. We are now in the midst of an important cultural change as increasing numbers of people agree with environmentalists that nature is fragile, interconnected, organically whole, and vulnerable to harm from non-natural forces. It is still too early to know for sure that this cultural change will fundamentally affect the environmental health sciences. But some environmental epidemiologists are designing innovative ways to study the effects of industrial toxins on public health, ways that are less reductionist than traditional epidemiology and less reflective of the old pre-environmentalist assumptions that nature is basically strong and sturdy. As a consequence, there are now new reasons to expect that environmental health research will show a positive correlation between a community's diseases and its exposure to industrial pollution.

It is important to point out that the authors of these new studies are not necessarily passive receivers of environmentalist ideas. Many of the scientists I have referred to in this paper are active participants in the environmental movement. (They work for environmental organizations; they write for publications that explicitly identify with the movement's goals; they speak at movement events.) This state of affairs seldom gets attention from scholars examining the effect of culture on science. Social constructivists tend to portray scientists as living in a sea of unexamined cultural assumptions that they involuntarily replicate in their research. But in periods of social change, when the old assumptions are contested, scientists are more likely to pay attention to the ideas guiding their work. If they find incongruities between what they hold true about the world and the regular practices in their field, then they are apt to search for new ways to conduct their investigations. In the case of environmental epidemiology, we have seen scientists, many of whom publicly identify with the environmental movement, consciously trying to do studies that will show that great harm is likely to occur when people treat nature as a mere means to an end. That is, like all scientists, they assume their job is to describe reality to the best of their ability.

Recognizing the work that some epidemiologists are doing to develop a science more in keeping with environmentalist principles suggests two kinds of relations between culture and science. In one, described by scholars such as Keller, Haraway, Martin, and Krieger and Fee, scientists unconsciously design studies that reproduce undemocratic and inegalitarian values. The bias in their research goes largely unnoticed as long as the values are uncontested. In another, the kind I describe here, scientists struggle to invent ways to investigate the world that will be consistent with new democratic, egalitarian (or in this case, environmentalist) values. The bias in these investigations is more likely to be noticed both because the underlying values are new and because the results often imply the need for new public policies.[7]

Of course the results do not always do so. In the case of environmental epidemiology, if a suspect pollutant or group of pollutants is not in fact harmful to human health, even environmentalist investigators will eventually discover that it is safe, as long as their research projects are careful and honest. By the same token, careful studies on environmental pollutants by industry scientists sometimes show those pollutants to be hazardous. In other words, the actual properties of chemicals are not infinitely malleable by values. My point in this essay has been that values influence scientists, not that values predetermine the outcome of research.

7 There is a third possible relationship between scientific practices and culture. In this one, scientists unconsciously design studies reflective of democratic, egalitarian, environmentalist values. This relation happens, or will happen, when such values are so widely embraced by the general public that they become simple common sense and a science unreflective of them seems, to most people, to have a political agenda.

References

Arnold, S. F., et al. (1996). Synergistic Activism of Estrogen Receptor with Combinations of Environmental Chemicals. *Science, 272*, 1489-1492.

Been, V. (1994). Locally Undesirable Land Uses in Minority Neighborhoods: Disproportionate Siting or Market Dynamics? *Yale Law Journal, 103*(6), 1383-1422.

Berney, B. (1993). Round and Round it Goes: The Epidemiology of Childhood Lead Poisoning, 1950-1990. *The Milbank Quarterly, 71*(1), 3-39.

Bookchin, M. (1962). *Our Synthetic Environment*. New York: Knopf.

Botkin, D. B. (1990). *Discordant Harmonies. A New Ecology for the Twenty-First Century*. New York: Oxford University Press.

Brechin, S. R. and Kempton, W. (1994). Global Environmentalism: A Challenge to the Postmaterialist Thesis? *Social Science Quarterly, 75*(2), 245-269.

Brown, P. and Mikkelsen, E. J. (1990). *No Safe Place: Toxic Waste, Leukemia, and Community Action*. Berkeley: University of California Press.

Brulle, R. J. (2000). *Agency, Democracy, and Nature: The U.S. Environmental Movement from a Critical Theory Perspective*. Cambridge, MA: MIT Press.

Buffler, P. A. and Kyle, A. D. (1999). Carcinogen Risk Assessment Guidelines and Children. *Environmental Health Perspectives, 107*(6), A286-A289.

Carson, R. (1962). *Silent Spring*. Boston: Houghton Mifflin.

Colborn, T., Dumanoski, D., and Myers, J. P. (1997). *Our Stolen Future*. New York: Plume/Penguin Press.

Commoner, B. (1966). *Science and Survival*. New York: The Viking Press.

Commoner, B. (1972). *The Closing Circle: Man, Nature and Technology*. New York: Bantam Books.

Cortese, A. (1996). Endocrine Disruption. *Environmental Science and Technology, 30*(5), 213A-215A.

Cranor, C. F. (1990). Some Moral Issues in Risk Assessment. *Ethics, 101*, 123-143.

Cronon, W. (Ed.). (1995). *Uncommon Ground: Toward Reinventing Nature*. New York: W.W. Norton.

Cuoto, R. A. (1986). Failing Health and New Prescriptions: Community-based Approaches to Environmental Risks. In C. E. Hill (Ed.), *Current Health Policy Issues and Alternatives*. Athens: University of Georgia Press.

Dryzek, J. (1997). *The Politics of the Earth: Environmental Discourses*. New York: Oxford University Press.

Dubos, R. (1965). *Man Adapting*. New Haven: Yale University Press.

Dunlap, R. E. (1991). Public Opinion in the 1980s: Clear Consensus about the Environment. *Environment, 33*(2), 8.

Dunlap, R. E., Gallup, G. H., and Gallup, A. M. (1992). *The Health of the Planet Survey: A Preliminary Report on Attitudes on the Environment and Economic Growth Measured by Surveys of Citizens in 22 Nations to Date* (A George H. Gallopp Memorial Survey). Princeton, NJ: The George Gallup International Institute.

Epstein, S. S. (1978). *The Politics of Cancer*. San Francisco: Sierra Club Books.

Erickson, K. (1994). *A New Species of Trouble: Explorations of Disaster, Trauma, and Community*. New York: W.W. Norton.

Feyerabend, P. K. (1975). *Against Method*. London: New Left Books.

Gamson, W. A., and Modigliani, A. (1989). Media Discourse and Public Opinion on Nuclear Power: A Constructionist Approach. *American Journal of Sociology, 95*(1), 1-37.

Gibbs, L. M. (1982). *Love Canal: My Story*. Albany: State University of New York Press.

Goehl, T. J. (1997). Playing in the Sand. *Environmental Health Perspectives, 105*(6), 564-565.

Goldsteen, R. L. and Schorr, J. K. (1991). *Demanding Democracy After Three Mile Island*. Gainsville: University of Florida Press.

Gottlieb, R. (1993). *Forcing the Spring: The Transformation of the American Environmental Movement*. Washington, D.C.: Island Press.

Gough, M. (1986). *Dioxin, Agent Orange: The Facts*. New York: Plenum Press.

Gould, S. J. (1981). *The Mismeasure of Man*. New York: W.W. Norton.

Greenland, S. (Ed.). (1987). *Evolution of Epidemiologic Ideas: Annotated Readings on Concepts and Methods*. Chestnut Hill, MA: Epidemiology Resources, Inc.

Griffith, J. D., Duncan, R., and Hulka, B. S. (1990). *Biological Markers in Epidemiology*. New York: Oxford University Press.

Haraway, D. (1987). Animal Sociology and a Natural Economy of the Body Politic. In S. Harding and J. F. O'Barr (Eds.), *Sex and Scientific Inquiry*. Chicago: University of Chicago Press.

Harding, S. G. (1986). *The Science Question in Feminism*. Ithaca: Cornell University Press.

Harlow, S. D. and Linet, M. (1989). Agreement Between Questionnaire Data and Medical Records: The Evidence for Accuracy of Recall. *American Journal of Epidemiology, 129*(2), 232-248.

Haynes, R. C. (1997). The Road to Justice. *Environmental Health Perspectives, 105*(9), 920-922.

Hays, S. P. (1987). *Beauty, Health, and Permanence: Environmental Politics in the United States, 1955-1985*. New York: Cambridge University Press.

Hook, G. E. R. and Lucier, G. W. (1997). Synergy, Antagonism, and Scientific Process. *Environmental Health Perspectives, 105*(8), 784.

Keller, E. F. (1987). *A Feeling for the Organism: The Life and Work of Barbara McClintock*. New York: W.H. Freeman.

Krewski, D. and Thomas, R.D. (1992). Carcinogenic Mixtures. *Risk Analysis, 12*(1), 105-113.

Kriebel, D., et al. (2001). The Precautionary Principle in Environmental Science. *Environmental Health Perspectives, 109*(9), 871-876.

Krieger, N. and Fee, E. (1994). Man-made Medicine and Women's Health: The Biopolitics of Sex/Gender and Race/Ethnicity. *International Journal of Health Services, 24*, 265-283.

Krimsky, S., and Plough, A. (1988). *Environmental Hazards: Communicating Risks as a Social Process*. Dover, MA: Auburn House.

Kuhn, T. (1962). *The Structure of Scientific Revolutions*. Chicago: University of Chicago Press.

Latour, B. (1990). *We Have Never Been Modern*. New York: Harvester Wheatsheaf.

Leopold, A. (1966). *A Sand County Almanac: With Other Essays on Conservation from Round River*. New York: Oxford University Press.

Levine, A. G. (1982). *Love Canal: Science, Politics, and People*. Lexington, MA: Lexington Books.

Longino, H. E. (1990). *Science and Social Knowledge: Values and Objectivity in Social Inquiry*. Princeton: Princeton University Press.

Martin, E. (1991). The Egg and the Sperm: How Science Has Constructed a Romance Based on Stereotypical Male-female Roles. *Signs: Journal of Women in Culture and Society, 16*(3), 485-501.

Mazur, A. (1998). *A Hazardous Inquiry: The Rashomon Effect at Love Canal*. Cambridge: Harvard University Press.

McKinney, J. D. (1997). Interactive Hormonal Activity of Chemical Mixtures. *Environmental Health Perspectives, 105*(9), 896.

Milbrath, L. W. (1984). *Environmentalists: Vanguard for a New Society*. Albany: SUNY Press.

NAACP-Flint Chapter vs. John Engler, Governor, State of Michigan (Circuit Court for the County of Genesee, MI 1997).

Nash, R. F. (1989). *The Rights of Nature: A History of Environmental Ethics*. Madison: University of Wisconsin Press.

National Research Council. (1983). *Risk Assessment in the Federal Government: Managing the Process*. Washington, D.C.: National Academy Press.

National Research Council. (1991). *Environmental Epidemiology: Public Health and Hazardous Waste* (Vol. 1). Washington D.C.: National Academy Press.

National Research Council. (1993). *Pesticides in the Diets of Infants and Children*. Washington, D.C.: National Academy Press.

National Research Council. (1996). *Science and Judgement in Risk Assessment*. Washington, D.C.: National Academy Press.

Natural Resources Defense Council. (1989). *Intolerable Risk: Pesticides in Our Children's Food*. New York: NRDC.

O'Brien, M. H. (2000). When Harm is Not Necessary: Risk Assessment as Diversion. In R. Hofrichter (Ed.), *Reclaiming the Environmental Debate: The Politics of Health in a Toxic Culture*. Cambridge: The MIT Press.

Ozonoff, D., and Boden, L. I. (1987). Truth and Consequences: Health Agency Responses to Environmental Health Problems. *Science, Technology and Human Values, 12*(3), 70-77.

Paigen, B. (1982). Controversy at Love Canal. *Hastings Center Report, 12*(3), 29-37.

Perera, F. (1987). The Potential Usefulness of Biological Markers in Risk Assessment. *Environmental Health Perspectives, 76*(3), 141-145.

Proctor, R. N. (1995). *Cancer Wars: How Politics Shapes What We Know and Don't Know About Cancer*. New York: Basic Books.

Rauber, P. (1998). New! Improved! Destroys the Environment! *Sierra, 83*(3), 56-59.

Rochon, T. R. (1998). *Culture Moves: Ideas, Activism, and Changing Values*. Princeton: Princeton University Press.

Rosenbaum, W. A. (1995). More Choice: Risk Assessment. *In Environmental Politics and Policy*. Washington, DC: Congressional Quarterly Press.

Rothman, K. (1990). A Sobering Look at the Cluster Busters' Conference. *American Journal of Epidemiology, 132*(supplement 1), s6-s13.

Sander, G. (Ed.). (1987). *Evolution of Epidemiologic Ideas: Annotated Readings on Concepts and Methods*. Chestnut Hill, MA: Epidemiology Resources, Inc.

Schmidt, C. W. (2001a). A Growth Spurt in Children's Health Laws. *Environmental Health Perspectives, 109*(6), A267-A273.

Schmidt, C. W. (2001b). The Lowdown on Low-dose Endocrine Disruptors. *Environmental Health Perspectives, 109*(9), A420-A421.

Silbergeld, E. K. (1993). The Risks of Risk Assessment. *New Solutions, 3*(2), 43-44.

Szasz, A., and Meuser, M. (1997). Environmental Inequalities: Literature Review and Proposals for New Directions in Research and Theory. *Current Sociology, 45*(3), 99-120.

Tal, A. (1997). Assessing the Environmental Movement's Attitudes Toward Risk Assessment. *Environmental Science and Technology, 31*(10), 470A-476A.

Tesh, S. N. (1988). *Hidden Arguments: Political Ideology and Disease Causality*. New Brunswick, NJ: Rutgers University Press.

Tesh, S. N. (2000). *Uncertain Hazards: Environmental Activists and Scientific Proof.* Ithaca: Cornell University Press.

U.S. Environmental Protection Agency. (1994). *Health Assessment Document for 2,3,7,8-Tetracholodibenzo-p-dioxin and Related Compounds (DRAFT)*. Washington D.C.: U.S. EPA.

U.S. Environmental Protection Agency. (1999). *Report of the Title VI Implementation Advisory Committee: Next Steps for EPA, State, and Local Environmental Justice Programs* (No. EPA #100-4-99-004). Washington, D.C.: The National Advisory Council for Environmental Protection and Technology.

U.S. General Accounting Office. (1991). *Superfund: Public Health Assessments Incomplete and of Questionable Value* (No. GAO/RCED-91-178). Washington, D.C.: General Accounting Office.

United Church of Christ/Commission on Racial Justice. (1987). *Toxic Wastes and Race in the United States: A National Report on the Racial and Socio-Economic Characteristics of Communities with Hazardous Waste Cites.* New York: United Church of Christ.

Vainio, H., and Husgafvel-Pursianen, K. (1995). Elimination of Environmental Factors or Elimination of Individuals: Biomarkers and Prevention. *Journal of Occupational and Environmental Medicine, 37*, 12-13.

Van Doren, P. M. (1996). The Effects of Exposure to "Synthetic" Chemicals on Human Health: A Review. *Risk Analysis, 16*(3), 367-376.

Verchick, R. R. M. (1996). In a Greener Voice: Feminist Theory and Environmental Justice. *Harvard Women's Law Journal, 19*(2), 23-88.

White, L., Jr. (1967). The Historical Roots of Our Ecological Crisis. *Science, 155*(3767), 1203-1207.

Zavestoski, S., et al. (2002). Science, Policy Activism, and War: Defining the Health of Gulf War Veterans. *Science, Technology & Human Values, 27*(2), 171-205.

2

LOOKING UPSTREAM

Virginia Ashby Sharpe, Ph.D.*

The gaps between different cultural views of risk are not the kind that can be bridged with quantitative methods.

—*Alistair Woodward, 1999:365*

It is the social feelings that matter, not exposure to a supposedly toxic material environment. The material environment is merely the indelible mark and constant reminder ... of one's social exclusion and devaluation as a human being.

—*Richard G. Wilkinson, 1996:215*

Introduction

Sandra Steingraber opens her beautiful and powerful book, *Living Downstream*, with the following story about a village along a river: "The residents who live here, according to parable, began noticing increasing numbers of drowning people caught in the river's swift current and so went to work inventing ever more elaborate technologies to resuscitate them. So preoccupied were these heroic villagers with rescue and treatment that they never thought to look upstream to see who was pushing the victims in" (Steingraber, 1998:xxii).

* Virginia Ashby Sharpe is Director of the Integrity in Science Project at the Center for Science in the Public Interest (CPSI), a consumer advocacy organization in Washington, DC. Before her move to CSPI, she was Deputy Director of the Hastings Center in Garrison, NY. The aim of the Integrity in Science Project is to advocate for greater scrutiny of the commercialization of science and the role of industry in science-based policy. Dr. Sharpe received her B.A. from Smith College and her Ph.D. in philosophy and bioethics from Georgetown University. Her areas of research include ethical issues in the structure and delivery of health care, integrity in science, environmental justice, children's environmental health, women's health issues, and the science, politics, and ethics of wolf restoration. She is the treasurer of Feminist Ethics and Social Theory (F.E.A.S.T.), a professional organization dedicated to promoting feminist ethical perspectives on philosophy; moral, social and political life; law; and public policy.

The metaphor of upriver events and downstream effects offers at least two important insights. One is that proximate causes are not necessarily the only or even the most important ones in understanding a problem or its possible solutions. The second is that the most visible effects of a problem, though often the starkest and most repugnant, are not the only evidence that we have of the problem. In this paper, I urge us to look upstream from environmental inequalities to see what might be required for environmental justice as it has been richly defined for this volume. Specifically, if we are to make good on the vision of justice captured in Bunyan Bryant's definition, we will need to look beyond the current stories of cause and effect that motivate much of the institutional and professional attention to the issue of disproportionate environmental risk and burden.

In what follows, I attempt to do this by drawing on epidemiological evidence that has been collected over the last 30 years concerning the relationship between justice, health, and human development. I will make use of some of this evidence to shed light on the goals of environmental justice.

Beginning with Aristotle's formal conception of justice that "equals are treated equally and unequals may be treated unequally," I distinguish between inequality in an absolute or moral sense and inequality in a relative sense referring to material differences between people. Because liberal democracies are built on the assumption of moral equality between people (no person is unequal in the absolute sense), their task is to determine which material or relative inequalities are unjust or unfair. The argument given here is that a just, flourishing, and healthy society is one that sustains human capabilities by reducing the relative income disparities. Given this, I argue that social policies aimed at redistribution of wealth will be required to achieve environmental justice in the broadest sense.

Causes and Effects

The most heated debates in the environmental justice literature focus on two questions. One is whether racial and economic minorities in and outside the U.S. bear a greater risk of exposure to potentially harmful toxins than do whites and others who are politically and economically advantaged. The other debate affirms the premise of disproportionate burden and centers on whether these differential risks are the result of discrimination. The first debate is about effects; the second is about cause.

Effects

Quantitative risk assessment is one of the principal tools in the debate about effects and has played a major role in setting the terms of that debate. In its 1983 report, *Risk Assessment in the Federal Government: Managing the Process*, the National Academy of Sciences established quantitative risk assessment as the authoritative method for establishing the factual basis for environmental decision-making. One of the report's major recommendations was that agencies maintain a "clear conceptual distinction between the assessment of risks and considerations of risk management alternatives, that is, the scientific findings and policy judgments embodied in risk assessment, should be distinguished from the political, economic, and technical considerations that influence the design and choice of regulatory strategies" (National Academy of Sciences, 1983:7). Putting aside questions about the legitimacy of such a distinction (e.g., whether the factual and evaluative dimensions of risk can be neatly separated, and whether a methodological reliance on technical expertise *de facto* excludes a community-based approach to risk management (Burke, 1996), risk assessment applied to the question of disproportionate burdens on minority communities has led to evidentiary battles over the health impacts of, for example, exposure to dioxins, arsenic, and petrochemicals in "cancer alley". These contests over the accuracy of data have led to either infinite delay on the management side or temporary stopgap measures that leave communities feeling cheated and disenfranchised.

In his controversial book *The Promise and Peril of Environmental Justice*, Christopher Foreman argued that studies offered to substantiate claims of disproportionate environmental impacts on minority and low-income communities are highly questionable, having severe methodological and evidentiary limitations (Foreman, 1998). Foreman disputes any proven causal relationship between industrial activities and adverse health effects on minority communities except for lead exposure in minority children and chemical exposure in farm workers. In the end, Foreman suggests that "health" understood in the more inclusive sense of "quality of life" may better describe the aspirations of those fighting for environmental justice (Foreman, 1998:88). I will return to this point later in the chapter. For now, it is enough to point out that the notion of "quality of life" substantially broadens the scope of relevant "effects" beyond the standard biophysiological targets of risk assessment.

Causes

Anyone who has written, read about, or been active around environmental racism is familiar with the debate about whether certain land uses, for example, really *are* evidence of racism. The debate essentially comes down to whether it can be proven that the siting of a locally unwanted land use (LULUs) in a minority community is discriminatory. This determination is required if legal redress is to be sought under the equal protection clause in the 14th Amendment to the U.S. Constitution. A valid equal protection claim in an environmental justice lawsuit requires proof that the defendant intended to discriminate against the plaintiff. The best example of this debate is "which came first, the dump or the minority community?" The argument is that if the dump came first and the minorities moved in afterwards on the basis of affordability, this does not constitute racism or discrimination because these people made a voluntary choice to move into the neighborhood (Been, 1993:1014).

The data I will provide on what is known as "capability deprivation" (Sen, 1999:20) reveal that injustice is something that arises from economic and political factors more subtle and far reaching than whether a particular land use is intentionally racist. One of the obvious problems with the argument that the location of a dump in a minority community is not racist because minorities voluntarily chose to move or stay there is it assumes that "residential mobility" and the "dynamics of the housing market" (Boerner and Lambert, 1994:16) are somehow benign or morally neutral. However, understanding the afflictions of inequality means recognizing not simply the harms associated with intentional discrimination or even the immediate and proximate dangers of toxic materials, but also the "toxicity of social circumstances and patterns of social organization" (Wilkinson, 1996).

Justice and Equality

In *Nicomachean Ethics*, Aristotle provides us with one of the earliest and most influential articulations of justice in the philosophical tradition. In its most general sense, he says, justice means that equals are treated equally and unequals may be treated unequally (Aristotle, 1131a:20-30). How this abstract principle has been filled in and translated into public policy is nothing less than the history of political philosophy, economics, and the ongoing battleground of local, national and international politics. For Aristotle, the question of justice is fundamentally an ethical question about what constitutes a good, healthy, and flourishing society. In trying to make sense of what Aristotle might mean by a just society allowing for unequal treatment, it is helpful to make a distinction between equality in the *absolute* sense and equality in the *relative* sense.

Absolute Inequality

If we say that "X is not equal to Y" in the absolute sense we are making a judgment that Y is somehow superior to X because Y has some characteristic that X does not have. Throughout human history we have drawn boundary lines around the moral sphere or the sphere of moral consideration. Those inside the sphere are considered to be equal by virtue of some shared characteristic such as white skin and male gender (the U.S. Constitution's basis for excluding people of color and white women from full citizenship) and property ownership (the basis for excluding non-property owners from voting and other forms of political participation). Those lacking particular qualifications are seen as morally inferior and therefore not entitled to equal treatment or consideration.

One of the great moral triumphs of liberal democracy is its premise that human dignity and self-determination are by themselves a sufficient basis for inclusion in the moral sphere. The antidote to the exclusion of people based on arbitrary characteristics of race, class, religion, gender, religion, and sexual orientation is the doctrine that all humans are morally equal by virtue of their dignity and autonomy. This philosophical conception of moral equality has been the basis for the guarantee of civil and political rights in the United States and around the world. It is also the basis by which we judge actions and policies to be racist, classist, sexist, bigoted, prejudiced, or discriminatory. In the context of environmental injustice, appeals to the equal protection clause succeed on the basis of a compelling argument that the defendant's actions stemmed from such a belief.[1]

Relative Inequality

To say that two people are not equal *relatively speaking* is to say that they are differently situated. The key moral question here is which differences of situation are morally important. That is, which inequalities, for example of health, income, material circumstances, opportunity, gender, ethnicity, or age, are unjust or unfair and which are not. In our country Medicare and Medicaid

1 Equal protection claims are predicated on the assumption that racism is "a discrete and hostile act." As Laura Pulido has observed, however, this narrow definition of racism misses the fact that racism and white privilege are structural phenomena that saturate our institutions. Thus, to combat environmental racism, it is not enough to look for it in intentional acts.(See Pulido, 2000).

which are intended to assure healthcare access to the elderly and the poor, respectively, the Americans with Disabilities Act (ADA) which is intended to assure equal access and opportunity to the disabled, and affirmative action which is intended to assure equal citizenship, access, and opportunity to those historically disenfranchised from political, civil, and economic participation are all policies seeking to remedy relative inequalities that are seen to be unfair or unjust. The ADA, for example, establishes that it is unfair to be excluded from access to a job for which you are qualified simply because you can't walk up the stairs to the office. The pressure to abandon these policies, to curtail affirmative action, and to cut back Medicaid are often, by contrast, based on the belief that inequalities in income and opportunity are *not* unjust and therefore require no remedy. This view is best reflected in the libertarian axiom that such inequalities may be "unfortunate but they are not unfair" (Nozick, 1974).

In the libertarian philosophy that undergirds much of conservative laissez-faire capitalism, the solution to relative inequalities is not redistribution, as in a "welfare state," but rather market transactions that allow people the liberty to remove themselves from undesirable situations. This view shows up in environmental justice literature in a number of ways.

First, a free-market libertarian would likely argue that those who move into areas environmentally degraded by dumps, toxic sites, and so forth do so voluntarily and freely. If, as libertarians believe, justice is freedom and freedom is not violated, then there is no injustice. Second, if people freely accept compensation for bearing particular burdens — such as living near an undesirable land use or selling their toxic home or land to a polluting company, then their liberty has been respected, and again there has been no injustice done. From this perspective, the solution to relative inequalities is not regulation or redistributive social practices, but discrete market transactions that respect individual liberty. A third way that free-market libertarianism shows up in environmental justice debates is grounded in this philosophy's emblematic assumption that one is free to do anything as long as it does not harm or pose undue risk on someone without his or her consent. Giving absolute priority to the principle of liberty in this way places the all important burden of proof on aggrieved parties to prove that they have been involuntarily harmed or placed at risk. The issue of the burden of proof is another important battleground in the debate over environmental justice.

Following this libertarian approach, a free-market, anti-regulatory philosophy favors placing the burden on potential claimants to prove harm or undue risk. The rationale here again is that liberty is paramount, and restrictions to liberty constitute unjust interference. In the case of a siting decision, for example, a company subscribing to this philosophy would assert that its liberty must be unrestrained — its activities unregulated — unless it can be proven that its activities are dangerous. Environmental justice advocates including Robert Bullard, Bunyan Bryant, and others (Bullard, 1994; Bryant, 1995; Earth Charter, 2002; Steingraber, 1997) articulate a precautionary principle that essentially shifts the burden of proof, requiring that the proponents of an activity (such as a power generating plant, an incinerator, a hazardous waste facility, or a nuclear power plant) prove that it is safe or will not cause significant harm. As John Bailar (Bailar and Bailar, 1999) and others have observed, the obstacles to proving either harm or safety are enormous. These include determining the scope of the impact(s) (who or what will be affected: children, adults, property, animals, ecosystems, future generations, etc?); the nature and magnitude of impact(s) (great or minimal? causing disease, death, or reduced quality of life?); the scale of the impact(s) (short-term, long-term?); the probability of the impact(s) (likelihood?); and the acceptable level of harm or safety (value trade-offs such as jobs vs. a healthy environment).

Those who argue for a more precautionary approach believe that given what we know about the hazards of modern industrial life, it no longer makes sense that the enormous obstacles to proof should be borne by the public — a fact only underscored by the apparently unequal distribution of burdens. Supporters of a preventive or precautionary approach also argue that the current burden of proof has provided an opportunity for infinite delay as adversaries spend years contesting the meaning of data. As Bryant has argued, "causality arguments or issues of certainty are often used to rationalize inaction, particularly when it has been economically or politically expedient to do so" (Bryant, 1995:10). We have ample evidence of such delays in the debate over dredging PCBs from the Hudson River and the harms associated with cigarette smoking. Though I believe that we as a nation should move toward the adoption of a more precautionary approach to the introduction of new technologies and the production and siting of known hazardous materials, I also believe that the debate about the burden of proof as well as many of the ongoing debates over the empirical evidence linking exposure to adverse health effects represent an impasse in the environmental justice literature. I'm not suggesting that risk assessment is unimportant or that a broader public policy conversation about the burden of proof should not go forward. What I am suggesting, however, is that we need a new perspective on these debates to move us toward the achievement of a more just and healthy society, and one that includes more than environmental risk factors and the impact of biophysiological insults. In other words, to have a more robust understanding of environmental justice we need to look at the conditions "upstream" that broadly determine the health of society.

In the service of this broader conception of "the environment," "environmental risk factors," and "environmental health," I'd like to make good on my promise to share data on "the social determinants of health" — data that challenge the prevailing assumption of an inherent tension between progress and social justice and between economic efficiency and equity; data that help us to understand what is at stake in relative inequality.

The Social Determinants of Health

The 1974 World Population Conference in Bucharest, Romania represented a turning point in the global understanding of the relationship between population and development. For decades, the working assumption of Western development experts was that population growth was a cause, if not the cause, of underdevelopment. On the basis of this assumption, national and international policy promoted population control initiatives, sometimes coercive ones, as the means to economic growth and progress. At the conference, Third-World delegations turned this assumption on its head. Population growth, they argued, was not the cause of underdevelopment, it was the consequence (Conroy, 1981). Empirical evidence from Kerala, India, for example, gave rise to the view that underdevelopment was the result of systemic inequalities which in turn led to uncontrolled population growth. The evidence established that population growth would be reliably curbed only by the eradication of infant mortality and inequities in income and improved education and economic participation. In Kerala, healthcare and nutrition initiatives, property ownership by women, and programs to eliminate illiteracy, especially among women, resulted in zero population growth. In other words, women's increased social and political participation meant they were able to develop capabilities other than childbearing as a means of social participation. The evidence from Kerala indicated that the enhancement of social justice for women and children was the best means by which to slow population growth and to enhance overall life expectancy (Ratcliffe, 1977; Sen, 1999).

Since then, evidence has mounted that just as social factors such as gender equity, literacy, and maternal and child health services influence the rate of reproduction, so do social factors influence the life expectancy of groups both within and between societies. More specifically, the evidence suggests that greater equity in society also produces greater overall health.

For over a century, epidemiological studies — that is, studies of health and disease in populations rather than individuals — have shown that differences in social position are closely related to health and longevity within societies.

For example, in a developed country, the wealthy may have a life expectancy two to four times higher than the poor (Wilkinson, 1996; Daniels, et al., 1999). A conclusion long drawn from these data was that the wealthier the person or society, the healthier it would be. If we were to chart this conclusion on a graph, we would show that as income increased, so too would life expectancy (Figure 1). This conclusion has, in part, provided support for arguments that increases in income alone will improve health status. It was not until international comparisons were conducted that we began to understand that the relationship between health and income is more complex.

Figure 1: The conventional wisdom about the relationship between wealth and health (life expectancy)

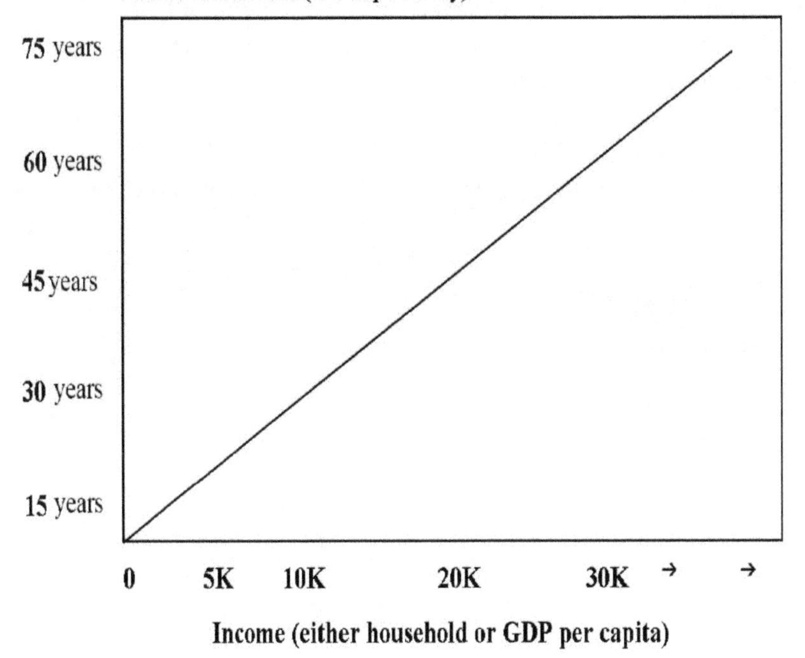

The 1998 United Nations Human Development Report showed that once a country passes a threshold level of income, its entire population "can be more than twice as rich as another without being any healthier"(Wilkinson, 1996:3) (Figure 2). The difference in per capita gross domestic product (GDP) between the United States and Costa Rica, for example, is roughly $21,000. However, Costa Rica's life expectancy exceeds that of the United States. Likewise, Cuba has a life expectancy on par with the U.S., but a per capita GDP roughly one-fifth of our country. These and similar data amassed over the last 30 years by eight research groups in ten different sets of data indicate that there is something other than wealth that produces relatively healthier societies and something other than income poverty that produces relative illness. Cross-national comparisons show that health disparities are correlated with relative disparities in socioeconomic status. What matters most in the achievement of health in a society is the size of the gap between its rich and poor members, that is, the relative income inequality of the society. The wider the gap, the lower the overall life expectancy. The narrower the gap, the higher the life expectancy. In some of the most striking research, for example, an analysis of the relationship between the poorest 20 percent of the population and the richest five percent showed that the higher the income of the richest or the wider the income differences within a society, the higher infant mortality rates were for the society overall (Wilkinson, 1996). The healthiest societies, by contrast, were the most egalitarian societies.

Figure 2: The relationship between country wealth and life expectancy

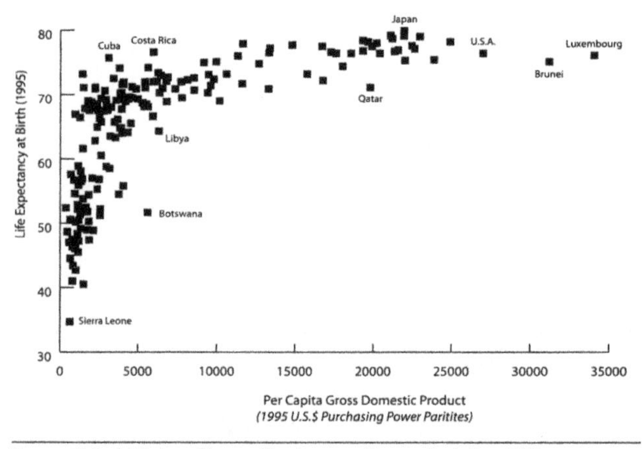

Source: United Nations Human Development Report Statistics, 1998.

From: Daniels, N., Kennedy, B. Kawachi, I. Why justice is good for our health: The social determinants of health inequalities. *Daedalus* 1999, 128(4) 215-252.

Additional research has shed light on the specific ways in which social inequalities adversely affect the overall health of a society by creating and systematically depriving an underclass. In the United States, "the most inegalitarian states with respect to income distribution invest less in public education, have larger uninsured populations, and spend less on social safety nets" (Daniels, et al., 1999:223). Similarly, as Figure 3 shows, homicide rates among states in the U.S. correlate with the percentage of total household income received by the least well off 50 percent. In 1990, Louisiana and Mississippi — the states where the poor receive the smallest share of its state's total household income — had the highest homicide rates. By contrast, the lowest homicide rates occur in states with the most egalitarian distribution of income.

Figure 3: The relationship between income distribution and homicide among the states of the USA in 1990

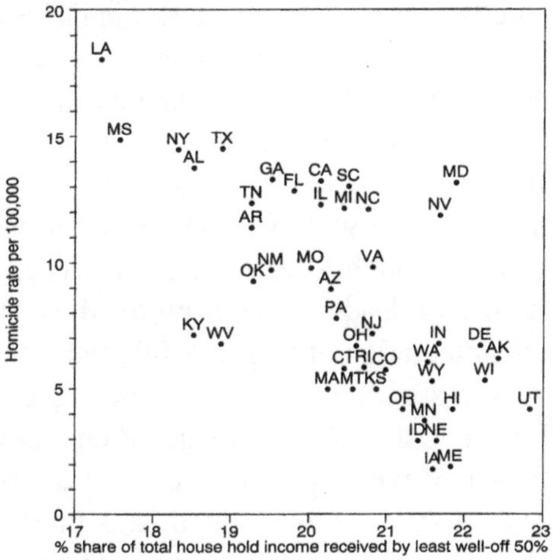

From: Wilkinson, R. 1996.*Unhealthy Societies: The Afflictions of Inequality.* New York: Routledge, p. 157.

What these data indicate is that in societies where basic needs of food, clothing, shelter, and sanitation have been met, health differences are explained by relative deprivation within the society. Since basic needs have been met, this deprivation refers not to material necessities, but to what Amartya Sen has called "capabilities" or the various political, economic, and social freedoms that enable people to lead lives that they have reason to value. These deprivations of the underclass reinforce and promote a loss of social cohesion and undermine the overall health of society.

It might be useful at this point to provide an example not from social science, but from literature. In his brilliant 1940 novel *Native Son*, Richard Wright paints a searing picture of the destructive force of racism and classism through the tragic intersection of the lives of Bigger Thomas, a young, poor black man, and the Daltons, a wealthy white family. At the beginning of the book, we see Bigger, his mother, and two siblings waking up in their one room, rat-infested apartment. The apartment is in Chicago's "Black Belt" — the only area of the city where white real estate owners will rent to black people. Bigger has a job interview that night with Mr. Dalton, and his mother's anxiety makes it clear that the well-being of the family depends on Bigger's taking the job. Mr. and Mrs. Dalton are privileged by wealth, race, and social position. They see it as their obligation to help the less fortunate make something of themselves. They offer Bigger a job as their chauffeur, replacing another black man whom they had helped put through night school. Mary, the Dalton's daughter, a spoiled and naive, but well-meaning college student believes that communism will resolve racial and economic divisions. Without understanding Bigger's vulnerability as a black man in a white society and as a poor black employee to a wealthy family, Mary flouts social taboos and insists on treating Bigger as if there were no differences between them, sitting in the front seat of the car with him and making him eat with her and her boyfriend at a restaurant in Bigger's neighborhood. Through a series of events, Bigger's fear, shame, confusion, and marginalization leads to the death of Mary Dalton. Her death not only results in the disintegration of Bigger's life, but also creates a frenzy of fear, distrust, and social disruption in Chicago. The tragic irony of the story lies in the fact that Mr. Dalton, though he extends his charity to Bigger, is also the owner of the South Side Development Company, the real estate company from which the Thomas family rents their squalid apartment for eight dollars a month, more than whites are charged for comparable housing. When at the coroner's inquest, Mr. Dalton is asked why he doesn't simply charge blacks less rent rather than compensating some with charity, he says that it would be "unethical" to undersell his competitors (Wright, 1940:278). When he is further asked whether he thought conditions under which the Thomas family lived in his rental apartment might in some way have contributed to the death of his daughter, he says, "I don't know what you mean" (Wright, 1940:279). In his final statement to the court hearing Bigger's trial, Bigger's lawyer reiterates the upstream conditions of American society in 1940 that culminated in the death of Mary Dalton. "Taken collectively, [American Negroes] are not simply twelve million people; in reality they constitute a separate nation, stunted, stripped, and held captive *within* this nation, devoid of political, social, economic, and property rights" (Wright, 1940:333). Those who today argue that market forces such as residential mobility bring poor residents voluntarily to environmentally degraded areas would do well to reflect on the ways in which today's market conditions similarly force particular housing choices.

The Civil Rights Movement and subsequent legislation from the 1960s and 1970s has provided the basis for equal opportunity for people of color, the poor, and women in this country. During this same period, it has been argued that many of the burdens of industrial development — the so-called "externalities" of waste, noise, odor, poor housing, fragmented neighborhoods, and illness — have fallen disproportionately on these groups. As I mentioned earlier, Christopher Foreman and others have argued that other than lead exposure in minority children and chemical exposure in farm workers, studies to substantiate claims of disproportionate environmental impacts on minority and low-income communities are highly questionable having severe methodological and evidentiary limitations (Foreman, 1998). Foreman acknowledges that it may be "quality of life" rather than "health" narrowly understood that best describes the aspirations of those fighting for environmental justice (Foreman, 1998:88).

Foreman's distinction between health and quality of life is important because it highlights a pervasive and often implicit assumption that health is reducible to the absence of disease. This definition of health is, of course, a by-product of our medical paradigm. If we think about health within the broader public health and development paradigms, however, we get a much richer conception of what it would mean to be healthy both as a society and as an individual.

From the perspective of public health and development, health is not simply the absence of disease, but rather it is the use of one's human capabilities to lead a life that one has reason to value (Sen, 1999). Evidence from public health and development literature indicates that psychosocial factors such as political inclusion, opportunities for utilizing economic resources, stress, and literacy are the major determinants of health both for individuals and societies. In other words, the most significant risk factors for illness and premature death are social in nature with poorer health outcomes closely linked to inequalities in the distribution of wealth and opportunity.

What then does this have to do with environmental justice? First, this analysis of the social determinants of health tells us that the causal story of environmental health risks is not reducible to an empirically established linkage between exposure to chemical A and adverse health effects. It is these determinations, of course, that are precisely the aim of environmental risk assessment. To know that racial and economic minorities are burdened by environmental inequities is enough to know that they are disproportionately subject to adverse social conditions that limit quality of life and human capabilities. This would certainly include living and working in environments degraded by industrial siting, pollution, or crime, or compromised by political exclusion. These data also tell us that "environment" means more than the air we breathe, the water we drink, and the ground in which our food is grown. As Dana Alston proclaimed at the First National People of Color Environmental Leadership Summit, "The issues of the environment do not stand alone by themselves. They are not narrowly defined. Our vision of the environment is woven into an overall framework of social, racial, and economic justice... the environment for us is where we work, where we live, and where we play" (Gottlieb, 1993:5, quoting Alston).

Second, this analysis of the social determinants of health calls into question the separation of scientific risk assessment from risk management and public health approaches. Unlike risk assessment which is technocratic, pollution-specific, and often focused on a single hazard, public health looks at broad community health indicators and community-based solutions. If as Sen, Wilkinson, and others have argued, participation, capacity-building, and social cohesion are essential ingredients in a flourishing society, then enhanced community involvement in environmental risk management may contribute directly to overall improvements in social welfare and quality of life.

Conclusion — Treating (Relative) Unequals Unequally

Earlier in this chapter, I indicated that according to Aristotle, a just society is one where equals are treated equally and where unequals may be treated unequally. We are now in a position to understand what this might mean. In Aristotle's day, slavery was an unquestioned part of the social order, and women were not granted citizenship. Therefore, for Aristotle, there were people who were unequal in the absolute sense by virtue of their ethnicity, gender, and socioeconomic status.

In modern democratic societies, we have rejected the idea of the absolute inequality of people. The premise of American democracy is that all people are created equally. This fact about our moral equality provides a basis on which to make sense of our relative inequality — those very real material and historical factors that differently situate us. The data that I have referred to on the social determinants of health indicate that it is not the wealthiest countries that have the best health; it is the countries that have the smallest income differences between rich and poor. Inegalitarian societies, those with larger relative income differences, are less socially cohesive and suffer more of the corrosive effects of social and economic divisions. Relative inequality in this sense adversely affects not only those who have the short end of the stick, but also the health of society as a whole. For Aristotle, the question of justice is ultimately a question about what constitutes a good, healthy, flourishing society. Given the data that we have examined, it seems that the most pressing problem in and between societies is the alleviation of relative inequalities. This will require treating unequals unequally in John Rawls' (1971) sense of seeking policies that achieve the greater advantage of the least well off. In other words, and contrary to a free-market libertarian approach, without a redistribution of income and welfare advantages including social and environmental benefits to the least well off, society as a whole will not flourish.

I'd like to make three final observations. First, the evidence on the social determinants of health suggest that our habit of pitting justice (equity) and progress (growth, development, efficiency) against one another is a false dichotomy. Efficiency and growth are not ends in themselves; they are means to ends. The benefits of economic growth are not direct; they are indirect. The challenge for society, therefore, is the conversion of income into human development. These data suggest that efficient growth is achieved when there is greater equity (Wilkinson, 1996).

Second, assessing the harmful effects of environmental agents should be based on the notion of health that derives from public health, not from medicine. This will require incorporating variables from the United Nations Human Development Index into our analyses of risk and harm. It will also require a more community-based approach to risk characterization and management.

Third, the orientation of policymakers should not simply be directed at rectification of past discrimination, but rather to the type of society that authenticates social cohesion and participation. Only if we take seriously the dramatically unsustainable effects of relative inequality will we be able to move forward together (Dworkin, 2001).[2]

---

2 This paper draws substantially from Virginia A. Sharpe's "Environmental Justice and the Social Determinants of Health" in *A Quest for Environmental Justice* (Rowman and Littlefield). Thanks to participants in the Goodwin-Niering Center's "A Quest for Environmental Justice" conference as well as participants and commentators in the University of Michigan's "Environmental Crisis or Crisis of Epistemology" conference for helpful feedback on this paper.

References

Alston, D. (1991, October). *Moving Beyond the Barriers*. First National People of Color Environmental Leadership Summit. Washington, D.C.

Aristotle. (1985). *Nicomachean Ethics* (T. Irwin, Trans.). Indianapolis, IN: Hackett Publishing Company.

Bailar, J. C. and Bailar, A. J. (1999). Risk Assessment: The Mother of All Uncertainties. In A. J. Bailar (Ed.), *Uncertainty in Risk Assessment of Environmental and Occupational Hazards*. New York: The New York Academy of Sciences.

Been, V. (1993). What's Fairness Got to Do With It? Environmental Justice and the Siting of Locally Undesirable Land Uses. *Cornell Law Review, 78*, 1001-1085.

Boerner, C. and Lambert, T. (1994). *Environmental Justice?* (No. Policy Study 21). St. Louis, MO: St. Louis Center for the Study of American Business.

Bryant, B. (1995). Issues and Potential Policies and Solutions for Environmental Justice: An Overview. In B. Bryant (Ed.), *Environmental Justice: Issues, Policies, and Solutions*. Washington, DC: Island Press.

Bullard, R. D. (1994). Environmental Justice for All. In R. Bullard (Ed.), *Unequal Protection: Environmental Justice and Communities of Color*. San Francisco: Sierra Club.

Burke, T. A. (1996). Back to the Future: Rediscovering the Role of Public Health in Environmental Decision Making. In C. R. Cothern (Ed.), *Handbook for Environmental Risk Decision Making: Values, Perceptions and Ethics*. Chelsea, MI: Lewis Publishers.

Conroy, M. E., Kelleher, K., and Villamizar, R. I. (1981). The Role of Population Growth in Third World Theories of Underdevelopment. In D. Callahan and P. Clark (Eds.), *Ethical Issues Of Population Aid: Culture, Economics and International Assistance*. New York: Irvington Booms.

Daniels, N., Kennedy, B. P., and Kawachi, I. (1999). Why Justice is Good for Our Health: The Social Determinants of Health Inequalities. *Daedalus, 128*(4), 215-252.

Dworkin, R. (2001, April 14). Race and the Uses of Law. *New York Times*, pp. A-17.

Earth Charter. Retrieved with no date from http://www.earthcharterusa.org/ecdraft.html.

Foreman, C. (1998). *The Promise and Peril of Environmental Justice*. Washington, DC: Brookings Institution Press.

Gottlieb, R. (1993). *Forcing the Spring: The Transformation of the American Environmental Movement*. Washington, DC: Island Press.

National Academy of Sciences. (1983). *Risk Assessment in the Federal Government: Managing the Process*. Washington, DC: Proceedings of the National Academy of Sciences.

Nozick, R. (1974). *Anarchy, State and Utopia*. New York: Basic Books.

Pulido, L. (2000). Rethinking Environmental Racism: White Privilege and Urban Development in Southern California. *Annals of the Association of American Geographers, 90*(1), 12-40.

Ratcliffe, J. (1977). Poverty, Politics and Fertility: The Anomaly of Kerala. *Hastings Center Report, 7*(1), 34-42.

Rawls, J. (1971). *A Theory of Justice*. Cambridge, MA: Harvard University Press.

Sen, A. (1999). *Development as Freedom*. New York: Anchor.

Steingraber, S. (1997). *Living Downstream*. New York: Vintage Books.

United Nations Development Programme. (1990). *Human Development Report 1990*. New York: Oxford University Press and subsequent yearly reports. http://www.undp.org/hdro/report.html.

Waldmann, R. J. (1992). Income Distribution and Infant Mortality. *Journal of Economics, 107*(4), 1283-1302.

Wilkinson, R. G. (1996). *Unhealthy Societies: The Afflictions of Inequality*. New York: Routledge.

Woodward, A. (1999). Uncertainty in Risk Characterization and Communication. Discussion. *Annals of the New York Academy of Sciences, 895*, 365-6.

Wright, R. (1940). *Native Son*. New York: Harper & Brothers.

3

ENVIRONMENTAL ETHICS AND ENVIRONMENTAL JUSTICE

John Callewaert, Ph.D.

(Environmental Justice is) (t)he fair treatment and meaningful involvement of all people regardless of race, color, national origin, or income with respect to the development, implementation, and enforcement of environmental laws, regulations, and policies. Fair treatment means that no group of people, including racial, ethnic, or socioeconomic groups, should bear a disproportionate share of the negative environmental consequences resulting from industrial, municipal, and commercial operations or the execution of federal, state, local, and tribal programs and policies (USEPA, 1997).

Introduction

One of the most salient debates in environmental policy today centers around racial and class biases in environmental protection and exposure to environmental risk. For more than a decade, community groups, activists, policymakers, and others have discussed such biases under the framework of environmental justice. Environmental justice is both a social movement and a field of study that seeks to address the unequal distribution of environmental benefits and harms and asks whether procedures and impacts of environmental decision-making are fair to people they affect. In the U.S., a primary issue for those concerned about environmental justice is that some groups, most often communities of color and low-income, face a

---

John Callewaert is the Integrated Assessment Program Director with the Graham Environmental Sustainability Institute at the University of Michigan. Previously, he was Director of the Institute for Community and Environment and Associate Professor at Colby-Sawyer College. Callewaert completed his Ph.D. in the Resource Policy and Behavior program within the School of Natural Resources and Environment at the University of Michigan. Areas of interest include environmental ethics, environmental policy, environmental sociology, community-based research, and service learning.

disproportionate exposure to environmental health risks such as air and water pollution, and environmental hazards such as landfills, incinerators, sewage treatment plants, and polluting industries.

Evidence of such disproportionate exposure is found in numerous empirical studies (Lester, Allen and Hill, 2001; Liu, 2001; Mohai and Bryant 1992; Newton, 1996). In an analysis of 64 studies, Benjamin Goldman (1994) found an overwhelming body of empirical evidence that people of color and lower incomes face disproportionate environmental impacts in the U.S. All but one of the 64 studies (98 percent) found environmental disparities either by race or income, regardless of the kind of environmental concern or the level of geographic specificity examined (Goldman, 1994).

Given such compelling evidence, environmental justice considerations have emerged as a major part of environmental discourse over the past decade. Taylor (2000b) notes that while there has been much written on the environmental justice movement, attention has primarily been focused on case studies analyzing the spatial distribution of environmental hazards and on policy formulation. Little attention has been paid to the ideological and historical foundations of the environmental justice movement and how these relate to the dominant environmental discourse (Camacho, 1998; Melosi, 1995; Taylor, 1993; Taylor, 1997a).

For example, Koppes (1988) asserts that equity (equal distribution of the development of resources rather than control by a few elites), efficiency (management of natural resources), and esthetics (preservation of nature without development) were the three ideals that dominated American environmentalism during the Progressive era. Koppes claims that over time, equity has been pursued less consistently that the other two ideals. Using the benefits of efficiency programs for redistribution purposes always aroused political opposition, and efficiency-oriented bureaucracies usually had little sympathy for such troublesome issues such as equity (Koppes, 1988). The environmental justice movement represents a rejection of such views and seeks to place equity back into environmental discourse and decision making.

Because of the efforts to reinsert equity considerations within environmental discourse, the environmental justice movement is transforming the way mainstream environmentalists, people of color, and low-income people think about and relate to the environment. In addition, many within the environmental justice movement openly criticize the traditional or mainstream American environmental movement because of a general failure to consider the social dimensions of environmental issues (Bullard, 1993; Foreman, 1998; Hurley, 1995; Westra and Lawson, 2001). As present, it is no longer considered appropriate for mainstream environmentalists to define and analyze environmental issues without considering the social justice implications of the problem.[1] The environmental justice movement amplifies and clarifies the connections between environmental and social justice and emphasizes that these connections are inseparable (Taylor, 2000b).

The purpose of this paper is to examine the origins and possible connections between contemporary environmental ethics and environmental justice. It is my contention that while there is a lack of exchange between the two areas, there are benefits to considering how ethical reflection can clarify notions of environmental justice and how environmental justice can expand the range of issues considered by environmental ethics. I will first provide a brief overview of environmental justice and environmental ethics. This will be followed by an exploration of perceptions of equity among environmental justice stakeholders (community groups, government, and industry) from a qualitative study of three environmental justice complaints filed with the Office of Civil Rights of USEPA. Considering these notions of justice is one way to demonstrate how environmental ethics and environmental justice can inform each other. Finally, several other areas of explorations will be identified.

Environmental Justice Overview

Civil rights, academic communities, and environmental groups to a certain degree first identified environmental inequities in a focused way in the 1970s. One of the earliest references to the concept of environmental justice was at a 1976 national conference entitled "Working for Environmental and Economic Justice and Jobs." This five-day conference was held at a United Auto Workers Education Center in Black Lake, Michigan and gathered over 300 union officials, ecology activists, and community leaders interested in exploring their common interests (Hill, 1976).

An incident in 1982, in Warren County, North Carolina, is often cited as the event that propelled environmental injustice and more specifically environmental racism into public awareness in the U.S. In Warren County, a community mobilized in opposition to a state proposed landfill for polychlorinated biphenyl (PCB) contaminated soil in a predominantly African American community. Grassroots opposition followed the siting decision and

1 Noted are recent developments of environmental justice initiatives by many environmental groups, government agencies, and private organizations. See the following websites: the Ford Foundation (http://www.fordfound.org/), the Sierra Club (http://www.sierraclub.org/environmental_justice/index.asp), USEPA (http://www.epa.gov/compliance/environmentaljustice/index.html), and the National Wildlife Federation (http://www.nwf.org).

grew into a movement that took on the atmosphere of a civil rights campaign (Hartley, 1995). The events of Warren County have been repeated in many communities across the country. There are hundreds of environmental justice organizations within the United States addressing a wide range of environmental concerns at the local, national, and international levels (Bullard, 1992; Taylor, 2000a). Together these efforts comprise the environmental justice movement.

Most scholars understand environmental justice to be a recent development of the past few decades. Other scholars, such as Harold Platt (2000) push back the origins of the intersections of race, class, power, and environmental concerns to the public health initiatives of the late 19th Century as typified in the work of Jane Addams in the slums of the near west side of Chicago. For the most part these efforts generally were contested under the rubric of "social" as opposed to "environmental" problems (Gottlieb, 1993). Nevertheless, because of its emphasis on race, class, and the environment, and its questioning of the goals and objectives of mainstream environmentalism, the environmental justice movement is playing a historic role in reintroducing equity into public and academic debates over environmental policy (Melosi, 1995).

The past decade has also seen the development of several policy initiatives and legal outcomes that have advanced the cause of environmental justice (Gaylord and Bell, 2001; Gerrard, 1999; Lester et al., 2001; Liu, 2001). One of the most significant events came in February 1994 when President Clinton issued Executive Order 12898, which requires that each federal agency must make environmental justice part of its mission. In addition, Executive Order 12898 created an interagency workgroup on environmental justice to coordinate the environmental justice plans of all affected federal agencies.

For its part, USEPA has established an Office of Environmental Justice and each USEPA regional office has an Environmental Justice Coordinator. Some regional offices of USEPA, such as Region V, have targeted Superfund sites as their priority environmental justice program (US Environmental Protection Agency, 1997). From the beginning, USEPA has been concerned about the implications of a strong environmental justice movement. A 1991 internal agency memo describes the formation of several environmental justice network organizations as "early signs that long-simmering resentment in the minority and Native American communities about environmental fairness could soon be one of the most politically explosive environmental issues yet to emerge." The memo urged the agency to make its goal of "substantial investment in environmental equity and cultural diversity an unmistakable matter of record with mainstream groups before activists enlist them in a campaign that could add the agency to industry and local officials as a potential target" (Crampton, 1991).

One of the most widely discussed policy initiatives has been USEPA's 1998 *Interim Guidance for Investigating Title VI Administrative Complaints Challenging Permits* (Corporate Watch, 1999; Mank, 1999). Drawing on the 1964 U.S. Civil Right Act, the guidance established a mechanism for processing environmental justice complaints alleging discriminatory effects resulting from the issuance of pollution control permits by state and local governmental agencies that receive USEPA funding (USEPA, 1998). USEPA currently provides several billion dollars of federal funding under 44 different programs to about 1,500 recipients, including virtually all state or regional siting or permitting agencies. From September 1993 to 2002 USEPA received more than 100 environmental justice complaints under Title VI.[2]

While federal environmental justice initiatives began in the early 1990s under USEPA administrator William Reilly and were expanded by Carol Browner, the issue has not been abandoned by the Bush administration. In August of 2001 Christine Todd Whitman issued an internal EPA memo stating that USEPA has a firm commitment to the issue of environmental justice and its integration into all programs (Whitman, 2001). In addition, the National Academy of Public Administration (NAPA) issued a report for USEPA on strategies for improving the integration of environmental justice into permitting procedures. The report stressed that environmental justice efforts need to be implemented as part of the agency's core mission (NAPA, 2001). Resolution of key environmental justice conflicts and a firm application of environmental justice policies, however, will be the true test of USEPA's commitment to environmental justice.

Environmental Ethics Overview

The origins of environmental ethics go back much further than the past few decades. Just as elements of the environmental justice movement can be seen in earlier aspects of social equity discourse, reasoned accounts of how people should live their lives and regard nature find their origin in the creation stories and early philosophies of many cultures (Hargrove, 1989; Callicott, 1997; Westra, Robinson and Oelschlaeger, 1997). Contemporary considerations of environmental ethics are connected with the rise of the environmental movement in the 1960s and 1970. Three influential sources for environmental ethics at that time were Aldo Leopold's "Land Ethic," which explicitly claims that the origins of ecological problems are philosophical (Callicott, 1989); Garrett

2 See http://www.epa.gov/ocrpage1/docs/t6stsep2001.pdf. (No retrieval date).

Hardin's consideration of ethical and environmental dimensions of human population growth in his article "Lifeboat Ethics" (1974); and Lynn White's seminal piece on the influence of religious beliefs in generating the modern environmental crisis "The Historical Roots of Our Ecological Crisis (1967). Initially most activities in the 1970s focused on the debate around White's and Hardin's theses and primarily addressed issues from historical, theological, and religious perspectives (Cobb, 1995; Linzey, 1976). In time, others worked to establish the philosophical foundations of the field (Birch and Cobb, 1981; Hargrove, 1989; Norton, 1991; Rolston, 1975).

Following the initial work of the 1970s and through the next two decades, the field of environmental ethics expanded to consider a wide range of issues and foci. Several notable developments include the deep ecology movement (Naess, 1973), social ecology (Bookchin, 1971, 1990), ecofeminism (Merchant, 1983; Reuther, 1975; Warren, 1994),and animal rights (Regan, 1982, 1983; Singer, 1975) as well as considerations of economics (Sagoff, 1988), policy (Shrader-Frechette, 1988; Caldwell and Shrader-Frechette, 1992), wilderness (Snyder, 1990) and sustainable development (Engel and Engel, 1990). Only recently has there been discussion of issues that can be identified as environmental justice considerations (Dobson, 1998; Figueroa, 1999; Hargrove, 2001; Jamieson, 1994; Westra and Lawson, 2001). Like the environmental justice movement which has worked to identify itself as distinct from the mainstream environmentalism, so too has environmental ethics worked to establish itself as much more than a curiosity of mainstream philosophy (*A Very Brief History of the Origins of Environmental Ethics for the Novice*, 2002).

Divergence and Complementarity

At first glance it would seem that environmental ethics and environmental justice would complement each other. In general, both are seeking to address normative standards related to the environment. Furthermore, given the social implications of some of the early work in environmental ethics such as the essays by Hardin and White, one could expect that environmental justice would have developed as a topic consideration within environmental ethics. However, a focus on more immediate human-oriented or anthropocentric goals, as opposed to more generalized environmental values, is characteristic of the environmental justice movement.[3] As such, environmental justice has been a marginal topic of discussion within ethical and philosophical discussions of environmental issues,

3 However, it should be noted that many of the 17 Principles of Environmental Justice developed at the First National People of Color Environmental Leadership Summit (October 27, 1991) incorporate both ecocentric and anthropocentric values.

which have tended to focus more on animal rights, wilderness issues, and value theories of nature (Hargrove, 2001). In addition, Hargrove notes that because of the emphasis on holism in environmental ethics, which stresses the good of the whole or the system, there is little regard for the individual in environmental ethics literature. As evidence of the marginal role of environmental justice discourse within environmental ethics literature, by 2002 a review of articles in the online bibliography of International Society for Environmental Ethics identified only 30 or so articles that directly worked with environmental justice themes from more than 5000 records in the entire bibliography.[4] In some cases, the term "environmental justice" has been employed, but it concerns justice due to non-human species as a result of environmental degradation rather than the disproportionate burden of environmental problems across human communities (Wenz, 1988; Stern and Dietz, 1994).

There is also ambiguity in environmental justice discourse about the use of "justice." While the environmental justice movement has been very successful in identifying and bringing about public awareness regarding the problems of environmental injustice such as disproportionate environmental health risks and cumulative impacts, a clearly defined normative standard of justice for environmental justice has not yet been articulated. Similarly, despite the frequent use of terms such as "justice," "equity," and "injustice" in environmental justice discourse, there has been little theoretical discussion of what is meant by such terms. For example, does environmental justice mean strict equity in environmental conditions and standards? If so, what problems might occur with such an approach? If environmental justice is not strict equity, then what are other methods of ensuring justice in environmental decision-making?

Scholars such as Bullard (1994) have considered various dimensions of equity such as geographical equity, the location and spatial configuration of communities and their proximity to environmental hazards; procedural equity, the extent that governing rules, regulations, evaluation criteria, and enforcement are applied in a nondiscriminatory way; and social equity, the role of sociological factors such as race, ethnicity, class, culture, lifestyles, and political power in environmental decision-making. Others scholars such as Taylor (1997b) have noted that members of the environmental justice movement speak of justice as it relates to the notions of equity, impartiality or equality, and sharing and partnership. Also, a distinction is made between two kinds of justice; 1) distributive justice, the ways in which members of

4 *International Society for Environmental Ethics Bibliography*. Retrieved with no date from http://www.cep.unt.edu/bib/index.

a society properly distribute the benefits and burdens of social cooperation; and 2) corrective, communicative, or retributive justice, the concern with the way individuals are treated during a social transaction (Taylor, 1997b). Despite these insights, there has not yet been an adequate consideration of the abundant scholarly and philosophical literature addressing equity and justice (Foreman, 1998; Liu, 2001; Opotow and Clayton, 1994). Furthermore, this lack of inquiry into conceptions of justice, equity and ethics has serious implications for the effective articulation of environmental injustice claims and the implementation of policy initiatives and other efforts seeking to address environmental injustices.

One explanation for this lack of inquiry is the theoretical divergence mentioned above. Another possible reason for the lack of philosophical inquiry into environmental justice is that as Charles Mills (1997) claims, philosophy has remained remarkably untouched by the debates over issues related to multiculturalism and ethnic diversity. Furthermore, Mills claims that both demographically and conceptually, philosophy is one of the "whitest" of the humanities. African Americans constitute only about one percent of philosophers in North America, and there are even fewer Latino, Asian American, and Native American philosophers.[5] From this perspective, issues such as environmental justice and environmental racism, which primarily affect people of color, are not addressed because there are few people of color within philosophy to examine these issues or environmental justice is not an area of interest for other philosophers in general.

Case Studies

While environmental justice and environmental ethics may be distinct, I believe the two issues can help inform, expand, and strengthen each other. Environmental ethics has the potential to clarify and focus the ethical and moral claims found in environmental justice discourse, and environmental justice can expand and deepen the social dimensions of environmental ethics as it has done for mainstream American environmentalism. Examining the operative notions of justice and equity within environmental justice discourse will be a good method for studying the possible connections between the two topics. To do that, research material from a qualitative analysis of three environmental justice case

5 A 1994 report on American philosophy, Status and Future of the Profession, revealed that "only one department in ten (28 of the 456 departments reporting) has any (tenure-track) African American faculty, with slightly fewer having either Hispanic American or Asian American (tenure-track) faculty (17 departments in both cases). A mere seven departments have any (tenure-track) Native American faculty." *Proceedings and Addresses of the American Philosophical Association, 70* (1996): 137

studies will be analyzed. The three cases all involve complaints that were filed under the United States Environmental Protection Agency's *Interim Guidance for Investigating Title VI Administrative Complaints Challenging Permits*.

There are a variety of explanations and understandings of environmental justice. Although there is a relative consensus concerning the definition of the problem of environmental injustice, there remains considerable disagreement regarding its causes and possible solutions (Sandweiss, 1998). There are also diverse underlying ethical frameworks and value systems that are operative with key environmental justice stakeholders (community groups, industry, and government). The primary purpose of the case study analysis was to examine the competing conceptual frameworks of environmental justice. In addition, the study focused on the significance of existing environmental justice policies such as the *Interim Guidance* and state agency initiatives in determining the outcome of specific claims of environmental injustice.

For the research project, standard methods were followed for qualitative research as developed and outlined by Glaser and Strauss (1967), Charmaz (1988), Denzin and Lincoln (1994), and Patton (1990). The primary data collection methods used were one-on-one semi-structured interviews with members of community groups, industry executives, and government administrators for each of the selected complaints. Participants were identified by reviewing the official complaint documents filed with USEPA and by reviewing media sources to identify key individuals related to each case and from each stakeholder group. A total of nine, one-hour interviews were conducted. More interviews would have been desirable, but many of the representatives from the permitting agencies and industry were not willing to be interviewed citing concerns about the legal ramifications of the Title VI complaints. However, in the absence of interviews many of the people contacted offered written responses to the study questions or other printed material.

All interviews were tape-recorded with the consent of participants. Following the interviews, the recordings were transcribed. To complement the data gathered from the interviews, numerous documents associated with each of the complaints were gathered. These documents included historical accounts of the communities from public libraries and newspaper stories of key events and individuals. In addition, Freedom of Information Act requests were submitted to each of the state environmental permitting agencies (the Arizona Department of Environmental Quality, the Illinois Environmental Protection Agency, and the Ohio Environmental Protection Agency) and USEPA's Office of Civil Rights in order to conduct a comprehensive file review of documents related to each of the complaints. These requests provided copies of hearing transcripts, correspondence between the stakeholders, press releases, and state agency responses to the complaints. In total, more than 200 documents were collected. All of the research documents were converted to word processing files by using an optical character recognition scanner and then organized and analyzed using Atlas.ti[6], a qualitative data management software package. At least one site visit was made for each of the cases. This provided opportunities to conduct in-person interviews, gather the related documents, attend public hearings, and visit each of the communities.

The three complaints were selected from the complete list of active Title VI complaint cases and held the greatest potential for examining notions of equity and justice. All three exemplified long-established communities that had experienced conflict with local government and industry officials over environmental concerns for several years. As such, the three cases provided ample information from a variety of sources (personal interviews, official records, compliance reports, media accounts, etc.). The study design was unique in that it focused on identifying the perspectives of the primary stakeholders – community groups or individuals, government agencies, and industry. Previous work has mainly involved the community perspective or the impact of environmental injustice. This is logical as communities of color and low-income communities bear the brunt of environmental hazards. However, it is also important to examine the perspectives of other stakeholders in order to understand the full range of barriers and strategies for resolving environmental injustices. Site visits, data collection ,and stakeholder interviews were conducted in the summer of 1999.

One case concerns the complaint that was filed by the Alum Crest Acres Association and the Southside Community Action Association following an explosion in 1997 of a 8,500 gallon kettle of formaldehyde, phenol, and sulfuric acid at a Georgia-Pacific resins facility on the south side of Columbus, Ohio. Neighbors of the plant complained about its safety for years, and Ohio Environmental Protection Agency records confirm there were eight major spills at the plant since 1976 (Ohio EPA, 1997; Edwards, 1997). Residents filed the complaint following Ohio EPA's decision to repermit the facility following the explosion. The complaint was filed in May 1998 and was accepted by USEPA for investigation in February 2000.

Another case involves the complaint filed in October 1998 by The Paper, Allied-Industrial, Chemical and Energy Workers International Union (PACE), and residents of Rillito, Arizona against the Arizona Department

6 Muhr, Thomas. 1997. *Atlas.ti: The Knowledge Workbench for Visual Qualitative Data Analysis, Management and Theory Building*. Berlin: Scientific Software Development..

of Environmental Quality for permitting the expansion plans of the Arizona Portland Cement Company. Workers and residents were concerned about the expansion plans as Arizona Portland Cement was fined $367,840 for violating state and county hazardous waste laws. The company was caught burning benzene contaminated waste oil for fuel (Yozwiak, 1996).

The third case involves a complaint filed in September 1997 against the Illinois EPA for multiple permitting decisions related to an incinerator in Robbins, Illinois. The complaint was filed by the South Cook Environmental Action Coalition – a citizens' environmental group comprised of residents of Robbins and surrounding communities. Constructed in 1994, the incinerator in Robbins has been plagued by numerous permitting violations including several uncontrolled fires. Representative Jesse L. Jackson, Jr., whose congressional district includes Robbins, stated that the facility's smokestack towers over an archipelago of aging communities "like the Washington monument of Chicago's south suburbs" (Jeter, 1998). USEPA accepted the complaint for investigation in October 1998.

Table 1 (next page) provides demographic information on each of the communities. Using the permitted facilities as a focal point, 0-1 mile, 0-2 mile, and 0-5 mile radii comparisons show that the percentage of people of color (predominantly African Americans) is highest in the 0-1 mile radius and in general decreases as one moves out from the facility. At nearly every level of comparison, however, the percentage of people of color is higher than the state or national rates, which according to USEPA (1997) guidelines, defines the community as a minority community for evaluating environmental justice concerns.

With this basic overview of each case, particular notions of justice and equity will now be examined with regard to environmental justice. A good place to start is by examining some fundamental understandings of environmental justice. USEPA offers the following definition for environmental justice:

> The fair treatment and meaningful involvement of all people regardless of race, color, national origin, or income with respect to the development, implementation, and enforcement of environmental laws, regulations, and policies. Fair treatment means that no group of people, including racial, ethnic, or socioeconomic groups, should bear a disproportionate share of the negative environmental consequences resulting from industrial, municipal, and commercial operations or the execution of federal, state, local, and tribal programs and policies (USEPA, 1997:16).

Table 1

Demographic Comparisons:
One, Two, and Five-Mile Radii from Facilities with State and National Percentages

	0-1 Mile		0-2 Miles		0-5 Miles			
Population By Origin	Total	Perct.	Total	Perct.	Total	Perct.	State	National 50 States/D.C.
COLUMBUS							OH	
White	940	21%	10347	57%	123269	66%	87%	76%
Total People of Color	3628	79%	7674	43%	63873	34%	13%	24%
RILLITO							AZ	
White	145	46%	528	72%	4898	84%	72%	76%
Total People of Color	173	54%	209	28%	937	16%	28%	24%
ROBBINS							IL	
White	1545	17%	28698	62%	196826	54%	75%	76%
Total People of Color	7772	83%	17915	38%	169481	46%	25%	24%

SOURCE: 1990 Census. People of Color figures represent total population figures minus the White, non Hispanic figures. The Hispanic category is defined by the U.S. Census Bureau as an ethnic category, not as a race. Hispanic may include counts from any of the Census race categories including White. 1990 census data are presented as those were the data available when the complaints were filed. Also, USEPA's Environmental Justice Query Mapper (http://www.epa.gov/compliance/whereyoulive.html) has not yet incorporated 2000 census data.

As discussed above, in an effort to establish an environmental justice policy framework, USEPA presented the *Interim Guidance* in 1998. To support this policy framework, USEPA used Title VI of the U.S. Civil Rights Act of 1964, which states the following:

> No person in the United States shall, on the ground of race, color, or national origin, be excluded from participation in, be denied the benefits of, or be subjected to discrimination under any program or activity receiving Federal financial assistance (42 USC. 2000d to 2000d-7).

These federal initiatives clearly demonstrate a rights-based notion of social justice. Fairness, impartiality, equity, and the right to participation in environmental decision-making processes are the cornerstones of these policy initiatives. Despite the broad anti-discriminatory language in USEPA's environmental justice definition and Title VI regulations, the agency avoided enforcing Title VI statutes against state or local recipient agencies from the early 1970s until the early 1990s. Expressing a strong utilitarian perspective, the agency argued that terminating funding to a discriminating recipient under Title VI would undermine its primary goal of providing financial assistance to state and local agencies to reduce pollution. USEPA maintained this approach even though other federal agencies enforced Title VI (Colopy, 1994; Fisher, 1995; Willoh and Collins, 1996). Even with the introduction of the *Interim Guidance* in 1998, USEPA maintained that though facially-neutral policies or practices that result in discriminatory effects violate Title VI regulations, such activities can be permitted if they are justified and there are no less discriminatory alternatives (US Environmental Protection Agency, 1998).[7]

In 2002, in addition to receiving more than 100 environmental justice complaints in the past decade under Title VI, USEPA has also received sharp criticism for developing an ambiguous and problematic policy. Criticism has come from both proponents who believe the policy is too narrow and opponents of environment justice who believe the policy is too broad (USEPA, 1999). In analyzing the data from the three Title VI complaints identified for this study, it is clear that competing conceptions of justice are directly related to this criticism.

For example, some common understandings of environmental justice on the part of community members include a wide range of factors such as fairness or the equal right to environmental quality, environmental protection, and access to resources. The notion of equitable environmental quality was expressed by one community member in Ohio who filed a Title VI complaint on behalf of his neighborhood organization:

> Fairness. In other words, equitable distribution of the good and bad. If there are good things coming out of these industries, share it with everybody, the whole community. If there are bad things, if these things are really necessary for the good of the community relative to jobs, let everybody share the emissions equitably rather than, you know, I'm going to put it just in this

7 The Interim Guidance does not provide an example of a policy or practice that would be justified. However, a Title VI Advisory Committee considered this issue at length. Several members of the Committee put forth the view that the overall social good contributed by a facility should serve as justification for its disproportionate adverse effects. The Committee offered examples of a permit covering a facility that is necessary to national defense or a permit renewal application for an existing sewage treatment plant. In the second example, the social good of avoiding waterborne disease could not be satisfied by facilities at a greater distance from the community of concern and the disparate impact posed by the facility would therefore be justified. Other members of the Committee opposed the idea of using either economic benefits or the broader public good to justify discrimination in any context arguing that the health of a community comprised of a protected class should never be sacrificed to secure more attenuated benefits for society at large. USEPA. 1999. Report of the Title VI Implementation Advisory Committee: Next Steps for EPA, State, and Local Environmental Justice Programs, EPA 100-4-99-004 ed. Washington, D.C.: The National Advisory Council for Environmental Protection and Technology, p. 92.

> area and these people are the ones we are asking to give up any potential…, suffer any consequences of these… rather than sharing it with other areas too. (Community Source[8] [PD 8: 1174-1185[9]])

A long-time opponent of the Robbins incinerator highlighted the need for equal environmental protection:

> Equity for people of color. Being entitled to the same environmental protection and the same access to opportunity that everyone else has. (Community Source [PD 1: 1056-1060])

A third community source emphasized the importance of equal access to opportunities and resource:

> Simply put, environmental justice means insuring that poor communities have the same resources and opportunities that wealthy communities have always had. (Community Source [PD 238: 4245])

Fairness as a common assumption on the part of community activists has also been by identified by several other environmental justice researchers and writers (Capek, 1993; Davy, 1996; Gibbs, 1982; Levine, 1982).

State environmental permitting agencies, however, primarily understand environmental justice in terms of procedural equity. An agency can only consider issues from the perspective of the procedural mandates (environmental health standards, emissions criteria, public notice, etc.) that it has been given. If these procedures are met, the agency cannot deny a permit because of other concerns such as cumulative or disproportionate impacts. For example, the llinois Environmental Protection Agency responded in the following way to public concerns related to the waste-to-energy incinerator in Robbins.

> The Illinois EPA strives to prevent adverse human health or environmental effects of activities governed by the Environmental Protection Act from being disproportionately imposed on minority and low-income populations. Within context of existing law, the Illinois EPA lacks authority to reject (the) permit

---

8 Following the confidentiality protocols established for this research project, participant names will not be connected with quotes. Instead, all quotes will be referenced by the stakeholder group to which the participant or material has primary affiliation (community source, government source, or industry source). All interview participants signed consent forms agreeing to this and other confidentiality protocols.

9 (PD 8: 1174-1185) is the reference for the research document from which this quote is taken. "PD" refers to primary document, thus "PD 8" denotes primary document number 8 and "1174-1185" references the specific line numbers of primary document 8 that are associated with this quote.

> application unless issuance of the permit would result in a violation of the Environmental Protection Act or a Board regulation. (Government Source [PD 185: 64-93])

This passage highlights the conflicting nature of state agency approaches to environmental justice. While stressing the goal of preventing disparate impacts, the agency notes that it lacks the authority to do anything about these problems if they fall outside of existing regulatory standards.

Most industry or business stakeholders understand environmental justice from the perspective of the market. The occurrence of areas of disparate environmental impact is due not to a lack of equity or procedural justice, but rather to a market rationality in which industry seeks access to infrastructure, resources, labor, and land allowing it to maximize profits. According to this perspective, if such areas are predominantly communities of color or low-income, it is because residents have also sought out access to things as cheap housing and employment. This view is articulated in the following two quotations. The first quote is from comments made by the Arizona Chamber of Commerce on the *Interim Guidance*, and the second is from the Environmental Justice Report of the Arizona Department of Environmental Quality.

> As stated earlier, the Chamber strongly believes that the root cause of "disparate impact" and claims of "environmental racism" are economic, not sociological. Accordingly, the aims of the environmental justice movement will be met best by encouraging, rather than discouraging, safe and environmentally-sound economic development in communities with large minority and/or low-income populations. (Industry Source [PD 74: 318-327])

> First, many employees of these firms are people of color. These individuals have lived in close proximity to industrial hubs for many years. Low wages, transportation, as well as individual customs, have kept them in these areas. (Government Source [PD 17: 26-30])

It is clear there are multiple as well as competing conceptions of justice operative within environmental justice discourse. Community stakeholders focus on group equity. They want to ensure that their communities do not bear an unfair burden of environmental problems. Government stakeholders focus on other issues. There is a concern for individual equity as articulated in the Title VI language from the *Interim Guidance*. However, the USEPA definition of environmental justice focuses on group or community equity, and this focus has been overridden by a broader social agenda that places greater importance on the work of state regulatory agencies. This is demonstrated by the fact that in 2002 USEPA has not ruled in favor of any of the communities that have filed Title VI environmental justice complaints. Finally, industry and business groups understand environmental justice in terms of market forces and question any policy initiatives that seek to address environmental injustices. Further examination of these multiple conceptions is critical to resolving environmental injustice because as Rasinski, Smith, and Zuckerbraun (1994) note, public conflicts over environmental issues often results from differing conceptions of how to best achieve social justice. In the following section three theories of justice and their relation to environmental justice are considered.

Theories of Justice and Environmental Justice

Several scholars (Davy, 1996; Liu, 2001; Perhac, 1999; Wenz, 2001) note that there are three primary theories of ethics and justice that have application to environmental justice – contractarianism, utilitarianism, and libertarianism. The work of John Rawls, particularly his theories of justice and social ethics as presented in *A Theory of Justice* (1971), provides the clearest contemporary exposition of contractarianism. Rawls builds a theory based on equal liberty and equal opportunity so that "each person possesses an inviolability founded on justice that even the welfare of society as a whole cannot override" (1971:3). Rawls offers two principles of justice within his model of the social contract. The first principle is that "each person is to have an equal right to the most extensive basic liberty compatible with a similar liberty for others." The second principle (Rawls terms this the "difference principle") is that "social and economic inequalities are to be arranged so that they are both (a) reasonably expected to be to everyone's advantage, and (b) attached to positions and offices open to all" (Rawls, 1971:60).

Utilitarian justice assumes that social arrangements have to provide for the greatest happiness for the greatest number. The goal is to achieve the greatest possible balance of benefits over harms for society as a whole (Liu, 2001). Libertarian justice assumes that social arrangements have to provide for unrestrained interactions among free individuals (Davy, 1996). Libertarianism emphasizes freedom of individuals. People should be able to do whatever they want in the absence of force or fraud, as long as they respect the equal right of others to do the same (Liu, 2001; Wenz, 1988). Davy (1996) summarizes the three concepts as follows:

- Contractarianism – “Justice is what is beneficial to the poor, or: Minimize pain!”
- Utilitarianism – “Justice is what is beneficial to the most, or: Maximize happiness!”
- Libertarianism – “Justice is what is beneficial to the strong, or: Maximize liberty!”

Reviewing the material from the three cases, community groups generally espouse a contractarian view of social justice when seeking to address environmental injustice. Demands for fairness and equity mirror Rawls’ contractarian view that each person in society deserves an equal right to basic liberties. Community groups also voice opposition to the social and economic inequalities created by environmental injustice. As much of the research suggests, communities of color and low-income experience disproportionate exposure to environmental hazards and generally do not directly benefit from the industrial or waste management activities that they oppose.

Government stakeholders primarily follow a utilitarian perspective. In general, state agencies pursue procedural justice with the overall objective of benefiting the broader public good. As noted in the quotes above, government stakeholders often have no authority to entertain a complaint or community concern that falls outside of procedures, rules and regulations. Over time, this process leaves community groups feeling they have been abandoned by government agencies that fail to address broader community concerns about health and the environment.

Business or industry groups most closely reflect a libertarian perspective and chafe at command and control strategies. In general, industry stakeholders believe that the market must be allowed to take its course and that justice is best determined through the market. Improving environmental conditions of high-risk populations will require a new conception or definition of justice. Justice cannot be solely left to the market, nor can it be relegated to environmental rules and regulations. A failure to broaden and form a new definition of justice that is more conclusive will tear at the social fabric as people struggle to protect their families against environmental harm. There is a fundamental struggle between three different ethical perspectives, and it must be dealt with if we expect the kind of change that will provide long-term protection to high-risk communities.[10]

---

10 Many thanks to Bunyan Bryant, Ph.D. of the School of Natural Resources and Environment at the University of Michigan for his insights and comments on this section.

What then is the best way to resolve these competing notions of environmental justice in order to promote effective policy? Davy (1996) notes it is often assumed that injustice can be remedied by dispensing justice, but is there a form of justice that can or should satisfy all stakeholders? Furthermore, given the reality of the multiple conceptions of environmental justice it is inevitable that dispensing one form of justice would only enrage the stakeholders that hold a competing conception of justice (Davy, 1996). It is interesting to note that in addition to there being a uniform opinion of the primary theories of social justice that can be applied to environmental justice there is also uniformity in rejecting the theories for being unable to adequately address environmental injustice (Davy, 1996; Perhac, 1999; Wenz, 2001). None of the theories can adequately serve as a unified framework to deal with environmental justice issues (Liu, 2002:43).

Some have suggested that a way to resolve environmental injustice is to shift away from a particular normative paradigm such as contractarianism, utilitarianism, or libertarianism and instead focus on the issue of risk (Foreman, 1998; Lester et al., 2001; Perhac, 1999). Lester, Allen, and Hill claim that with a risk-based framework, siting decisions and allocations of cleanup funds would be driven by the threat or health risks posed by existing environmental hazards (2001:184). However risk-based decision-making is not a panacea for assessing environmental injustice. There are many questions about the inherent assumptions of risk assessment, and there are limits to what can be known about long-term or cumulative impacts (Andrews, 2000; Ringquist, 2000:252). Today's flawless solution can quickly become tomorrow's "asbestos" or another Warren County catastrophe. In addition, there are enormous power differentials between various stakeholders in environmental disputes that could unfairly influence a risk assessment process (Callewaert, 2000; West, 1982, 1994). A community organization would rarely have access to resources and political influence that a government agency or corporation might have.

Instead of seeking an absolute standard of justice or decision-making I contend that the best strategy for addressing environmental injustice is to broaden opportunities for stakeholder input and dialogue. More efforts are needed to expand opportunities for democratic decision-making so that all parties involved are informed and can present their ideas for just solutions. This is not a simple call for more participatory democracy or procedural justice. In order to effectively address environmental injustices particular emphasis needs to be placed on empowering communities of impact so that their voices can be clearly heard. Such principles are most clearly outlined in Iris Young's (1990) *Justice and the Politics of Difference*. Thus one clear connection between environmental ethics and environmental justice can be found in considering the ethical and most appropriate public participation guidelines for contentious siting decisions.

In an analysis of the literature on what people think are fair procedures Tyler (2000:121) notes that four elements "are the primary factors that contribute to judgments about their fairness: opportunities for participation (voice), the neutrality of the forum, the trustworthiness of the authorities, and the degree to which people receive treatment with dignity and respect." In general, theorists conclude that the vital aspect of procedural justice judgments lies in the degree to which decision-making procedures allow for participation and the statement of each party's viewpoints, (Ebreo and Linn, 1996:1262). In addition, the work of Walsh, Warland, and Smith (1997) demonstrates that one effective way for environmental justice advocates to strengthen their voice is to join their concerns with those of other environmental advocates.

Several of the recommendations from the Title VI (*Interim Guidance*) Federal Advisory Committee report specifically address this call for greater stakeholder participation in decision-making. For example, the committee, which included community, industry, and government representatives, unanimously agreed that communities affected by environmental justice issues should not be treated by USEPA or other regulatory agencies as merely another stakeholder group. Given that communities face greater risks and negative impacts from the outcomes of the decision-making processes, their views and concerns should be given more status and recognition than other stakeholders. In addition, standards must be set to make decision-making processes more accessible to community members (U.S. Environmental Protection Agency, 1999).

Such principles would probably be most successfully implemented at the state and local levels where opportunities for public participation are more likely. Agencies currently provide public notices and hearings related to permitting decisions, yet many communities still fail to receive adequate notice of such events or residents may be limited in their ability to participate because of language, transportation, or scheduling difficulties.

Conclusion

Environmental justice and environmental ethics have been considered distinct areas of discourse. Through this paper I have sought to identify the ways in which these two areas can and need to inform each other. Environmental ethics was used to analyze perceptions of justice and equity within environmental justice discourse. The analysis revealed that primary stakeholders in environmental justice disputes hold competing conceptions of equity and justice. One unifying ethical framework for addressing this conflict was not identified. Rather a call for a more inclusive process for environmental decision-making was identified. Understanding the very different ethical perspectives is critical for the formation of effective policy. The analysis also demonstrated how environmental justice can expand the application of environmental ethics. Traditionally the discipline has focused more the non-human dimensions of environmental thought.

Identifying perceptions of justice and public participation are not the only areas for considering the overlap between environmental justice and environmental ethics. Other themes evident in the case study analysis and in other works that could be pursued include considerations of the rights of individuals versus the rights of communities or societies (Bullard 1994, Taylor 1997b, Westra 2001) and value theories of place, particularly wilderness versus urban or settled areas (Lawson, 2001). These themes and others could be explored further as part of an effort to expand conceptions of environmental ethics and clarify notions of environmental justice. The time is past when environmental issues could be considered apart from social equity issues and when the environmental dimensions of social equity concerns could be ignored.

References

Andrews, R. N. (2000). Risk-Based Decision Making. In N. Vig and M. E. Kraft (Eds.), *Environmental Policy in the 1990's*. Washington, D.C.: Congressional Quarterly Press.

Birch, C., and Cobb, J. B., Jr. (1981). *The Liberation of Life: From the Cell to the Community*. Cambridge: Cambridge University Press.

Bookchin, M. (1971). *Post-Scarcity Anarchism*. San Francisco: Ramparts Press.

Bookchin, M. (1990). *The Philosophy of Social Ecology: Essays on Dialectical Naturalism*. Toronto: Black Rose Press.

Bullard, R. D. (1992). *People of Color Environmental Groups Directory*. Flint, MI: Charles Stewart Mott Foundation.

Bullard, R. D. (1993). Anatomy of Environmental Racism and the Environmental Justice Movement. In R. Bullard (Ed.), *Confronting Environmental Racism: Voices from the Grass Roots*. Boston, MA: South End Press.

Bullard, R. D. (1994). Overcoming Racism in Environmental Decision-Making. *Environment, 36*(4), 10-44.

Caldwell, L. K., and Shrader-Frechette, K. (1992). *Policy for Land Law and Ethics*. Lanham, MD: University Press of America.

Callewaert, J. (2000). *Understanding the Multiple Conceptions of Environmental Justice: A Qualitative Analysis of Stakeholder Perceptions and Values Regarding The VI Environmental Justice Complaints*. Unpublished Dissertation, University of Michigan, Ann Arbor.

Callicott, J. B. (1989). *In Defense of the Land Ethic: Essays in Environmental Philosophy*. Albany, N.Y.: State University of New York Press.

Callicott, J. B. (1997). *Earth's Insights*. Berkely, CA: University of California Press.

Camacho, D. (1998). *Environmental Injustices, Political Struggles: Race, Class, and the Environment*. Durham, NC: Duke University Press.

Capek, S. (1993). The Environmental Justice Frame: A Conceptual Discussion and Application. *Social Problems, 40*(1), 5-24.

Charmaz, K. (1988). The Grounded Theory Method: An Explication and Interpretation. In R. Emerson (Ed.), *Contemporary Field Research: A*

Collection of Readings. Prospect Heights, IL: Waveland Press.

Cobb, J. (1995). *Is It Too Late? A Theology of Ecology*. Denton, TX: Environmental Ethics Books.

Colopy, J. (1994). The Road Less Traveled: Pursuing Environmental Justice Through Title VI of the Civil Rights Act of 1964. *Stanford Environmental Law Journal, 13*, 126-189.

Corporate Watch. (1999). *The Corporate Backlash Against Environmental Justice*. Retrieved January 15, 2000, from http://www.corpwatch.org/trac/gallery/ej/ejflyer.html

Crampton, L. (1991). Environmental Equity Communication Plan. In G. Binder (Ed.). Washington, DC: U.S. Environmental Protection Agency.

Davy, B. (1996). Fairness as Compassion: Towards a Less Unfair Facility Siting Policy. *Risk: Issues in Health, Safety, and Environment, 7*(2), 99-108.

Denzin, N., and Lincoln, Y. (1994). *Handbook of Qualitative Research*. Thousand Oaks, CA: Sage Publications.

Dobson, A. (1998). *Justice and the Environment: Conceptions of Environmental Sustainability and Dimensions of Social Justice*. Oxford: Oxford University Press.

Ebreo, A., Linn, N., and Vining, J. (1996). The Impact of Procedural of Justice on Opinions of Public Policy: Solid Waste Management as an Example. *Journal of Applied Psychology, 26*(14), 1259-1287.

Edwards, R. (1997, September 11). Chemicals Had Ingredients for Volatile Reaction. *The Columbus Dispatch,* p. B4.

Engel, J. R., and Engel, J. G. (Eds.). (1990). *Ethics of Environment and Development: Global Challenge, International Response*. Tucson, AZ: University of Arizona Press.

Figueroa, R. M. (1999). *Debating the Paradigms of Justice: The Bivalence of Environmental Justice.* Unpublished Dissertation, University of Colorado, Boulder, CO.

Fisher, M. (1995). Environmental Racism Claims Brought Under the Title VI of the Civil Rights Act. *Environmental Law, 25*(2), 285-334.

Foreman, C. (1998). *The Promise and Peril of Environmental Justice*. Washington, DC: Brookings Institution Press.

Gaylord, C., and Bell, E. (2001). Environmental Justice: A National Priority. In L. Westra and B. E. Lawson (Eds.), *Faces of Environmental Racism: Confronting Issues of Global Justice*. London: Rowman and Littlefield.

Georgia Pacific Resins Plant Site History. (1997). Ohio EPA.

Gerrard, M. (1999). *The Law and Environmental Justice: Theories and Procedures to Address Disproportionate Risk*. Chicago, IL: American Bar Association.

Gibbs, L. M. (1982). *Love Canal: My Story*. Albany: State University of New York Press.

Glaser, B. G., and Strauss, A. L. (1967). *The Discovery of Grounded Theory: Strategies for Qualitative Research*. New York: Aldine de Gruyter.

Goldman, B. (1994). *Not Just Prosperity: Achieving Sustainability with Environmental Justice*. Paper presented at the Corporate Conservation Council, Synergy '94 Conference, Washington, D.C.

Gottlieb, R. (1993). *Forcing the Spring: The Transformation of the American Environmental Movement*. Washington, DC: Island Press.

Hardin, G. (1974). Lifeboat Ethics: The Case Against Helping the Poor. *Psychology Today, 8*(1), 24-126.

Hargrove, E. (1989). *Foundations of Environmental Ethics*. Englewood Cliffs, NJ: Prentice Hall.

Hargrove, E. (2001). Foreword. In L. Westra and B. E. Lawson (Eds.). *Faces of Environmental Racism: Confronting Issues of Global Issues of Global Justice*. Lanham, MD: Rowman & Littlefield.

Hartley, T. (1995). Environmental Justice: An Environmental Civil Rights Value Acceptable to All World Views. *Environmental Ethics, 17*(3), 277-289.

Hill, G. (1976, May 4). Woodcock Calls for an Alliance of Labor and Environmentalists. *The New York Times*.

Hurley, A. (1995). *Environmental Inequalities: Class, Race, and Industrial Pollution in Gary, Indiana, 1945-1980*. Chapel Hill, NC: The University of North Carolina Press.

International Society for Environmental Ethics Bibliography. Retrieved with no date from http://www.cep.unt.edu/bib/index.

Jamieson, D. (1994). Global Environmental Justice. In R. Attfield and A. Belsey (Eds.), *Philosophy and the Natural Environment* (pp. 199-210). Cambridge: Cambridge University Press.

Jeter, J. (1998, April 11). Poor Town That Sought Incinerator Finds More Problems, Few Benefits: Environmentalists, State, Neighbors Foil Cash-for-trash Plan. *The Washington Post,* p. A3.

Koppes, C. (1988). Efficiency, Equity, Aesthetics: Shifting Themes in American Conservation. In D. Worster (Ed.), *The Ends of the Earth*. Cambridge: Cambridge University Press.

Lawson, B. (2001). Living for the City: Urban United States and Environmental Justice. In L. Westra and B. E. Lawson (Eds.), *Faces of Environmental Racism: Confronting Issues of Global Justice*. London: Rowman and Littlefield.

Lester, J., Allen, D., and Hill, K. (2001). *Environmental Injustice in the United States: Myths and Realities*. Boulder, CO: Westview Press.

Levine, A. G. (1982). *Love Canal: Science, Politics, and People.* Lexington, MA: Lexington Books.

Linzey, A. (1976). *Animal Rights: A Christian Assessment of Man's Treatment of Animals*. London: SCM Press.

Liu, F. (2001). *Environmental Justice Analysis: Theories, Methods, and Practices*. Boca Raton, FL: Lewis Publishers.

Mank, B. (1999). Title VI. In M. Gerrard (Ed.), *The Law and Environmental Justice: Theories and Procedures to Address Disproportionate Risk.* Chicago, IL: American Bar Association.

Melosi, M. (1995). Equity, Eco-Racism and Environmental History. *Environmental History Review, 19*(3), 1-16.

Merchant, C. (1983). *The Death of Nature: Women, Ecology, and the Scientific Revolution*. New York: Harper and Row.

Mills, C. (1997). *The Racial Contract*. Ithaca, NY: Cornell University Press.

Mohai, P., and Bryant, B. (1992). Environmental Racism: Reviewing the Evidence. In B. Bryant & P. Mohai (Eds.), *Race and the Incidence of Environmental Hazards: A Time for Discourse*. Boulder, CO: Westview Press.

Muhr, T. (1997). *Atlas.ti: The Knowledge Workbench for Visual Qualitative Data Analysis, Management and Theory Building*. Berlin, Germany:

Scientific Software Development.

Naess, A. (1973). The Shallow and the Deep, Long-range Ecology Movement: A Summary. *Inquiry, 16*, 1-16.

National Academy of Public Administration. (2001). *Environmental Justice in EPA: Reducing Pollution in High-Risk Communities Is Integral to the Agency's Mission*. Washington, D.C.: National Academy of Public Administration.

Newton, D. (1996). *Environmental Justice: A Reference Handbook*. Santa Barbara, CA: ABC-CLIO.

Norton, B. (1991). *Toward Unity Among Environmentalists*. New York: Oxford University Press.

Ohio EPA. 1997. Georgia Pacific Resins Plant Site History.

Opotow, S., and Clayton, S. (1994). Green Justice: Conceptions of Fairness and the Natural World. *Journal of Social Sciences, 50*(3), 1-11.

Patton, M. Q. (1990). *Qualitative Evaluation and Research Methods*. Newbury Park, CA: Sage Publications.

Perhac, R. (1999). Environmental Justice: The Issue of Disproportionality. *Environmental Ethics, 21*(1), 81-92.

Platt, H. (2000). Jane Addams and the Ward Boss Revisited: Class, Politics, and Public Health in Chicago, 1890-1930. *Environmental History Review, 5*(2), 194-222.

Rasinski, K., Smith, T., and Zuckerbraun, S. (1994). Fairness Motivations and Tradeoffs Underlying Public Support for Government Environmental Spending in Nine Nations. *Journal of Social Sciences, 50*(3), 179-197.

Rawls, J. (1971). *A Theory of Justice*. Cambridge, MA: Harvard University Press.

Regan, T. (1982). *All that Dwell Therein: Animal Rights and Environmental Ethics*. Berkeley, CA: University of California.

Regan, T. (1983). *The Case for Animal Rights*. Berkeley, CA: University of California Press.

Reuther, R. R. (1975). *New Women, New Earth: Sexist Ideologies and Human Liberation*. New York, NY: Seabury Press.

Ringquist, E. (2000). Environmental Justice: Normative Concerns and Empirical Evidence. In N. Vig & M. E. Kraft (Eds.), *Environmental Policy in the 1990s* (pp. 232-256). Washington, D.C.: Congressional Quarterly Press.

Rolston, H. (1975). Is There an Ecological Ethic? *Ethics: An International Journal of Social and Political Philosophy, 85*(1), 93-109.

Sagoff, M. (1988). *The Economy of the Earth.* Cambridge: Cambridge University Press.

Sandweiss, S. (1998). The Social Construction of Environmental Justice. In D. E. Camacho (Ed.), *Environmental Injustices, Political Struggles: Race, Class, and the Environment*. Durham, NC: Duke University Press.

Shrader-Frechette, K. (1988). Parfit, Risk assessment, and Imperceptible Effects. *Public Affairs Quarterly, 2*, 75-96.

Singer, P. (1975). *Animal Liberation*. New York: Random House.

Snyder, G. (1990). *The Practice of the Wild.* San Francisco, CA: North Point Press.

Status and Future of the Profession. (1996). *Proceedings and Addresses of the American Philosophical Association, 70*(2).

Stern, P., and Dietz, T. (1994). The Value Basis of Environmental Concern. *The Journal of Social Issues, 50*(3), 65-84.

Taylor, D. E. (1993). Environmentalism and the Politics of Inclusion. In R. Bullard (Ed.), *Confronting Environmental Racism: Voices from the Grassroots* (pp. 53-62). Boston, MA: South End Press.

Taylor, D. E. (1997a). American Environmentalism. *Race, Gender and Class, 5*(1), 16-62.

Taylor, D. E. (1997b). Women of Color, Environmental Justice and Ecofeminism. In K. J. Warren (Ed.), *Ecofeminism: Women, Culture, Nature*. Bloomington, IN: Indiana University Press.

Taylor, D. E. (2000a). Introduction. *American Behavioral Scientist, 43*(4), 504-507.

Taylor, D. E. (2000b). The Rise of the Environmental Justice Paradigm. *American Behavioral Scientist, 43*(4), 508-580.

Tyler, T. R. (2000). Social Justice: Outcome and Procedure. *International Union of Psychological Science, 35*(2), 117-125.

U.S. Environmental Protection Agency. (1997). *Interim Final Guidance for*

Incorporating Environmental Justice Concerns in EPA's NEPA Compliance Analyses. Washington, D.C.: U.S. Environmental Protection Agency.

U.S. Environmental Protection Agency. (1998). *Interim Guidance for Investigating Title VI Administrative Complaints Challenging Permits*. Washington, DC: U.S. Environmental Protection Agency.

U.S. Environmental Protection Agency. (1999). *Report of the Title VI Implementation Advisory Committee: Next Steps for EPA, State, and Local Environmental Justice Programs* (No. EPA #100-4-99-004). Washington, DC: The National Advisory Council for Environmental Protection and Technology.

A Very Brief History of Environmental Ethics. (2002). Retrieved January 18, 2002, from http://www.cep.unt.edu/novice.html.

Walsh, E. J., Warland, R., and Smith, D. C. (1997). *Don't Burn It Here: Grassroots Challenges to Trash Incinerators*. University Park, PA: The Pennsylvania State University Press.

Warren, K. (1994). *Ecological Feminism*. New York: Routledge.

Wenz, P. (1988). *Environmental Justice*. Albany, NY: State University of New York Press.

Wenz, P. (2001). Just Garbage. In L. Westra and B. E. Lawson (Eds.), *Faces of Environmental Racism: Confronting Issues of Global Justice*. London: Rowman and Littlefield.

West, P. C. (1982). *Natural Resources Bureaucracy and Rural Poverty: A Study in the Political Sociology of Natural Resources*. Ann Arbor, MI: University of Michigan, School of Natural Resources, Natural Resources Sociology Lab.

West, P. C. (1994). Natural Resources and the Persistence of Rural Poverty in America: A Weberian Perspective on the Role of Power, Domination and Natural Resource Bureaucracy. *Society and Natural Resources, 7*(5), 415-427.

Westra, L., and Lawson, B. E. (2001). *Faces of Environmental Racism: Confronting Issues of Global Justice*. London: Rowman and Littlefield.

Westra, L., Robinson, T. M., and Oelschlaeger, M. (1997). *The Greeks and the Environment*. London: Rowman and Littlefield Publishing.

White, L., Jr. (1967). The Historical Roots of Our Ecological Crisis. *Science,*

155(3767), 1203-1207.

Whitman, C. T. (2001, August 9). EPA's Commitment to Environmental Justice [USEPA Memo]. Washington, DC: U.S. Environmental Protection Agency.

Willoh, D., and Collins, T. (1996). Environmental Justice and TSD Siting Policies: Title VI is the Plaintiffs' Newest and Best Weapon, but Will It Succeed in Missouri. *Missouri Environmental Law and Policy Review, 3*, 285-334.

Young, I. M. (1990). *Justice and the Politics of Difference*. Princeton, NJ: Princeton University Press.

Yozwiak, S. (1996, Dec. 11). Oil Firm Fined $5.3 Million Over Waste Sent to Arizona. *The Arizona Republic,* p. A1.

4

POWER AND KNOWLEDGE IN REGULATING AMERICAN INDIAN ENVIRONMENTS:

THE TRUST RESPONSIBILITY, LIMITED SOVEREIGNTY, AND THE PROBLEM OF DIFFERENCE

Darren J. Ranco*, Ph.D.

...I will point out that acting as a limited sovereign and acting as a protected entity in the context of environmental regulation involve many of the same struggles. These struggles reveal how the United States, in this context through the EPA, controls Native American knowledge, culture, and identity. Thus, my emphasis in this paper is not on the status or beauty of Native American knowledge regarding the environment (cf. Callicott, 1989; Tsosie, 1996), but on the structures that limit their articulation.

Introduction

During the 1990s, American Indian Nations[1] assumed regulatory primacy over certain portions of federal environmental laws in the United States. As of March 1998, there were 146 Tribes that had been delegated authority over at least one Environmental Protection Agency (EPA) program (USEPA, 1998). This delegation authority, referred to as Treatment in the Same Manner as States (TAS), firmly embeds tribal governments within the

---

1 I will refer to Indian Nations as Tribes, Native Nations, and by their respective specific names in this paper.

* Darren J. Ranco is an Assistant Professor of Native American Studies and Environmental Studies at Dartmouth University. A member of the Penobscot Indian Nation, he has a Ph.D. in Social Anthropology from Harvard University and an MSEL from Vermont Law School. His research focuses on the ways in which indigenous communities in the United States resist environmental destruction by using local knowledge to protect cultural resources.

cooperative-federalist system of major environmental laws in the United States.[2] In this system, the Federal government sets base standards and the states (and now Tribes) set specific regulatory guidelines for polluting industries (Percival, 1996). With varying success, Tribes use these programs to control pollution within reservations and by developing tribally-based standards they are able to force neighboring states to cease dumping on Indian lands. To control the impacts of toxic waste on reservations, using tribally-based standards, is critical because these standards can adopt ceremonial and other culturally specific uses of resources (Galloway, 1995). Incorporating standards with culturally specific uses of resources is seen by many to be an important aspect of self-determination, sovereignty, and, therefore, tribal survival (Weaver, 1996).

To Tribes that have not developed their own standards, EPA has issued policy statements (USEPA, 1991; USEPA, 1994; USEPA, 2001) aimed at taking into consideration tribal health and natural resources. When EPA acts as the standard setter and regulatory enforcer in accordance with these policy statements, they reaffirm the legal principle known as the Trust Responsibility*. As the Trustee of Indian lands, the Federal government has a high fiduciary duty to protect tribal resources (Wood, 1994). As in the case of tribally produced regulations, these policies are supposed to apply not only when pollution is produced on and contained within Indian reservations, but also to situations where EPA actions or decisions may impact reservation lands and communities.

Neither of these regulatory methods for environmental protection—standard setting or trustee protection—are currently available to other environmental justice groups. They are both rooted in the unique legal relationship the United States has with Indian Nations. However, examining the operational aspects of these two forms of community-based environmental protection strategies is instructive to other environmental justice groups. While many communities of color have to fight in order to get heard in state and federal permitting processes (Cole and Foster, 2000), EPA has made it an

2 TAS authority started in the late 1980s when Tribes were specifically added into the federalist system of the major environmental laws as these laws were re-authorized. In 1988, the Clean Water Act (33 U.S.C Sec. 1251-1387 [1988]), the Safe Drinking Water Act (42 U.S.C. Sec. 300f-300j-26 [1988]), the Comprehensive Environmental Response, Compensation and Liability Act (42 U.S.C. Sec. 9601-9675 [1988]), and the Surface Mining Control and Reclamation Act of 1977 (30 U.S.C. Sec. 1235(k) [1988]) were all rewritten to include Tribes in this way. In 1990, the Clean Air Act was amended, and Tribes were given TAS status for a number of air pollution regulatory programs (104 Stat. 2464 [1990]) (cf. Goldtooth 1995).

* Trust Responsibility (TR) originated out of Indian treaties, statues, and executive orders. Congress had plenary power over Indian affairs, and TR in a narrow sense defines legal duties of the U.S. in managing prosperity and resources of Indian tribes.

explicit mission to always include Indian Nations—each of the methods of protection described above are rooted in a close consultation process (USEPA, 1994). As we shall see, however, being involved in a regulatory process may not be enough for many environmental justice groups and communities of color. It is to this end that I write this paper—should "getting to the table" be the ultimate goal for environmental groups, and how should this table be structured? In the following sections, I will offer two different table settings and how they are and are not successful. My focus will be on the ways in which each of these methods,standard setting or trustee protection, involves the control of knowledge in an ultimately unequal power relationship. To conclude, I will consider how this dilemma of structuring an appropriate regulatory table intersects with key debates in political philosophy around the "dilemma of difference"—the dilemma of how to make social policy in multi-cultural and multi-racial societies.

Sovereignty, Self-Determination, and the Trust Responsibility

The United Nations defines self-determination as a people's right to "freely determine their political status and freely pursue their economic, social and cultural development" (United Nations, 1976). This lofty idea must be met by the "domestic dependent nation" status that currently exists between the United States and Indian Nations (Wilkinson, 1987). There is no post-colonial scene for Indian Nations in North America, and the current political status of Native American groups is part of a colonial process yet to be "freely determined." This does not mean that the current political and legal status of Indian Nations is totally illegitimate or imagined—many Indian Nations have culturally appropriate governments that provide services and protections rooted in legal rights retained from time immemorial (O'Brien, 1986). However, at least as many Native communities are not represented by culturally or socially relevant governments, and whatever administrative units exist within these communities must be viewed as colonial impositions (Alfred, 1999).

The current operational and legal status of an Indian Nation, the struggle for Native sovereignty—the legal and political control of activities within Indian controlled territory—continues to be the primary focus for indigenous groups in North America and across the globe. In the struggle for environmental protection, it is critical to legitimize environmental standards, which often exceed the standards of the Nation-State and surrounding governments. In addition to its obvious legal underpinnings, Native sovereignty is a shared political discourse that indigenous groups use with governmental entities that have the most interest in keeping them part of a larger Nation-State.

Arguments for reclaiming indigenous sovereignty abound in the legal literature about Indian Nations in the United States, Canada, and the rest of the world (cf. Kickingbird, 1977; Barsh and Henderson, 1980; Wilkinson, 1987; Morris, 1992; Nanda 1981). Generally, the sovereignty argument is based on a notion of the universal human right to self-determination for all people. Self-government, embedded within the legal-judical notions of sovereignty as a political goal, has also been critiqued by scholars of Native American Studies (Deloria and Lytle, 1984; Boldt and Long, 1984; Barsh, 1980; Alfred ,1999). These arguments focus on the fact that because "sovereignty" is a non-Native, universalizing legal concept that fails to reflect indigenous values, it is therefore an inappropriate political goal for Native American indigenous groups. Supporting this thesis, some scholars have pointed out that the administrative and mechanical aspects of sovereignty are further means of native control (Nelson and Sheley, 1985). For the purpose of this paper, we must keep in mind that the current state of tribal sovereignty in the United States places tribal programs firmly under the control of Congress, which has unilateral control over tribal governments (Pommersheim, 1995). Thus, in the context of the framework established by federal environmental laws, tribal sovereignty, in any real Western sense, or in a culturally appropriate way, does not currently exist.

In fact, the idea of the trust "protection" itself is rooted in the arrangement of sovereignty that defines Federal-Tribe relations. Even though the Trust Doctrine is prominent in Indian law, it remains amorphous (Chambers, 1975; O'Brien, 1986). While the Trust Responsibility has been recognized by courts, Congress, and the executive branch (Chambers, 1975, Wood, 1994), the seeds of the trusteeship are traceable to the first cessions of Indian land to the Federal government (O'Brien, 1986; see also Wood, 1994). Nearly all Native people in this country, including those in Alaska and Hawaii, share in common a loss of their land to the impulses of an immigrant majority with a colonialist, capitalist persuasion. The vast cessions of land to the U.S. government by Native people were premised on federal promises that they could continue their way of life on homelands of smaller size, free from the intrusions of the majority society. Most fundamentally, the modern form of the trust obligation is the Federal government's duty to protect this separatism by protecting tribal lands, resources, and the native way of life (O'Brien, 1986).

The federal duty to protect the separatism of Tribes was often expressed in treaties negotiated between the Federal government and Indian Nations. At the time of early treaty negotiations in the late 18th Century, Indian Nations were still relatively powerful and autonomous, and the treaties expressly recognized their sovereignty (O'Brien, 1986). Many treaties also contained express assurances that the Federal government would "protect" the Tribes (Wilkinson, 1987:15-6). While individual treaties differed from tribe to tribe, they were all oriented toward ensuring the perpetual availability of a sustained land base and a sustained cultural existence of Indian Nations (Wilkinson, 1987). Nearly all the treaties promised a permanent homeland, and many included assurances of continued rights to fish, hunt, and collect plants for subsistence and trade.[3] The vast majority of the treaties contained federal promises to provide food, clothing, and services to the Tribes (Wilkinson, 1987). Several treaties also provided that the Federal government would ensure the Tribes' peaceful existence even if it meant restraining a hostile non-Indian population.[4]

I point to the common history of limited tribal sovereignty and the Trust Responsibility to show that these are not inherently contrary, and neither are fully cognizant of tribal or United Nations notions of self-determination, real or imagined. In the following sections, I will point out that acting as a limited sovereign and as a protected entity in the context of environmental regulation involves many of the same struggles. These struggles reveal how the United States, in this context through the EPA, controls Native American knowledge, culture, and identity. Thus, my emphasis in this paper is not on the status or beauty of Native American knowledge regarding the environment (cf. Callicott, 1989; Tsosie, 1996), but on the structures that limit their articulation.

---

3 See Treaty with the Walla Walla, June 9, 1855, art. I, 12 Stat. 945, 946 (guaranteeing right to fish, hunt, gather roots and berries, and pasture stock off reservation); Treaty with the Nisqually, Dec. 26, 1854, art. III, 10 Stat. 1132, 1133 (guaranteeing right to fish at all "usual and accustomed grounds and stations"); Treaty with the Menominee, Feb. 8, 1831, 7 Stat. 342, 345 (allowing hunting and fishing on ceded lands), also cited in Wood 1994:1569.

4 See Treaty with the Northern Cheyenne and Northern Arapahoe, May 10, 1868, art. I, 15 Stat. 655, 655 ("If bad men among the whites, or among other people subject to the authority of the United States, shall commit any wrong upon the person or property of the Indians, the United States will . . . cause the offender to be arrested and punished according to the laws of the United States, and also reimburse the injured person for the loss sustained."). These were known as "bad men" clauses, also cited in Wood 1994:1569.

FIGURE1: DIOXIN DISCHARGE LIMITS FOR LINCOLN PULP & PAPER

1993 Draft Permit	
<3 yrs	1 mg/day & 20 ppq daily at WWTP
3-5 yrs	109 ug/day & Report ppq daily max at WWTP
1997 Final Permit	
During First Year	109 ug/day & 10 ppq daily max at WWTP
After First Year	109 ug/day & 10 ppq daily max at WWTP
	10 ppq daily max at Bleach Plant

mg=milligram
ug=microgram
ppq=parts per quadrillion

notes:

Discharges at the WWTP (wastewater treatment plant) occur after dilution.

Measurements at the Bleach Plant occur directly after processing.

The Penobscot Indian Nation and the Trust Responsibility[5]

The primary residential part of the Penobscot Indian Nation's (Nation) reservation called Indian Island is 35miles downstream from the Lincoln Pulp and Paper bleached kraft mill (LP&P) where high quality paper is manufactured and bleached, and in the process dioxin is formed and discharged into the Penobscot River. For decades, the river has been contaminated with 2,3,7,8-tetrachlorodibenzo~p~dioxin, more commonly known as TCDD or dioxin (see Graham, 1992). Dioxin, a volatile toxin, is formed as a by-product by various industrial processes that involve the mixing of chlorine and organic materials under conditions of heat and pressure such as in the cases of herbicide production, solid waste incineration, metal smelting, and the bleaching of paper

5 Data for this section were gathered during roughly two years of ethnographic fieldwork from 1997-1999 at the Penobscot Indian Reservation in Maine and at the Boston Office of EPA. For the complete study see Ranco, 2000.

(Lakind and Rifkin, 1990; Webster, 1990). Because the Penobscot River's source of dioxin contamination emanates from LP&P's discharge pipes, a fish consumption advisory has been issued by the State of Maine as a result of the high dioxin levels in the river below LP&P. The advisory warns people not to consume more than 12 fish meals per year (8 oz. per meal) of fish caught in the 56 mile area of the river between Lincoln Pulp and Paper and Penobscot Bay. Many reservation islands, including Indian Island, are downstream of the mill.

On January 23, 1997, in an attempt to combat this grim fact, EPA issued the LP&P National Pollution Discharge Elimination System (NPDES), which is designed to replace the company's permit issued March 28, 1985. The unique aspect of the permit is that it has the most stringent dioxin limits ever imposed on a Kraft Paper Mill in the United States (USEPA, 1997a).

In consultation with EPA, the Nation strongly urged the Agency to take into account its Trust Responsibility in writing LP&P's permit to discharge dioxin into the Penobscot River. The legal and moral discourses that surround the Trust Responsibility were used by the Nation to influence EPA to write a strict permit so that tribal health and natural resources would be protected. Between the initial draft permit in 1993 and the final draft permit in 1997, the Nation became a primary party in the permit review and comment process.

As you can see in Figure 1 on the previous page, the 1997 version of the permit sets very strict goals for LP&P. According to EPA's official statement that went with the final draft of the permit, the Agency "set the most stringent compliance method available to the agency, given the current approved analytical technology for dioxin," to assure that dioxin levels in the river meet water quality requirements. EPA estimates that these permit conditions, by measuring dioxin at the bleach plant before dilution, assure an "in stream dioxin level at least six times lower than could be assured by the draft [1993 version] permit's requirement to monitor non-detect at the wastewater treatment plant" (USEPA, 1997b:4). After writing such a strict permit which involved a lot of political will in the face of a very powerful industry in northern New England, EPA was quite surprised when the Nation appealed the permit arguing that EPA had not, in fact, met its Trust Responsibility to the Tribe. What went wrong? What did the Nation think was owed to them? In a letter from the Nation to EPA just weeks before the final draft permit was completed, this is clearly explained:

> The single most important issue for the Penobscot Nation with this permit is to be able to restore for our members as quickly as possible their right to fish in the Penobscot River for their individual sustenance in a manner that

> *poses no risk to their health....* As you know, we opposed the previous draft of this permit because it allowed for the continued discharge of dioxin into reservation waters and onto reservation land and in our view failed to protect our fishing rights.... Until EPA can assure that our members will be able to fully and safely exercise our fishing rights, we believe that EPA is violating its trust responsibility and the Clean Water Act (Penobscot Indian Nation, 1996:1-2).

The fact that this was written just weeks before the issuance of the final draft permit, leads one to believe that EPA should not have been surprised at all by the formal challenge. Yet the Agency felt like they had done as much as they could, given the circumstances, and they had certainly met the vague legal standard behind the Trust Responsibility. In the public notice that went with the final draft permit, the Agency stated that:

> EPA has met its trust obligation to the Penobscot Nation by limiting the Nation's dioxin exposure level of risk within the range of risks that EPA has determined to be *reasonable* in cases of other highly exposed tribal and non-tribal populations. In so doing, EPA has taken particular account of the fishing rights and consumption patterns of the Penobscot Nation and has consulted fully with it regarding the Agency's approach to its permit decision (USEPA, 1997b:19-20).

Whereas the Nation understands the Trust Responsibility as requiring a permit that "poses no risk," EPA maintains that it can fulfill this responsibility by assessing a "reasonable" risk for this situation. In order to understand these different perspectives, we must first understand how risk was assessed in writing the Lincoln Pulp and Paper permit.

Risk, Fish, and Consumption

In regulating toxic substances, EPA expresses risk in the amount of cancer deaths caused by the exposure to that substance.[6] Clearly, death caused by cancer from a particular substance is not the only health risk from exposure to these substances, but these are the only risks mandated by law that the Agency can take into consideration when regulating these substances (National Research Council, 1983; Graham, Green, and Roberts, 1988). A major variable in determining this risk is the amount of exposure to a particular substance. Generally, EPA uses national statistics on consumption rates and access to resources to determine the amount of exposure to a substance, and in turn it tries to protect the average citizen (National Research Council, 1983; Jasanoff

6 For an overview of the structural problems with the existing institutional arrangements that cause EPA to only consider cancer deaths as risk see Menell,1991: Coughlin,1996: and Heiman, 1996.

,1996). In this particular case, EPA did more than this. While the average rate of ingestion for fish in the U.S. is 6.5 grams/day, for this scenario the Agency looked for an ingestion rate that best reflected tribal uses. During the negotiations, EPA received a fish consumption survey that the Penobscot Nation had completed in 1991 of tribal members.

This survey, conducted during the first few years of the fish consumption warnings (see Figure 2) on the Penobscot River, revealed a fish consumption rate of 11 grams/day for the average tribal member. Tribal bureaucrats strongly urged

FIGURE 2: ATTENTION FISHERMEN

Fish caught in the Penobscot River below Lincoln– may contain traces of dioxin, a chemical suspected of causing cancer in humans.

For your health and safety when eating fish taken from these waters, the following advisory should be observed:

1. No more than two meals (eight ounces per meal) of fish taken from this section should be eaten each month.

2. Pregnant women and nursing mothers should avoid eating any fish taken from this stretch of the river. Dioxin may affect the pregnancy or be passed to infants through the breast milk.

3. When preparing fish, areas with the highest potential dioxin content should be trimmed away. These include skin, fat, belly meat, and dark fat along the backbone and lateral line. Broil, bake or barbecue fish on a rack so juices, which may contain dioxin-rich fats, will drip off. Don't fry the fish.

For further information contact:

Andrew Smith, Maine Department of Human services, Tel. (207) 289-5378
Barry Mower, Maine Department of Environmental Protection, Tel. (207) 289-3901
Dan Kusnierz, Penobscot Nation DNR, Tel. 827-7776 ext. 361
Clem Fay, Penobscot Nation DNR, Tel. 827-7776 ext. 361

the Agency to see that this rate, already lowered from traditional consumption patterns due to warnings posted along the river, did not reflect traditional members most exposed to dioxin, who either do not respond to surveys or were not around while the survey was conducted. Despite these objections, EPA could now set a standard based on the "average" Penobscot and did exactly that. In the final permit, the amount of dioxin discharged allows an additional cancer of one in a million in eating 11g/day, slightly more than one additional cancer in 100,000 at 144 g/day and almost three additional cancers in 100,000 at 336 g/day.

The agency is quite clear in the public record that they are not required to protect all highly exposed individuals to a one-in-a-million risk (USEPA, 1997b:20). If this is so, then what does the Trust Responsibility mean in this instance? In a joint letter from the Nations and the Bureau of Indian Affairs early on in the negotiations, the Tribe asks precisely this question:

> It is incumbent upon EPA in determining risk levels or in authorizing such discharges to not merely consider the risks to Penobscot Indian health resulting from consumption of such contaminated fish, but more importantly, to protect tribal members from such contamination. Thus, while calculated risks may fall within the 'acceptable bounds of risk EPA has authorized' under the Clean Water Act, such risks are not acceptable for a sub-population, traditionally dependent upon fish for sustenance. This is particularly crucial when, as here, the Federal government has a trust responsibility to protect the resources of that sub-population (Penobscot Indian Nation, 1993:3).

Here, during the permitting process, the Nation argued for a more direct relationship between the trust responsibility and natural resources, not what was "acceptable." In fact, tribal bureaucrats were constantly urging the Agency to rethink its risk assessment procedure, one that has developed over the last two decades to protect Agency decisions from challenges in the court (Jasanoff, 1990, 1992). Frequently, the facts of this case challenged some of the most basic assumptions about the ways in which EPA looks at risk. In comments the Nation offered to the Agency over the three-year long negotiation, other risks, beyond those associated with the ingestion of fish, were called to EPA's attention: What about exposure to dioxin-rich sediments while foraging for medicines and food along the river? Is it safe to build housewares from reeds growing along the river? Is it safe to swim near the discharge pipes? Thus, through EPA's bureaucratic process, local knowledge regarding the river was seen as unimportant in making any significant impacts on the facts of permit. In the next section, I will focus on how such knowledge is incorporated into a process and yet ultimately ignored by EPA.

Interacting Knowledge, Process, and Bureaucracy

The problems associated with fairness and difference in environmental regulation strike to the core of American civic culture (Jasanoff, 1987, 1996). American democracy and economic development have not developed to account for special situations adequately, especially when the market economy is threatened by the needs of a particular group. And yet there are situations when special considerations must be accounted for, and how this is handled explains a lot about the state-making process.

It took over three years for the Agency to use an ingestion rate of 11 grams instead of 6.5 grams in its risk analysis of the LP&P permit. Clearly this was not the only issue being resolved here. The *process* itself was a way for the Agency to fulfill its moral and legal duties to the Penobscot Indian Nation, and for that matter Lincoln Pulp and Paper. In a direct exchange between the Tribe and the Agency in the final draft permit, we see the Tribe arguing for a particular risk assessment procedure, and the Agency answering in a way that has nothing to do with risk and everything to do with procedure:

> NATION: "It is our belief that it is up to the EPA to protect tribal consumers of fish at the 90th, 95th, and 99th percentiles. We certainly hope that EPA will consider our concerns when deciding whether to issue the discharge permit" (Penobscot Indian Nation, 1996:2).

> EPA: "EPA has taken particular account of the fishing rights and consumption patterns of the Penobscot Nation and has consulted fully with it regarding the Agency's approach to its permit decision" (USEPA, 1997b:21).

To understand how EPA believed its efforts were in good faith and fulfilled the Trust Responsibility, even though it remains unclear if the tribal resources will be protected, we must understand something about the nature of the agency. Throughout the late 1970s and 1980s, many of the scientific pronouncements by the Agency had come under attack by a variety of groups, both for and against the protection of the environment (Jasanoff 1990, 1992). In response to this, the Agency began to legally insulate itself by going outside of the government for an "independent" affirmation of agency policies.

With respect to its roles and responsibilities under the Trust Responsibility to Indian Nations, the Agency reacted in this familiar way. The Agency bent over backwards by inviting and exposing affected parties to participate in the permit writing process, and in some ways this is how it insulated itself from lawsuits and political disfavor. Although the Nation was completely involved in the writing of the permit, it was not convinced that the permit would actually protect tribal members from cancer or preserve its treaty fishing rights.

As we can see from the Penobscot example, the ultimate problem that Tribes face is getting the EPA to recognize and enforce local, different standards that will assure tribal cultural survival. Through a series of court cases, EPA not only has insulated its decision making process, but has also argued that it is "acceptable" to expose certain populations to a greater amount of risk (Ranco, 2001).[7] Although the data were fundamentally flawed in this case, EPA nonetheless tried to allow tribal fishermen the same amount of risk as the average citizen. The hurdle to overcome was monumental: How would the Tribe have persuaded an agency like EPA to protect tribal health and resources in a way that would meet tribal perspectives on risk or, more importantly, is this something that the United States or other Nation-States should guarantee?

Many of the detractors to quantitative risk assessments have pointed out the judgment calls involved in the process that expose sub-populations, like the Penobscot Indian Nation, to greater risks (Kuehn, 1996). These detractors call for a rethinking of this kind of hidden expertise, what I and others refer to as the managerial discourse—a discourse that frames the ability to use its expertise to protect its citizens (Williams and Matheny, 1995). The response to this managerial impulse most often is a pluralist discourse in order to argue for social regulation. Mark Sagoff has argued for decisions about the environmental management of risk that are "reasoned, intelligent," the product of "open-minded deliberation," and more importantly "countenances qualitative evidence, including evidence about common purposes and beliefs" (Sagoff, 1988:12-14, 220-24). Kristin Shrader-Frechette (1988) argues that "assessments of multi-attribute risks should be the products of social, ethical, cultural and legal rationality—not merely the projects of a bounded scientific rationality" (Shrader-Frechette, 1988:117). Neither of these solutions would necessarily help the Penobscot Nation in this case. As we have seen, EPA's control comes from both controlling the process and the scientific findings. An open-minded deliberation would merely force the Agency to work towards a political middle ground, one that the Nation could not agree with in this case. It should be clear in this case that procedural justice is not acceptable when different knowledge bases are involved.

What we are faced with, therefore, is a fundamental problem of difference with the bureaucratic apparatus of the modern Nation-State. The pluralist

---

7 See Dioxin/Organochloride Center v. Clarke (57 F.3d 1524 [9th Cir. 1995]), Natural Resources Defense Council (NRDC) v. EPA (16 F. 3d 1395 [4th Cir. 1993]), and Ohio v. EPA (997 F. 2d 1520 [D.C. Cir. 1989]).

discourse, the urge to include all perspectives in the state apparatus, is insufficient to protect a culture in this case, as it is in many others. Following Eileen Guana (1998) and James Anaya (1997), Christine O'Neill points to the problems of "inclusion":

> Norms favoring just or due process are widely held and well integrated into the fabric of many societies, including the United States.... Inclusion is not the remedy... What is necessary here is more than simply the inclusion of Native Americans in a process already cast by the majority or dominant culture. The entire process itself might need to be recast in order not to suppress or transform Native Americans' different cultural experiences (O'Neill, 2000:94).

O'Neill is particularly sensitive to the fact that the deck is stacked against Native American cultures procedurally and substantively because they are "different," especially in the environmental arena. In the conclusion, I will take up these themes again and cast them more fully in the context of the United States and the rights of groups in general. First, however, I will examine how the cooperative federalism of environmental law overcomes some of these problems of pluralism.

Acting as a Semi-Sovereign: Cooperative Federalism and the Pueblo of Isleta

While the Penobscot Indian Nation sought the Trust protection from the Unites States in a water pollution case, the Pueblo of Isleta, in its role as a limited sovereign, sought a similar kind of protection. In the mid 1990s, seeking protection from pollution originating in the State of New Mexico, the Pueblo of Isleta set its own water quality standards that the EPA, as the federal regulator, must enforce. How this process works is explained in the Clean Water Act (CWA). In most circumstances, if a federally recognized Indian Tribe has achieved treatment-as-a-state (TAS) status from the Environmental Protection Agency pursuant to the Clean Water Act, they can set water quality standards (WQS) to protect its resources (see 33 U.S.C. § 1377[e] and 40 C.F.R. § 131.8[a]). Because tribal governments have section 510 (TAS) authority in the Clean Water Act, the downstream Tribe's Water Quality Standards may be more stringent than the state's WQS for the same water body. In that instance, the state's permit probably would not be helpful in determining whether the (upstream) state-based discharge will comply with the tribal WQS.

Cognizant of such situations, the CWA directs EPA to determine if a proposed discharge "may affect" the quality of the waters of any state other than the one in which the discharge is made (33 U.S.C. § 1341[a][2][1988]). Under section 518, that directive requires EPA to determine whether a proposed federally permitted discharge in an upstream state may affect the water quality of downstream Tribe with approved WQS (56 F. R. 64,876-90 [1991]). If EPA so determines, then EPA must notify the "affected" Tribe of the proposed discharge (40 C.F.R. § 121.13 [1994]) and provide the Tribe with a copy of the permit application and supporting documentation (40 C.F.R. § 121.14).

The Tribe then evaluates the proposed discharge to determine if it will cause a violation of tribal WQS, and if so, the Tribe may object and request a hearing (33 U.S.C. § 1341(a)(2) [1988]). The permitting agency has a mandatory duty to hold a public hearing upon receiving a timely request from the downstream Tribe (Id.). If EPA is not the permitting agency, EPA must evaluate the Tribe's objection and recommend to the permitting agency whether and under what conditions the license or permit should be issued (40 C.F.R. § 121.13). The permitting agency is not bound to accept EPA's recommendations, but it must condition the permit in a manner necessary to meet all applicable WQS, including the WQS of a Tribe downstream from the proposed discharge (33 U.S.C. § 1341 [a][2][1988]). If such conditions cannot ensure compliance with those WQS, the permitting agency may not issue the permit (Id.).

This process was upheld as a valid one according to the Tenth Circuit in *City of Albuquerque v. Browner* 97 F. 3d 415 (10th Cir. 1996). In *Albuquerque*, the court held that EPA had full authority to revise Albuquerque's permit for its wastewater treatment facility to meet the Isleta Pueblo's WQS. In this case, the Pueblo of Isleta set Water Quality Standards based on the tribal ceremonial use of the Rio Grande River which included, in the Tribe's standards, "immersion and intentional or incidental ingestion of water" (*City of Albuquerque v. Browner* 97 F.3d 428). By approving the ceremonial use designation, EPA, in effect, allowed the Pueblo to use its own understanding of the importance of water as a basis for establishing standards under a federal regulatory program. Moreover, the Pueblo's promulgation of strict water quality standards demonstrated its willingness to use its sovereign authority to protect the purity of the river water beyond the level of protection provided by the State of New Mexico. Also, the Tenth Circuit's decision in *City of Albuquerque* indicated judicial willingness to support the important regulatory role that Congress and EPA have created for Tribes. The important practical outcome of this case was that EPA, after approving the Pueblo's standards, had to ensure that the *City of Albuquerque* would not violate these standards. To do this, EPA ordered

Albuquerque to design and implement more treatment for its wastewater treatment plant (Dussias, 1999:659). The cost of upgrading Albuquerque's sewage treatment works was estimated as high as $250 million over 10 years.

While this was a definitive victory for the Pueblo of Isleta and Tribes across the country, the process of "sovereignty" in this case has some significant costs. EPA must approve the WQS, ensuring that they meet the scientific principles EPA has laid out in its regulations—hardly an expression of sovereignty. Also, EPA support for the development of Tribal programs has only recently begun, and Tribal capacity in the monitoring and regulatory programs that EPA helped states set up in the early 1970s "are over 22 years behind the states" (Goldtooth, 1995:147). The Indian Programs in EPA remain under-funded and place Tribal governments at a distinct disadvantage in respect to states (Ranco, 2000). While EPA does provide grants for the development of water monitoring programs on Indian reservations, this money is generally not enough to develop and implement WQS. Thus, while legally an option to all Federally Recognized Tribes, establishing WQS has become a program pursued by mostly wealthier, larger Tribes with a government bureaucracy capable of adopting and implementing the full array of EPA programs. As we shall see in the following sections, the operational aspects of sovereignty that allow Indian Nations to regulate in this manner are also a means of controlling knowledge and identity.

The Problem of Difference in the Nation-State

> The indigenous demand for cultural survival does pose a problem for the state…most liberal democracies prefer in the long run to phase out ethnicity rather than to accommodate it…the demand for indigenous rights is incompatible with this program (Maybury-Lewis, 1997:145).

As I pointed out in the above sections, the prospects for incorporating tribal concerns into the EPA bureaucracy are not good. Many of the problems that Indian Nations in the United States and Canada face are along these lines. On the one hand, Tribes present their rights as sovereign partners in a Nation-State by maintaining their distinct cultural traditions and yet may be required to employ forms of sovereignty which look like, and do not challenge, the theory of rights in their resident Nation-State. When Tribes do not act as sovereigns in the United States, the Federal government is supposed to protect their resources, but as we have seen in the Penobscot case, the Federal government, and not the Tribe, determines the terms of this protection. When Tribes rely on other sovereign entities, they are subject to their theory of rights and because tribal situations represent special circumstances, tribal protection will never be central to the practice of these other sovereignties.

These circumstances pose a series of dilemmas for Indian Nations. In the context of the Penobscot and Pueblo of Isleta cases, and with other Indian Tribes in the United States, the Trust Responsibility and partial sovereignty are powerful tools to ensure cultural and governmental survival. In relationship to environmental justice groups, I would say the same basic problem exists in getting community members a place at the table (Cole and Foster, 2000). How far these tools can be pushed, and when, is a crucial question that can only be answered with an appreciation of how modern Nation-States preserve rights through the operation of their bureaucracies. Before I make some suggestions about what can be learned from these cases, I will first explore the problems and issues of indigenous people, and by extension environmental justice issues, pose for liberal-democratic Nation-States like the United States.

Essentially, the Penobscot Indian Nation was arguing that EPA, as an arbiter of the Trust Responsibility, take actions that would protect, or at least not harm, their culture. This is the same position many environmental justice groups face—how can bureaucracies that protect those in the dominant culture from environmental insults also be used to protect those in subordinate cultures. By appealing to the Federal government to settle a dispute between them and the State of New Mexico, the Pueblo of Isleta was asking for the same kind of protection. As I have pointed out in other work (Ranco, 2000), the Penobscot Nation's particular view of risk encompassed a sense of history and culture that EPA was unable to recognize, and this is why they challenged the draft permit. The disagreements over the legal issues flow from this experience and knowledge base, which is so closely tied to day-to-day interactions with the environment. It is thus impossible to articulate the different bases of knowledge claims without acknowledging the power scene within which they are produced. We are thus left with the question of whether or not it is possible or desirable for a Nation-State like the United States to protect the knowledge and culture of semi-sovereign groups like the Penobscot Indian Nation and the Pueblo of Isleta. Charles Taylor (1994) offers an original perspective of this problem in his essay, "The Politics of Recognition." Ostensibly addressing the dilemma of multi-culturalism, Taylor discusses the philosophical origins of contemporary liberal democracies and the possibility of such states acknowledging differences in the practice of their governments.

Taylor points to two possibilities in the liberal tradition for dealing with this problem of difference. The demand for recognition, animated by the ideal of human dignity, points both to the protection of the basic rights of individuals as human beings and to acknowledgement of the particular needs of individuals as members of specific cultural groups. In his response to Taylor, Walzer (1994) suggests that this tension articulates two forms of liberalism. One form of liberalism "is committed in the strongest possible way to individual rights and, almost as a deduction from this, to a rigorously neutral state, that is, a state without cultural or religious projects" (Walzer, 1994:99). The second kind of liberalism "allows for a state committed to the survival and flourishing of a particular nation, culture, or religion, or of a limited set of nations, cultures, and religions—so long as the basic rights of citizens who have different commitments or no such commitments at all are protected" (Walzer, 1994:99). Walzer and Taylor agree that the United States is strongly in the first camp of liberalism. To take the second kind of liberalism seriously, the state would be "called upon to take responsibility for everyone's (cultural) survival" (Walzer, 1994:102).

Taylor and Walzer give us important insights into the operation of liberal-democratic Nation-States. They remind us of the potential problems Nation-States face when they start to establish rights based on groups, not individuals. In addition, the state made up of multi-ethnic societies would have to defend collective as well as individual rights and in effect guarantee the circumstances under which ethnic groups can thrive (Walzer, 1982; also cited in Maybury-Lewis, 1997). Walzer is critical of this approach, arguing that it is possible only under tyranny (Walzer, 1982). He, like others (Maybury-Lewis, 1997; Taylor, 1994), holds out hope by arguing that liberal Nation-States can help cultures flourish by administratively making it easier on them with decentralization and federalism. While sympathetic to this type of administrative fix, Maybury-Lewis (1997) follows Habermas (1994) in maintaining that the state cannot guarantee the cultural survival of the minorities within it. The best it can do is "ensure that the rights of minorities are protected in such a way that they have a reasonable opportunity to ensure their own continuity...[and] make administrative arrangements to accommodate it" (Maybury-Lewis, 1997:155). What is "reasonable" will always be open to debate, and as we can see in the cases above, it may prove the difference between life and death. Additionally, it is striking that these arguments for and against the protection of racial and cultural minorities ignore the very real relationships between power and state knowledge, let alone the historical injustices that produce the current systems of dominance.

Administrative fixes such as those endorsed by Walzer, Maybury-Lewis, and others are already, at least partially, in place with Indian Nations in the United States. While they do not exist for environmental justice groups or other at-risk groups, the problems are similar when environmental justice groups are successful at getting their voice heard—being heard by an official body hardly ever solves the overall problem of excessive pollution and health risks (Cole and Foster, 2000). The ability for many Indian Tribes to act as sovereigns fulfills the federalist dream—and yet, the problem of difference remains. Many Tribes are either legally unable to assert themselves as sovereigns or to the terms that recognize sovereignty. This is the case in the United States because there is always the specter of federal control. As John Comaroff reminds us:

> Nothing is as likely to ensure that humans will assert (or invent) their differences than being made aware...of the indifference of the state to their predicament. Nor is it hard to understand why, when faced with such indifference, subordinated groups should stress their cultural distinctiveness in agitating against empowerment (Comaroff 1996:174).

In some ways, the pluralist impulse, so much a part of the liberal tradition, is supposed to cure the disease of indifference. EPA is quite comfortable with the idea of including Tribes in the decisions that impact their lands, and they did so in the Penobscot and Isleta cases. But Comaroff is saying something more profound about identity politics, and how states and citizens are engaged in a process of mutual alienation. In the Lincoln permit writing process, both EPA and the Penobscot Nation were caught in an identity play that made it virtually impossible for them to overlook their asserted differences.

Conclusion: Knowledge, Bureaucrats, and the Search for Self-Determination

As we have seen in the Penobscot case, the Trust Responsibility is a high ideal rarely met in any particular governmental action impacting Indian Tribes. Even when a state does recognize the legitimacy of indigenous groups as limited sovereigns, as it did in the Pueblo of Isleta case, it is hardly ever on its own terms consistent with the tenets of self-determination which would allow for the indigenous group to define its own political status. Elizabeth Povinelli (1997) in her work on aboriginal Australians has made a powerful observation along these lines. She points out that state recognition of multiculturalism and other methods of viewing the world "is a double gesture." On the one hand it "makes visible a particular set of social formations and subjectivities which necessarily have, more or less, a relationship to social reality" in any particular historical or geographical moment. On the other hand, it "constructs the interiors and edges of legitimacy—the boundary past which, say, the 'special rights' of native title turn into the 'equal rights' that the state provides some minorities" (Povinelli 1997:20). Rather than relativizing notions of law or rights, the promise of the Trust Responsibility, or recognition of the semi-sovereign status of indigenous groups in general, serves, as Justice Brennan put it, "to re-entrench and reaffirm the 'genius' of Western common law as against all other forms of law and society, including the indigenous law it has just recognized" (Povinelli 1997:20). Similarly, when an environmental justice group gains access to a state regulatory process, it is almost always in the terms that the state has set up—the same state that allows, and maybe even endorses, the fact that certain groups are over-burdened with pollution and sickness.

Despite this pessimistic view on the recognition of indigenous rights by Nation-States, Povinelli argues for a theory of state practice that leaves some hope for those of us who take the recognition of rights by states seriously. Povinelli sees the practice of the state in the day-to-day transactions of its functionaries—those who we lovingly called bureaucrats. In relating to the Australian High Court's ruling in *Mabo and Others v. The State of Queensland*, she finds hope that the ruling may open up state practices that are appreciative of other cultural practices, but this all comes down to whether or not bureaucrats are open to such considerations. As she states:

> (The) question remains whether this land commissioner and other land commissioners and native title tribunals will recognize these forms of cultural difference as within the difference recognizing intent of the law, or whether they will recognize a plurality of differences as possible in relation to the same material space (Povinelli 1998:610).

Following Povinelli, we cannot immediately assume that an arrangement of sovereigns or semi-sovereigns precludes a "plurality of differences." The possibility exists for us to recognize and support other forms of political organization, environmental protection, and knowledge production. In the context of Indians and environmental issues, it must start with indigenous ideas of environmental management and political practice. This may or may not require the full implementation of legal sovereignty on Indian reservations, although it should be a clear option for Indian Nations. Actually, the challenge is far greater. Self-determination is a much broader project than sovereignty. It involves people defining for themselves the ways in which they will interact with other people, arrange their communities, and protect themselves—what "legitimate" knowledge they use and why. Focusing on state model arrangements—the administrative fixes—distracts us from this basic, but critical principle. Hopefully, the policy makers of the future will be able to recognize the plurality of differences that are required to ensure self-determination for all people.

References

Alfred, T. (1999). *Peace, Power, and Righteousness: An Indigenous Manifesto.* New York: Oxford University Press.

Anaya, J. (1997). Ethnic Group Rights. In I. Shapiro & W. Kymlicka (Eds.), *Ethnicity and Group Rights*. New York: New York University Press.

Appadurai, A. (1990). Disjuncture and Difference in the Global Cultural Economy. *Peace Culture, 2*(2), 1-24.

Barsh, R. L., and Henderson, J. Y. (1980). *The Road: Indian Tribes and Political Liberty*. Berkeley: University of California Press.

Barsh, R. (1986). The Nature and Spirit of North American Political Systems. *American Indian Quarterly, 10*(2), 181-198.

Bee, R. L. (1999). Structure, Ideology, and Tribal Governments. *Human Organization, 58*(3), 285-294.

Boldt, M., and Long, J. A. (1984). Tribal Traditions and European-Western Political Ideologies: The Dilemma of Canada's Native Indians. *Canadian Journal of Political Science, 17*(3), 537-553.

Brightman, R. A. (1993). *Grateful Prey: Rock Cree Human-Animal Relationships*. Berkeley: University of California Press.

Callicott, J. B. (1989). American Indian Land Wisdom? Sorting Out the Issues. In J. B. Callicot (Ed.), *In Defense of the Land Ethic: Essays in Environmental Philosophy*. Albany: State University Press of New York.

Chambers, R. P. (1975). Judicial Enforcement of the Federal Trust Responsibility to Indians. *Stanford Law Review, 27*(5), 1213-1248.

Cole, L. W., and Foster, S. R. (2000). *From the Ground Up: Environmental Racism and the Rise of the Environmental Justice Movement*. New York: New York University Press.

Comaroff, J. L. (1996). Ethnicity, Nationalism, and the Politics of Difference in an Age of Revolution. In E. Wilmsen & P. McAllister (Eds.), *The Politics of Difference: Ethnic Premises in a World of Power*. Chicago: University of Chicago Press.

Coughlin, S. S. (1996). Environmental Justice: The Role of Epidemiology in Protecting Unempowered Communities from Environmental Hazards. *The Science of the Total Environment, 184*(67-76).

Deloria, V., and Lytle, C. (1984). *The Nations Within*. Austin: University of Texas Press.

Douglas, M., and Wildavsky, A. (1982). *Risk and Culture: An Essay on the Selection of Technical and Environmental Dangers*. Berkeley: University of California Press.

Dussias, A. M. (1999). Asserting a Traditional Environmental Ethic: Recent Developments in Environmental Regulation Involving Native American Tribes. *New England Law Journal, 33*(2), 653-689.

Feld, S., and Basso, K. H. (1996). *Senses of Place*. Santa Fe, NM: SAR Press.

Foucault, M. (1980). *Power/Knowledge: Selected Interviews and Other Writings, 1972-1977*. New York, NY: Pantheon.

Frickey, P. P. (1990). Congressional Intent, Practical Reasoning, and the Dynamic Nature of Federal Indian Law. *California Law Review, 78*, 1137.

Galloway, W. C. (1995). Tribal Water Quality Standards Under the Clean Water Act: Protecting Traditional Cultural Uses. *Washington Law Review, 77*, 177-202.

Goldtooth, T. B. K. (1995). Indigenous Nations: Summary of Sovereignty and Its Implications for Environmental Protection. In B. Bryant (Ed.), *Environmental Justice: Issues, Policies, and Solutions* (pp. 138-148). Washington, D.C.: Island Press.

Graham, J. D., Green, L., and Roberts, M. (1988). *In Search of Safety*. Cambridge: Harvard University Press.

Graham, J. (1992). *Public Hearing.* Paper presented at the Proposed Chapter 584: Surface Water Toxics Control Program and Interim Statewide Criteria for Dioxin, Augusta, ME.

Gramsci, A. (1971). *Selections from the Prison Notebook.* New York: International Publishers.

Grinde, D. A., and Johansen, B. E. (1995). *The Ecocide of Native America: Environmental Destruction of Indian Lands and Peoples*. Santa Fe, NM: Clear Light Publisher.

Guana, E. (1998). The Environmental Justice Misfit: Public Participation and the Paradigm Paradox. *Stanford Environmental Law Journal, 17*(3), 3-88.

Habermas, J. (1994). Struggles for Recognition in the Democratic Constitutional State. In C. Taylor (Ed.), *Multiculturalism* (pp 107-148). Princeton: Princeton University Press.

Harris, S., and Harper, B. (1997). A Native American Exposure Scenario. *Risk Analysis, 17*(6), 789-795.

Heiman, M. K. (1996). Waste Management and Risk Assessment: Environmental Discrimination through Regulation. *Urban Geography, 17*(5), 400-418.

Hughes, J. D. (1983). *American Indian Ecology*. El Paso: Texas University Press.

Jasanoff, S. S. (1987). Contested Boundaries in Policy-Relevant Science. *Social Studies of Science, 17*(2), 195-230.

Jasanoff, S. S. (1990). *The Fifth Branch: Science Advisers as Policymakers*. Cambridge, MA: Harvard University Press.

Jasanoff, S. S. (1992). Science, Politics, and the Renegotiation of Expertise at EPA. Osiris, 7: 1-23. *Osiris, 7*, 1-23.

Jasanoff, S. S. (1996). The Dilemma of Environmental Democracy. *Issues in Science and Technology, 13*(1), 63-75.

Kickingbird, K., et al. (1977). *Indian Sovereignty*. Washington, D.C.: Institute for the Development of Indian Law.

Krech, S. (Ed.). (1981). *Indians, Animals, and the Fur Trade*. Athens: University of Georgia Press.

Kuehn, R. R. (1996). The Environmental Justice Implications of Quantitative Risk Assessment. *Illinois Law Review, 38*(1), 103-178.

Lakind, J., & Rifkin, E. (1990). Current Method for Setting Dioxin Limits in Water Requires Re-Examinatian. *Environmental Science Technology, 24*(7), 960-981.

Martin, C. (1978). *Keepers of the Game: Indian-Animal Relationships and the Fur Trade*. Berkeley: University of California Press.

Maybury-Lewis, D. (1997). *Indigenous Peoples, Ethnic Groups, and the State*. Boston: Allyn and Bacon.

Menell, P. (1991). The Limitations of Legal Institutions for Addressing Environmental Risks. *Journal of Economic Perspectives, 5*(3), 93-113.

Meredith, H. L. (1993). *Modern American Indian Tribal Government and Politics*. Tsaile, AZ: Navajo Community College Press.

Moore, S. F. (1993). Moralizing States and the Ethnography of the Present American. *Ethnological Society Monographs Series, 5*, 55-77.

Morris, G. T. (1992). International Law and Politics: Toward a Right to Self-Determination for Indigenous Peoples. In M. A. Jaimes (Ed.), *The State of Native America* (pp. 55-86). Boston: South End Press.

Morris, W. (1998, July 31). Activists Seek Review of Richmond Facility. *West County Times*.

Nanda, V. (1981). Self-Determination Under International Law: Validity of Claims to Secede. *Case Western Journal of International Law, 13*(2), 42-96.

National Research Council. (1983). *Risk Assessment in the Federal Government: Managing the Process.* Washington, D.C.: National Academy Press.

Nelson, R., and Sheley, J. (1985). Bureau of Indian Affairs Influence on Indian Self-Determination. In V. Deloria (Ed.), *American Indian Policy in the Twentieth Century* (pp. 177-196). Norman: University of Oklahoma Press.

O'Brien, S. (1986). The Government-Government and Trust Relationships: Conflicts and Inconsistencies. *American Indian Culture & Research Journal, 10*(4), 57.

O'Neill, C. (2000). Variable Justice: Environmental Standards, Contaminated Fish, and "Acceptable" Risk to Native Peoples. *Stanford Environmental Law Journal, 19*(1), 3-120.

Penobscot Indian Nation. (1993). *Comments on Initial Draft Permit for Lincoln Pulp and Paper*. Indian Island, Maine: Department of Natural Resources.

Penobscot Indian Nation. (1996). *Joint Letter with Bureau of Indian Affairs Regarding Trust Responsibility and Fish Consumption.* Maine: Department of Natural Resources.

Penobscot Indian Nation Testimony in favor of LD 1577: An Act to Eliminate Paper Mill Dioxin and Restore Maine's Rivers, Maine State Legislature (1997).

Percival, R., et al. (1996). *Environmental Regulation: Law, Science, and Policy*. New York: Little, Brown, and Company.

Pommersheim, F. (1995). *Braid of Feathers: American Indian Law and Contemporary Tribal Life*. Berkeley, CA: University of California Press.

Povinelli, E. (1997). Reading Ruptures, Rupturing Readings: Mabo and the Cultural Politics of Activism. *Social Analysis, 41*(2), 20-28.

Povinelli, E. (1998). The State of Shame: Australian Multiculturalism and the Crisis of Indigenous Citizenship. *Critical Inquiry, 24*(2), 575-610.

Ranco, D. (2000). *Environmental Risk and Politics in Eastern Maine: The Penobscot Nation and the Environmental Protection Agency.* Unpublished PhD Dissertation, Harvard University, Cambridge, MA.

Robbins, R. (1992). Self-Determination and Subordination: The Past, Present, and Future of American Indian Governance. In M. A. Jaimes (Ed.), *The State of Native America* (pp. 87-121). Boston: South End Press.

Sagoff, M. (1988). *The Economy of the Earth: Philosophy, Law, and the Environmen*. Mary Knoll, NY: Orbis.

Sagoff, M. (1991). Zuckerman's Dilemma: A Plea for Environmental Ethics. *Hasting Center Report, 21*(5), 32-40.

Shrader-Frechette, K. (1988). Parfit, Risk Assessment, and Imperceptible Effects. *Public Affairs Quarterly,* 2(4), 75-96.

Taylor, C. (1994). *Multiculturalism: Examining the Politics of Recognition.* Princeton, NJ: Princeton University Press.

Tsosie, R. (1996). Tribal Environmental Policy in an Era of Self-Determination: The Role of Ethics, Economics, and Traditional Ecological Knowledge. *Vermont Law Review, 21*, 225.

U.S. Environmental Protection Agency. (1991). *Federal, Tribal, and State Roles in the Protection and Regulation of Reservation Environments.* Washington, D.C.: U.S. EPA.

U.S. Environmental Protection Agency. (1994). *Memorandum of Actions for Strengthening EPA's Tribal Operations*. Washington, DC: U.S. EPA.

U.S. Environmental Protection Agency. (1997a). *Joint Public Notice of the Lincoln Pulp and Paper Mill National Discharge Elimination System Permit*. Boston: Office of Ecosystem Protection, EPA-New England.

U.S. Environmental Protection Agency. (1997b). *Response to Public Comments*. Boston: Office of Ecosystem Protection, EPA-New England.

U.S. Environmental Protection Agency. (1998). *Treatment of Tribes in the Same Manner as States/Program Approval Matrix*. Washington, DC: U.S. EPA Office of Water.

U.S. Environmental Protection Agency. (2001). *Memorandum Re-affirming 1984 Indian Policy*. Washington, DC: U.S. EPA.

United Nations. (1976). *Covenant on Civil and Political Rights* (Vol. 999 (14668), 302 U.N.T.S.

Vecsey, C., and Venables, R. (1980). *American Indian Environments: Ecological Issues in Native American History*. Syracuse, NY: Syracuse University Press.

Walzer, M. (1982). Pluralism in Political Perspective. In M. Harrinton, J. Higham, E. Kantowicz and M. Walzer (Eds.), *The Politics of Ethnicity* (pp. 1-28). Cambridge: Belknap Press of Harvard University Press.

Walzer, M. (1994). Comment. In A. Gutman (Ed.), *Multiculturalism* (pp. 99-103). Princeton: Princeton University Press.

Weaver, J. (Ed.). (1996). *Defending Mother Earth: Native American Perspectives on Environmental Justice*. Maryknoll, NY: Orbis Books.

Webster, T. (1990). Why Dioxin and Other Halogenated Aromatic Hydrocarbons are Bad News. *Journal of Pesticide Reform, 9*(5).

Wilkinson, C. (1987). *American Indians, Time, and the Law*. New Haven: Yale University Press.

Williams, B., and Matheny, A. (1995). *Democracy, Dialogue, and Environmental Disputes: The Contested Languages of Social Regulation*. New Haven, CT: Yale University Press.

Wood, M. C. (1994). Indian Land and the Promise of Native Sovereignty: The Trust Doctrine. *Utah Law Review*, 1471-1569.

5

SCIENTIFIC KNOWLEDGE IN THE CONTEXT OF ENVIRONMENTAL JUSTICE

Mutombo Mpanya, Ph.D.*

While it may be the case that disproportionate exposure of people of color to excessive amounts of toxins is perhaps due to either malicious or racist behavior of the decision-makers, what is in fact happening may be something more profound. On the one hand there is a stratified and undemocratic society with extreme economic inequalities which affects people's perceptions and interests in environmental issues. On the other hand one is dealing with deep human limitations to grasp complex physical and social reality in a way that would be reflective of the totality of the social and the physical existence. The problem of environmental justice, therefore, will remain intractable because of these social and epistemological limitations and cannot be tackled or dealt with except by implementing more democratic and participatory processes that would bring together a multiplicity of perspectives to decision-making.

Introduction: Whose Knowledge?

Several years ago, a U.S.-based animal rights organization, Friends of Animals, approached the Ghanaian government about the possibility of releasing a number of retired laboratory monkeys into the forests

---

• Mutombo Mpanya, Ph.D., is originally from the Congo. He received most of his education in Management Engineering at the Free University of Brussels, Belgium. He earned a Ph.D. from the School of Natural Resources at the University of Michigan (1982). Mpanya has worked with international development agencies in several African countries for over 20 years. He served as coordinator of private volunteer organizations and activities at the Kellogg Institute of the University of Notre Dame from 1984 through 1989. He served as director of the International Environmental Studies Program at World College West in Novato, California.

of Ghana. In their plea for a haven for the former lab animals Friends of Animals assured Ghanaians that the monkeys were safe and would benefit the economy of local villages because of their appeal to tourists. As part of their appeal, Friends of Animals made payments to local officials, donated pencils and books to local schools, and made efforts to create a Ghanaian non-profit organization to manage the project.[1]

Nevertheless some Ghanaians, suspecting that the monkeys may have been exposed to HIV, Ebola, or other transmissible diseases, opposed their transfer. In response to this local opposition, the government of Ghana launched an inquiry and found that because of conflicting information it was impossible to ascertain whether or not the animals were indeed safe. In the end Ghana refused the monkeys. Ghanaian environmental activists speculate that the monkeys were probably shipped somewhere else in Africa or to another third world country. Friends of Animals, says Ghanaian political activist Salomon Agbenya, criticized the Ghanaian decision for not being based on "sound knowledge."

Whether in Africa, other third world countries, or here in the U.S., when people of color voice concerns related to issues of environmental injustice their perceptual and experiential knowledge is often dismissed as unsound or non-scientific. In the Ghanaian case, the community's suspicion, based on centuries old (lived) knowledge of inequitable relations between Africa and the Western world, was reduced to ignorance, backwardness, or superstition.

While the credibility of individual and community perceptions is frequently questioned, the notion of scientific objective knowledge in the context of environmental justice remains largely unchallenged. Often, when communities of color find themselves disproportionately and negatively impacted by environmental toxins they seek out authoritative (scientific) knowledge to justify their claims, assign responsibility, and challenge the corporate and governmental analysis, which often supports the environmental abuses. In this way victims of environmental racism are forced to utilize the very institutions that are associated with the injustices in the first place.

The space in which environmental injustice takes place is a space of political and epistemological conflict where knowledge is inseparable from corporate and political interests. In this paper I will first examine several different notions of knowledge as presented in the literature of environmental and science writers as well as that of philosophers and students of knowledge and society. Secondly, from these ideas I will look at how this knowledge

1 S. Agbenya, Personal Communication (no date).

functions when dealing with issues of environmental injustice. Thirdly, as a source of data, I will look at a variety of case studies, from both the U.S. and Africa, of communities confronting environmental racism and injustice. And finally, I will conclude with a discussion about the applicability of the findings and some policy recommendations.

Environmentalists

Many environmental thinkers make a distinction between two kinds of knowledge, scientific and indigenous, with the latter characterized as wholesome and the former as being the cause of much of today's environmental destruction.

Soule and Piper (1992) examine the disparate ways scientific and indigenous knowledge operates in relation to agricultural practices. Scientific knowledge, they say, is characterized by the identification of a limited set of variables intended to impact a single outcome. They trace this reductionist approach back to the work of Descartes and its agricultural applications to the work of Justin Liebig, the German chemist who discovered the indispensability of certain mineral nutrients, such as phosphorous, potassium and nitrogen, to plant growth. The strength of the scientific approach, say Soule and Piper, is in its ability to identify and locate critical factors in the face of immense complexity. But, they argue, there is a downside. Science's reduction has led people to believe they can control and improve upon nature and it has led to the attempted conquest of nature and our current ecological crises.

Soule and Piper contrast the analytic cause and effect approach of scientific knowledge with holistic, traditional, or indigenous approaches that are more appropriate for dealing with ecological complexity. Indigenous cultures mimic the behavior of the natural systems to develop sustainable agro-ecological systems. They use wild species. Their crops resemble natural communities. The plants they grow fit local precipitation and nutrient-cycles, preserve soil, and do not compete for nutrients with neighboring plants. Additionally, because many ecological processes extend beyond a single individual life span, indigenous ways of knowing incorporate long-range thinking into their agricultural practices compared with science's short-term result orientation.

Carolyn Merchant (1991) also identifies two kinds of thinking in relation to nature. These she calls mechanistic and organismic. The former, whose roots date back to the end of the Middle Ages, uses the notion of a machine as its guiding metaphor. Within the context of this mechanistic metaphor, the behavior of natural or social systems must be predictable, controllable, and subject to rational laws. This necessitates the rule of rationality over nature, society, and self. Nature is reduced to dead matter in motion, a system of inert parts to be externally controlled. This way of knowing nature, according to Merchant, places human beings outside of nature's scope and justifies the manipulation and domination of nature through scientific and technological means. Merchant sees the emergence of this view of nature as coinciding with the development of capitalism and affecting the notion of the self as the rational master of one's own feelings and passions. As such, the mechanistic view of nature is more than a framework in which to think about nature; it is also a way of wielding power over the natural and human world.

The organismic framework, on the other hand, uses the organism as its guiding metaphor for the understanding of nature. According to this view the universe is an integrated entity where everything is connected to everything else. This perspective is associated not only, as commonly thought, with Native American or other indigenous cultures but also, says Merchant, it can be traced back to Europe. In pre-modern Europe, she says, the natural universe was conceived of as a large organism. The movements of its parts were associated with the existence of a soul. Spirit moved through plants and animals. Stars and planets were alive. The earth was thought of as a nurturing mother. The water system was her blood, rivers and streams, her veins and veinlets. Soil was her skin and trees her tresses. Stones and metals emerged from her womb. Miners performed ceremonies before excavating her precious ore. The magician of pre-modern Europe was revered as a knower of nature who did not attempt to exert power over nature, but rather acted to protect nature and aid in its full manifestation. It is in this ancient organismic view, says Merchant, that the environmental movement has its roots.

Max Horkheimer (1972) explores issues of domination and social justice by examining the relationship between the political economy and scientific knowledge of the natural world. According to Horkheimer, scientific knowledge, or what he calls instrumental reason, dominates and controls nature by placing it in the service of human beings. And because instrumental reason denies the internal nature of human beings as well, it also leads to a manipulation of human consciousness and creates a situation of permanent struggle and social conflict.

Drawing upon the work of Marx, Horkheimer argues that scientific theories reproduce and reflect the ideology of dominant social groups and are therefore more representative of the politically constructed material world in which people live than any neutral, "objective" truth. This kind of "objective" knowledge, says Horkheimer, separates the human knowing subject from nature as the object of knowledge, which leads to both the domination of nature and the domination of humans. Science's knowledge of the natural world and the use of modern technology have, according to Horkheimer, led to the destruction of the natural world as well as increased social inequity, dehumanization, and totalitarian political control. Instead of using knowledge as an instrument of control and domination, Horkheimer suggests that knowledge should work towards the achievement of a just society and the fulfillment of human needs.

Max Oelschlaeger (1991) uses the works of Kepler, Galileo, Bacon, Descartes, and Newton to chronicle the development of scientific knowledge and its effects on nature. These authors trace a major shift from the notion of nature as an organism that was held in the Christian Middle Ages to that of nature as a mechanism. Kepler, in the tradition of classical physics, described the universe as a celestial machine comparable to a clock. Galileo defined as real, only those characteristics of the natural world that lend themselves to quantitative measurement and manipulation. Bacon saw humans as masters of the physical world and believed that through the application of scientific knowledge humans could restore the earth back to its initial purity. Descartes saw animals as machines lacking any sensibility. Newton completed the picture by comparing nature to mechanical forces interacting in accordance with mathematical laws.

In contrast with the mechanistic approaches to the knowledge of nature posited by Kepler, Galileo, Bacon, Descartes, and Newton, Oelschlaeger describes what he calls the systemic approach. For this he draws upon the work of Spinoza, a philosopher who recognized that humans are bound to, not separate from, the laws of nature. For Spinoza, life is a system of communications between the different elements of nature, a system in which humans, as inquiring subjects, are not separate from the rest of the world.

Like Oelschlaeger, David Abram (1996) also credits the origins of scientific objective knowledge with Descartes and Galileo. According to Abram it was Descartes who inaugurated the separation between the thinking subject and the outside material world and Galileo, through his equation of measurability with reality, who helped downplay subjective human experience and emphasized objectivity. Abram juxtaposes Descartes' and Galileo's views of science as human knowledge with Edmond Husserl's philosophy of phenomenology. Phenomenological knowledge is experiential knowledge. This kind of knowledge gained through familiarity with the world creates empathy, says Husserl, which allows the human subject to recognize the external world as a form of subject too. From this perspective the world of scientific knowledge is no longer a pure object, but rather is a miniature of mental experiences and perceptions brought together into a phenomenal world that we socially negotiate to constitute reality.

Husserl, says Abram, goes as far as to suggest that our phenomenological experiential knowledge of the world may find itself in conflict with scientific knowledge. In what he called the overthrow of scientific revolution, Husserl argued that the earth, not the sun, is the center of the phenomenal world. Lived experience may not agree with theoretical or scientific knowledge. And so, because for Husserl all human knowledge is rooted in our physical relation to the world, he proposes that scientific knowledge must also be rooted in our everyday, lived experience.

From Husserl, Abram moves on to Merleau-Ponty who viewed the human body as the site of all knowledge. Without the body, Merleau-Ponty argues there would be no way to experience the world or the self. Knowledge in this sense is a reciprocal interchange between the world and the body. Merleau-Ponty uses the notion of the body in an expansive and inclusive way that includes humans, plants, and animals. It is this larger body, he says, that gives rise to the individual identity *and* interdependence of the knower and the known.

In addition to philosophy, Abram also draws on history and anthropology for his analysis of knowledge. He distinguishes between animistic knowledge that integrates sensuous reality into the experience of knowing and alphabetical knowledge, which exists beyond the lived experience. Early forms of writing, according to Abram, relied on pictorial representation. After that came ideograms that dealt with specific aspects or qualities of the outside world. This pictorial form of writing though representative and therefore distanced from actual lived experience, nonetheless reinforced one's relation to the natural world. With the development of the alphabet and its symbolic economy, pictorial content was further abstracted and thus a greater divide was created between representation (written) and experience. Greek philosophy, says Abram, viewed alphabetic knowledge as *eidos*, an abstract, unchanging form or essence. Over time, written knowledge has replaced pictorial representations and oral stories that were imbued with the experience of the knower. Alphabetical knowledge, says Abram, has resulted in a severing of the relationship between the world and its knowing subject and created a psyche that is distanced from its lived experience.

Scientists

Environmental writers are not the only ones who recognize a polarization in knowledge and who believe there is more than one way of knowing the world around us. Among science writers, some such as Capra, Bohm, and Prigogine, see scientific knowledge itself as polarized. Others, such as Lewontin, concentrate on the role of scientific knowledge in society and see this polarization in the use of science as between the dominant class and the oppressed class.

Fritjof Capra (1996) connects knowledge, as a vision of reality, to environmental and social problems. Capra, drawing on the work of Thomas Kuhn, makes a distinction between two scientific paradigms, one he calls mechanistic, the other holistic. In the mechanical paradigm the environment is made of isolated parts; material progress and resources are unlimited; the human body is a machine; and life is a competition for existence. This mechanistic approach to the environment, says Capra, is responsible for today's environmental and social crises.

The holisticparadigm, which Capra associates with systems thinking, is a scientific knowledge characterized by four aspects. First, there is the assumption that the whole is not the sum of its parts. Second, processes and relationships are more important than fixed structures. Third, the emphasis is not on objectivity, but rather is on the relation to the human observer. And fourth, knowledge is not so much something firmly built; it is more like a changing metaphor. In this paradigm, which Capra refers to as an ecological paradigm, the physical world is a web of relations between interconnected elements.

Like Capra, David Bohm (2000) makes a distinction between what he calls mechanistic and non-mechanistic views of science. For Bohm, the mechanistic view sees the world as made of basic distinct elements independent of one another. The forces of interaction between these elements do not affect their basic nature. But, says Bohm, this approach to the knowledge of the physical world, even though still in use, has been challenged by other scientific theories such as relativity and quantum mechanics and more recently chaos theory and the study of complex dynamic systems.

In the non-mechanistic view, elements cannot be analyzed in isolation. Connections between elements and the whole are crucial. Bohm proposes a theory of "unbroken wholeness," a notion suggesting that the universe is an irreducible whole. According to this perspective, discrete particles are not the primary reality of the universe; rather it is the whole universe that manifests itself in each one of its parts. Bohm goes on to suggest that scientific, fragmentary, and analytical thinking has caused much of the disharmony we experience in society and that adopting a perspective of unbroken wholeness could help us overcome the separation between values and policy.

Ilya Prigogine (1997) talks about the science of dynamic systems such as celestial mechanics, thermodynamics, and fluid dynamics. He points out that already at the beginning of classical mechanics there were two notions of knowledge of the physical world. One, associated with Newton and Boltzmann, is an evolutionary knowledge with time-bound irreversible processes. The other, held by Leibniz and Laplace, viewed scientific knowledge as an all at once kind of knowing of the universe. In this perspective time becomes an illusion with no difference between the past, present, and future. For example, Laplace in his deterministic vision believed that if one knew all the laws of the universe one would then be able to precisely predict everything that would happen. These two knowledges can be described as deterministic and non-deterministic, or infinite and finite knowledge. Even though environmental and societal sciences deal with complex dynamic systems, they utilize finite knowledge to understand these systems. But because these systems are constantly evolving, they can be known only with limited predictability and are ultimately uncontrollable. This understanding forces us to move away from the notion of our relationship to nature as one of domination or control. Finite knowledge is at best reductionistic. Since reality is always changing, knowledge is only temporary or finite.

Biologist R. C. Lewontin (1992) defines science not only as a body of knowledge, but also as a set of methods and social institutions. Lewontin argues that science is influenced by the society in which it is embedded. Those who control the resources which science depends upon for its survival and production mold its ideas, methods, problems, and results. Thus, says Lewontin, science as a system of knowledge works in the interest of society's dominant classes. In its role as legitimizer and normalizer science's relationship to social ideology is clearly demonstrated in the relationship between Darwin's notion of survival of the fittest and the enactment of the 18th Century English Poor Laws that criminalized poverty. Generally, however, science's societal ideological influences are subtler. For example, prior to industrial capitalism, the individual was viewed as the creation of society, but today atomization and notions of individualism have infiltrated social explanations (psychology, sociology, economics) and replaced the notion of the socially made individual with the myth of the "self-made" human being.

Socialists and Philosophers

Lewontin's ideas echo those of many social scientists. Among students of knowledge and society like Vico, Lyotard, Foucault, and Althusser, there is a consensus that society has an impact on how and what we know. All agree that there is a relationship between knowledge and political power. Society decides what is worth knowing, how to know it, and why. Because society determines scientific practice, science is also beholden to the economic interests of the dominant class. Since profit, through increased surplus, is one of these interests, it should come as no surprise that science focuses its energies on improving technological efficiency and enhancing productivity.

Perhaps the earliest of the social scientists to examine the relationship between knowledge and society was Gianbattista Vico, who, in 1725 published *Sciencia Nova* (Bergin and Fisch, 1961). His goal was to apply the model of physical sciences to the world of nations. He began with the study of myths because he believed they represented the way in which human mental structures dealt with or represented the reality that they related to, cope with or struggle to understand. The myth represents a poetic wisdom or *sapienza poetica.* Once the myth is imposed on a reality as a model it becomes that reality. Humans, says Vico, have a tendency to recognize what they themselves have made up as true facts about the world. Humans create myths and institutions, and in turn these myths and institutions create humans. So, says Vico, knowledge, especially knowledge of society, may well be a human fabrication.

Jean-Francois Lyotard (1984) argues that the traditional notion of knowledge as an end in itself and as linked to the individual mind will change in our time. Knowledge will be computerized and sold. And nation states, he says, may go to war over the control of knowledge as they once fought over territory. He concludes that power and knowledge are the same thing, in that those who have power decide what knowledge is appropriate and worthwhile. The knowledge of which Lyotard speaks is not just a question of technical competence about what is true or efficient; it also includes the knowledge of social normalization for the purpose of control.

For Lyotard, scientific knowledge does not represent the totality of knowledge, but rather exists in competition with narrative knowledge. Narratives are popular stories, myths, legends, and tales that legitimize a given social order. In traditional societies narratives define the relationship of society to itself and to its environment. Scientific knowledge may also be in conflict with itself as when a new theory challenges a previously established one. Both narrative and scientific theories use didactics to insure their own reproduction. Lyotard argues that scientific knowledge, while in competition with narrative knowledge also relies upon it to advance its claims of supremacy. This is why government and industry spend large amounts of money to tell science's epic tale. There is the myth of science as the liberator of humanity, the myth of a better life, or the myth of science's battle against cancer. In these myths science is portrayed as hero.

Though knowledge is often presented as a form of liberation (as in emancipatory discourses of modernity) Foucault (1972) argues that knowledge, because it has the power to define others, is power over, and as such it stops being liberatory and becomes a form of surveillance, regulation, and discipline. Traditionally power exercised its will through physical constraint, but according to Foucault, a shift has been made towards the mental, intellectual, and cultural exercise of power. In his analysis of prison and mental health clinics he demonstrates how prior to the 18th Century brute force was utilized to control marginalized populations whereas in the modern world scientific and social science practices are predominately used to control populations. Constraints that were once enforced through violent means are now enforced through the production and internalization of certain forms of knowledge. In this way knowledge as power helps internalize the norms and values, rules and codes that prevail within the social order. It's a set of rules by which society lives that produces reality and creates objects of knowledge and rituals of truth. But Foucault also argues that this same knowledge can be used to challenge the existing social order.

Althusser (1969) drew on Marxist traditions that look at political economy, not so much as simply scientific knowledge, but representative of the ideology of the bourgeoisie. Because people get their ideas of what, why, and how to study from the society in which they live Althusser argues that all knowledge is therefore tainted by the ideology of the dominant members of that society. On the other hand Althusser also believed in the notion of a "real" or "objective" scientific knowledge that could reveal the ways in which knowledge is shaped or constructed by the dominant social class. Political economy as a critique of a bourgeois economy would be an example of such knowledge.

Theoretical Model: The Partiality of Human Knowledge

Though there are important differences amongst the above authors they all agree that there is more than one way of knowing. The environmental authors placed the scientific and non-scientific approaches to knowledge into a dualistic or binary opposition. The science writers identified a similar kind of dualism between analytical, mechanistic knowledge on one hand and holistic, ecological, and probabalistic knowledge on the other. All of the authors discussed agreed with the students of knowledge and society in that knowledge is directly related to and reflective of the interests of the society in which it is produced. As such, knowledge as representation can never fully exhaust the physical or human world it seeks to represent and is always, at best, partial.

Using this literature as a foundation, the following model emerges as a possible way of dealing with knowledge in the context of environmental injustice. First we must assume that human reality is made of physical and social components, and second we must assume that biological, ecological, and social interests define and affect both the experience of reality as well as how it is mentally represented in the form of knowledge. For example, in considering whether or not to release the monkeys into the forests of Ghana, Friends of Animals and the Ghanaians were dealing with radically different physical or experiential realities. Ghanaian knowledge of forests, monkeys, and the spread of diseases like Ebola or AIDS was different from that of the U.S.-based animal rights organization. The different social and political structures of Ghana and the U.S. also gave the Ghanaians and the Friends of Animals different mental frameworks from which to make their risk assessments. Friends of Animals were motivated by a concern for animal rights and operated within the framework of the "soundness" of scientific (Western) knowledge and Western middle-class environmental ethics. The Ghanaians, on the other hand, were operating from an experiential base with a long history of exploitation by the West and knowledge of animals as potential carriers of disease from Western experimental labs. It is important to note that the physical relationship of the Ghanaians to the potential risks was also radically different from that of Friends of Animals. Given these disparate realities, it's no surprise that Friends of Animals and the Ghanaians arrived at different conclusions about whether or not to ship the monkeys to Ghana.

We can also assume, as the case of the Ghanaians and Friends of Animals demonstrates, that experience and representation affect each other. With these assumptions, it becomes clear that human knowledge is partial. But partiality must be understood in several senses. As a mental model, knowledge is partial because it is forced to simplify and therefore represent only certain aspects of a more complex reality. This is partly the result of human limitation, but also because physical reality is ever changing and may evolve in ways the model cannot anticipate. This is precisely the point made by Soule and Piper (1992) about reductionism and by Prigogine (1997) about limited predictability. For Prigogine, a model can only say something about today's reality, not about how that reality might evolve.

Partiality also refers to the fact that as humans we have needs and interests. Abram (1996), based on the work of Husserl, argues that the human body is the seat of human experience, and therefore our biological and psychological needs affect the kind of knowledge we develop. But there may be aspects of the physical world that our bodies and technical instruments (as extensions of our bodies) may be unable to accurately detect. Sound vibrations may be beyond what we can hear, odors beyond what we can smell, and light beyond what we can see. Differences in physical variables that we may not be able to detect instrumentally may be undistinguishable from systematic or operational errors. According to Lewontin (1992), because humans live in societies that are stratified into diverse groups and classes, knowledge may represent the bias or "needs" of certain groups over others. Philosophically speaking one could say that every epistemic system says something not only about the world it intends (or pretends) to reveal, but also about the human physical and social conditions that produce that epistemic system.

Awareness of the conditions that shape knowledge is only possible in that moment of humility when knowledge catches itself through its own reflectiveness. This may be too much to ask in practical situations where knowledge of the world does not necessarily ascribe to the wisdom of self-knowledge. It is possible, however, to go from partiality to a multiplicity of the partials. We are not suggesting here a total knowledge of the type referred to by Laplace, but rather a holistic knowledge that brings some of the many voices, perspectives, and experiences together in a process of negotiation and decision-making. There will always be other theses and other theories, some of which may conflict while others are complementary. Conflict in environmental risk assessment and decision-making cannot be eliminated (Bernson, 1997). This, according to Bernson, is due to the number and variety of epistemic communities including scientists, technologists, economists, legal professionals, social and political scientists, politicians and the general public.

Case Studies

This background in environmental, scientific, and social science literature together with a model of the partiality of knowledge will help us understand how the characteristics of knowledge operate unsuccessfully or successfully in dealing with issues of environmental justice. But before we examine these specific cases of environmental injustice it is important that we have a minimal understanding of some of the chemicals involved and the places and people affected.[2]

Heavy metals such as mercury, lead, cadmium, and arsenic have higher densities than other common chemicals and are non-degradable. The mechanism of their toxicity comes from their affinity with sulfur, which is part of the chemical structure of enzymes essential to the metabolism of living organisms. Once they attach to the enzyme the latter can no longer properly perform its function, which impacts the health of the organism in a variety of ways.

2 The data in this section came from the following sources: B. Magnus Francis, Toxic Substances in the Environment (New York: John Wiley and Sons, 1994); Colin Baird, Environmental Chemistry (New York: W. H. Freeman and Company, 1995); Ben Selinger, Chemistry in the Marketplace (Toronto: Harcourt Race, 1998).

Pesticides are chemicals designed to kill or control unwanted organisms by interfering with their metabolic processes. Insecticides kill insects, herbicides kill plants, and fungicides kill fungi. Oxides of sulfur or arsenic have been used for thousands of years to kill insects. Organochlorine insecticides have been used since WWII. Organophosphate and carbamate insecticides came into use much later. These substances block the action of the enzymes that are required to transmit nerve impulses. Herbicides have also been used for centuries. However, several decades ago inorganic compounds were used to kill weeds by extracting water from their tissues. More recently, organic herbicides replaced the inorganic ones. Triazines and phenoxyherbicides are among the modern herbicides.

PCB's or polychlorinated biphenyls are not pesticides though they have some structural similarities as organochlorines. PCB's are chemically inert liquids that are difficult to burn, have low vapor pressure, and are good electrical insulators. From the 1950's until they were banned in the late 1970's, PCB's were used extensively in industries as cooling fluids, de-inking solvents, water-proofing agents, heat transfer fluids, etc. At high temperatures PCB's may form 2,3,7,8-Tetrachlorodibenzo-p-Dioxin (TCDD) or dioxin.

Radiation comes in three major categories: alpha, beta, and gamma. Alpha particles can be stopped by a sheet of paper. Beta particles can travel a long distance through the air. Gamma rays penetrate deeply and can destroy or change the genetic material in living organisms including humans. Radioactive materials may have a half-life of millions and billions of years. Chemical elements such as uranium, thorium, and radium are radioactive. Radioactivity has been used for over 200 years in the field of photography and more recently in archaeology for the dating of rocks and in biology for the dating of plants and animal remains. It has also been used to study sub-atomic particles. Perhaps the best known, and certainly the most devastating, use of radioactivity was the atomic bomb. Since the war, radioactivity has been used in the production of nuclear power and also in medicine.

Gasoline is a complex mixture of hydrocarbons and other chemicals. In the process of combustion gasoline produces nitric oxides. Though catalytic converters have been developed to control emissions of nitric oxides and carbon monoxide, 10-20 percent of the nitric oxide and carbon monoxide produced is released into the atmosphere. Before an engine has properly warmed up and during periods of sudden acceleration and deceleration bursts of emissions dump even higher percentages of pollutants into the air.

With respect to locations we will now look at several different cases, both in the United States and in Africa, and identify how the partial nature of knowledge results in difficulty anticipating negative impacts and in conflicting information about those impacts. We will also consider the strategic use of both scientific and traditional body-based and community-based knowledge for the purpose of confronting environmental injustice and racism.

The U.S. cases we will be looking at involve low-income minority communities. They include Hunter's Point, Richmond, and Midway Village in the San Francisco Bay Area, California; Anniston, Alabama; South Camden in Camden, New Jersey; West Harlem in Manhattan, New York; Mossville and Clacasieu Parish, Louisiana; and Shiprock, New Mexico. For the African case we will look at two large regions, Southern Africa and Eastern Africa.

San Francisco's Hunter's Point is a community of about 30,000 predominantly low-income African Americans. The neighborhood is home to two power plants, San Francisco's largest waste-water treatment facility, over 200 "hotspots" containing toxic substances, and two superfund sites (one federal and one state). One of the superfund sites, the 522 acre Hunter's Point Shipyard contains asbestos, PCB's, lead, a variety of solvents, and radioactive materials. In addition, there is a proposal to build a new power plant that would release 30 tons of toxic substance in the atmosphere annually to add to the 550 tons released by the two existing plants. Incidences of asthma and bronchitis in the children of Hunter's Point are exceptionally high, and cancer rates for women are among the highest in the world.[3]

Richmond, California, located just north of Berkeley, has a population of about 80,000 people, 50 percent of whom are African American. Historically, Richmond has been an industrial city that has hosted a number of companies including Vulcan Powder West, Santa Fe Rail, Kaiser Shipyard, Western Pipe and Steel, and others. Today perhaps the most important industries are petrochemical and chemical manufacturing facilities, the largest of which is Chevron (formerly Standard Oil). There are close to 40 chemical facilities operating in Richmond as well as landfills, toxic waste dumps, and incinerators.

---

3 The data about Hunter's Point in this section and in subsequent sections was taken from the following sources: Lisa Davis, "Fallout" (San Francisco Weekly, May 2-8, 2001); "Hunter's Point Shipyard" (Agency for Toxics Substances and Disease Registry, Jan 2001); Hunter's Point Fire Department Run Index for 2001; "Hunter's Point Shipyard" (Environmental Cleanup Newsletter July-Sept. 2001); "Fact Sheet: Bayview Hunter's Point" (Communities For a Better Environment Nov. 1998); "Why Do We Oppose the Expansion of Potrero Power Plant?" (No date. For more information contact: Communities for a Better Environment); Scott Winokur and Christian Berthelsen, "Power Plant Fight Intensifies: Potrero Hill Residents Battle Mirant." (San Francisco Chronicle, July 29, 2001); Eileen Hughes, "Hunter's Point Shipyard Parcel E Sampling and Analysis." (Tetra Tech EM Inc. Feb. 2002).

Spills and explosions occur several times a year. Residents in Richmond, especially the more impoverished Northern Richmond, nearest the industrial facilities, have complained for years about chronic health problems such as diabetes, asthma, and cancer.[4]

Midway Village is a housing project in Daly City, California. Composed of 150 units, the complex is occupied by approximately 1,200 mostly low-income African Americans. The Village was built in 1944 next to a Pacific Gas and Electric (PG&E) gas manufacturing facility that had been in operation since 1906. In 1980, it was discovered that the PG&E facility, known as the Martin Service Station, was contaminated with toxic chemicals including polynuclear aromatic hydrocarbons (PNA's or PAH's). The area was declared a superfund site in 1984, and in 1990 PG&E tests showed that the soil around the housing units was contaminated. Residents of Midway Village have complained of rashes, tumors, respiratory problems, bloody noses, genetic defects, and other health symptoms.[5]

West Anniston, Alabama is a community of about 10,000 mostly low-income African-Americans. The community is home to Swann Company that manufactured PCB's from the 1920's to 1977. Investigations led jointly by Monsanto and the Alabama Department of Environmental Management found the presence of PCB's in drainage ditches and in the soil of private residences. The community is also home to an unlined landfill that was used to dispose of hazardous wastes including PCB's. The landfill, mistakenly opened during

---

4 The data about Richmond in this section and in subsequent sections was taken from the following sources: "General Chemical May 2001 Bucket Result Summery" (Communities for a Better Environment); Shawn Masten, "Residents Plan to Seek Tests for Dioxin" (West County Times, Aug. 11, 1999); Shawn Masten, "Activists Want Blood Tested for Toxins" (West County Times, Dec. 7, 2000); Willie Morris, "Activists Seek Review of Richmond Facility" (West County Times, July 31, 1998); "Bay Area Dioxin Sources" (Communities for a Better Environment, July, 1999); "Chevron Fire, Richmond March 25, 1999 Richmond/San Pablo Bucket Brigade Results Summery Report." (Communities for a Better Environment, 1999); "Dioxins and Refineries: Analysis in the Bay Area, Aug. 2000." (Communities for a Better Environment. 2000); "Coalition Wants $60 Million From Chevron" (Bay City News Service, Dec. 1993); Willie Morris, "Chevron Will Give Neighbors $850,000" (West County Times, June 1994); Benjamin Pimentel, "Dioxin Fear For Richmond Residents" (San Francisco Chronicle, Aug. 12, 1999).

5 The data about Midway Village in this section and in subsequent sections was taken from the following sources: Melissa McMillan "Midway Village Housing Project: A Struggle for Environmental Justice." (No date. For more information contact: University of Michigan Environmental Justice Case Studies); Angelica Pence, "Ridding Midway Village of Tainted Soil—Again. (San Francisco Chronicle, August 25, 2001); Lisa Davis, "Fallout" (San Francisco Weekly. May 2-8, 2001); http://www.umich.edu/~snre492/Jones/midway.html.doc.

a groundbreaking event for a power plant, spilled additional hazardous waste in the community. West Anniston residents have complained of numerous health problems including asthma, reproductive deformities, and cancer. In the nearby Choccobocco River the large-mouth bass population was found to have extremely high levels of PCB's.[6]

West Harlem, a community of about 60,000 mostly low-income African Americans, is located in northern Manhattan. It is home to a Metropolitan Transportation Authority bus depot and the North River Sewage Treatment plant. The plant was built in 1985, occupies eight city blocks along the Hudson River, and processes over 170 million gallons of raw sewage a day. The plant was originally planned to be located in a white neighborhood but because of protest from the residents, the plant site was relocated to West Harlem. Residents of West Harlem find the plant's noxious odors so overbearing that they are unable to go out on their terraces or open their windows. Residents have complained of itchy eyes, shortness of breath, asthma, and bronchitis symptoms that they say are especially pronounced among children. [7]

Camden, New Jersey, located on the banks of Delaware River, has a population of 80,000 and has been an industrial city for over a half century. It has had numerous industries, including steel and a major transportation network. Today the waterfront neighborhood of South Camden hosts a regional sewage treatment plant, a trash-to-steam incinerator, two federal superfund sites, and other toxic waste sites. It is also home to the new Saint Lawrence Cement Company plant, which will add an additional 60 tons of dust into the air each year and close to 77,000 truck deliveries emitting diesel fumes and ground level ozone. South Camden's 2000 residents are predominantly poor

---

6 The data about West Anniston in this section and in subsequent sections was taken from the following sources: Robert D. Bullard, "South Camden Warriors Battle Environmental Racism: An Interview with Cassandra Roberts." (Environmental Justice Resource Center, Nov. 27, 2001); "Inside Story: Anniston Alabama" (Environmental Working Group, Jan. 2002); N. Beilef, "What Monsanto Knew" (The Nation, May, 2000); Katherine Dougan, "PCB's in Anniston's Soul, Air" (Anniston Star online, Feb. 2000); http://www.umich.edu/~snre492/jones/anniston.hotmail.

7 The data about West Harlem in this section and in subsequent sections was taken from the following sources: Amoruso Carol, "WE ACT For Environmental Justice." (Third Force, Dec. 31, 1997); Ashfield Benjamin, "Something Smells Like Environmental Racism" (Modern Times, Dec. 1993); Sarah E. Massey, "North River Sewage Treatment Plant."(New York: West Harlem Environmental Action, 2001): Michael Burger, "In the News: Bus Depots and Racism." (gothamgazette.com. April 19, 2002). Lorraine Woellert, " Pollution: Dumping on the Poor? Cement Plant that Stirred Up a Low Income Area May Be Shut Down." (Business Week Nov. 2001); http://www.umich.edu/~snre492/ny.hotmail.

people of color with an average income of 15,000 dollars a year. Over half of South Camden's residents have complained of respiratory problems.[8]

The communities of Mossville and Clacasieu Parish, Louisiana, located in Southwest Louisiana near the Texas border, are home to several chemical companies including Conoco, Condea Vista, and PPG. Over the years and specifically since 1997 these companies have released an increasing amount of toxins into the atmosphere. Among the chemicals detected in the air by Communities for a Better Environment, a non-profit organization, were benzene, carbon disulfide, methyl ethyl ketone, and xylene. Community residents have complained of burning eyes, nasal soreness, nosebleeds, sinus problems, ear infections, headaches, dizziness and tremors. A health survey conducted by the University of Texas found increased cases of stroke, heart disease, jaundice, and diarrhea.[9]

Shiprock, New Mexico is home to the Navajo Nation. Uranium mining began about 30 miles west of Shiprock around the Carrizo Mountain as early as 1918. The Vanadium Corporation of America and Kerr-McGee have been the major mining companies in Shiprock for many years. The Navajo Nation today complains of health damage and deaths to their people as a result of uranium mining. The Navajo Nation president has placed a moratorium on uranium mining. The Hopi and Dineh communities at Big Mountain are located in the Northern Arizona Black Mesa, south of the Grand Canyon. This region is rich in mineral resources. For years Peabody Western Coal Company has operated the largest coal mine in the world in this area. In 1974, the U.S. government partitioned the land between the Dineh (Navajo) and the Hopi and forced more than 12,000 Dineh to relocate in order to make room for coal mining. Many of those relocated were sent to Sanders, Arizona, which is the

---

8 The data about Camden, New Jersey in this section and in subsequent sections was taken from the following sources: Terry M. Richman, "New York State Tackles Environmental Justice" (Underberg-Kessler www.underberg-kessler.com/press, Oct, 2002); Lorraine Woellert, "Pollution: Dumping on the Poor? Cement Plant the Stirred Up a Low Income Area May Be Shut." (Business Week Nov. 2001).

9 The data about Mossville and Calcasieu Parish, Louisiana in this section and in subsequent sections was taken from the following sources: "US EPA Activity in Mossville, LA and Greater Calcasieu Parish 1998-2001" (United States Environmental Protection Agency, 2001); Gregory M. Zaius, "Health Consultation, Mossville, Calcasieu Parish, LA" (Agency for Toxic Substances and Disease Registry 2000); Greenpeace, "PVC: The Poison Plastic" (Greenpeace).

site of the second largest nuclear spill in U.S. history. This new land has also been poisoned by uranium mining.[10]

In Africa we will be looking at two regions: East Africa and the southern region of Africa. The south region of Africa[11] is made up of three countries: the Republic of South Africa, Zambia, and Zimbabwe. These countries have a combined total population of approximately 65 million people, more than 80 percent of whom are low-income and black. These countries, which represent the most industrialized part of black Africa, mostly host facilities that mine and process copper, gold, diamond, steel, iron ore, nickel, chromium, cobalt, zinc, and lead. They also have a large agricultural sector that produces cash crops such as tobacco, corn, cotton, wine, wheat, and fruit. These mining and agricultural industries use thousands of tons of toxic chemicals every year. Workers and community members close to these industries complain of eye irritation, bronchitis, asthma, tuberculosis, and other serious health conditions. Unfortunately, local environmental organizations have not yet proved strong enough to challenge the polluters and protect the local people and their land.

In East Africa[12] we will look at the countries of Ethiopia, Somalia, Kenya, and Tanzania. These four countries have a combined population of close to 130 million. The majority of this population is indigenous Africans. The economy of the region, unlike that of Southern Africa, is dominated by agricultural activities mostly in the form of cash crop production for export. Coffee is the most important of these crops, and other crops include sisal, sugar cane, cotton, bananas, and tea. There is also an important livestock sector in both

10 The data about Shiprock, New Mexico in this section and in subsequent sections was taken from the following sources: "Baseline Environmental Management Report 1996 Shiprock Site (New Mexico)" U.S. Department of Energy, Office of Environmental Management.

11 The data about the Southern region of Africa in this section and in subsequent sections was taken from the following sources: "Zimbabwe Hazards: Too Close to Home." (Zimbabwe Institute of Permaculture Research. Pesticide News, #37, Sept 1997); Katongo Chisupa, "Toxic Waste Dumping in Zambia." (Voices From Africa. Number 6, Part 2. UN Non-governmental Liaison Service, 2002); "DDT Fact Sheet" (Pesticide News, #40, June 1998); "Organophosphate Insecticides Fact Sheet" (Pesticide News, #34, Dec. 1996); Leslie London, "The Health Hazards of Organophosphate Use in South Africa." (Pesticide News, March 1995); "Environmentalists Call on South Africa to Reject Imports of Hazardous Waste" (Greenpeace, Sept. 2000); Tony Carnie, "South Africa Bucket Brigade Joins Battle for Clean Air," (no date, for more information contac Global Community Monitor); Joselito Laudencia, "South Africa Journal" (Apen Voices Volume 6:1 winter, 2001).

12 The data about East Africa in this section and in subsequent sections was taken from the following sources: "Pesticide 'Time-bomb' Ticking in Africa." (Africa Recovery, Vol 15 #1-2, New York: United Nations, 2002);"Somali West Imports" (TED Case Studies, 2002); Bill, Ellis, "Pesticide Dumping in Africa" (CSF Colorado, 2002).

Ethiopia and Somalia. According to M. K. C. Sridahar, a pesticide specialist, the use of pesticides in agriculture in this region has increased dramatically in the last three decades. At the same time the legal and illegal importation and dumping of toxic chemicals has increased. Additionally, more than 25 years of civil war in Somalia and Ethiopia have exacerbated these conditions. In certain communities, local populations have been exposed to toxic chemicals through drinking water, the food chain, the atmosphere, or direct physical contact. Pesticide residues have been detected in the tissues of plants, animals, and people in the last few decades, and cases of death directly related to toxic chemical exposure have been reported.

Unpredictable Impacts

Because scientific knowledge is partial and limited, it's not surprising that there are unanticipated and/or unintended consequences associated with chemical products as they interact with communities. The reductionist nature of this knowledge, which takes into account limited variables and focuses on a single outcome, makes it difficult to predict the behavior of complex systems. Soule and Piper (1992) have called this ability of science, to zero in on a specific aspect of reality, its strength, but argue that the price of this kind of reductionism is the loss of a broader, more holistic perspective. Prigogine (1997) as well says that because scientific knowledge is finite its ability to predict what will happen is limited. And Merchant (1999) and Horkheimer (1972) both argue that scientific knowledge, because of its mechanistic view of nature, is by design suited to serve the needs of industrial capitalism as an instrument of domination in which humans and other organisms are reduced to mechanisms and as such mere instruments of production. Given the reductionistic and mechanistic nature of scientific knowledge it may even be considered normal or expected that the health of humans and the wholeness of ecological systems would be neglected.

In Midway Village both PG&E and California State officials conceded that toxic substances had gotten into the earth in the early 1900's by a gas manufacturing plant that was later taken over by PG&E. Those who operated the facility at the time either did not consider or did not have knowledge of the long-term environmental behaviors of the products they were using and producing. Additionally, contractors who built the housing units used soil from a contaminated site to fill the marshland where the houses now stand. The gas manufacturer and the contractors did not predict the consequences of their actions and during the cleanup, the contractors didn't consider that the transportation of the dirt through the village would pose a health risk to the residents.

The notion that things are unpredictable assumes unknowability, but sometimes the unpredictability may be due to lack of care or priorities. The neighborhood in Anniston, Alabama that houses a landfill and the Monsanto facility has frequent and severe floods. During clean-up residents come into direct contact with chemical contamination. Clearly, the scientific knowledge that directed the location of the plant and the landfill did not take into account local ecological conditions, like flooding. Additionally technicians at the Monsanto Swann Plant failed to anticipate the effect of PCB's on living organisms—fish and humans.

Similarly in Shiprock, New Mexico, dirt from the uranium mining which contained radiation was disposed of on the sides of the mountains. When it rained the water carried it into the streams and onto the people's farms, and produce growing downstream was then contaminated by radiation.

The toxic history of Hunter's Point goes back to the end of WWII when the Navy organized a number of nuclear test experiments to study the effects of radiation from atomic explosions. Though the test proceeded, there was no knowledge of how to deal with the waste products. They were left with dangerous by-products and little understanding of how to cope with their environmental consequences. Ships involved in the experiment were brought to Hunter's Point for clean-up. Others boats were so badly contaminated that they had to be sunk off the San Francisco coast. In Hunter's Point the landfill had been used to dump a variety of hazardous wastes including nuclear waste, and organic and non-organic compounds such as chlorine, benzene, vinyl chloride, trichloroethylene, nickel, and PCB's. There was no foresight or concern on the part of the scientists that this site was too close to a large metropolitan area. Also in Hunter's Point, environmental contractors spilled a large amount of potassium permanganate and decided to pump this substance into the soil as a part of clean-up. They did not foresee the likelihood that this chemical could seep into the water and affect the aquatic life of the Bay; it did.

In Africa the situation is the same, or worse, than in the U.S. Little foresight has been used in regards to potential negative consequences in the use and the disposal of toxic chemicals. About 10 years ago there were already numerous cases of toxic waste dumping in Somalia. But conditions worsened during the war when facilities storing outdated pesticides were destroyed and chemicals spilled into drinking water resources. In rural Ethiopia, there are reports of over 3,000 tons of obsolete pesticides contaminating the food chain. Many local farming communities are engulfed in toxic fumes and dust. In Annabon, Equatorial Guinea, the island's fauna and flora has been destroyed by imported toxic and radioactive wastes.[13] Pesticides, dioxins and PCB's have entered the food chain and have affected the health of the people. In Zambia more than 300 tons of obsolete pesticides being stored in different parts of the country risk polluting the groundwater.[14] Additionally, Zambia's mining industry uses 300,000 metric tons of chemicals including cyanide, acid alkalis, peroxides, and heavy metals every year. Methods used by Zambia's mining companies to control the level of heavy metals in the waste stream have increased the pH of water, which has seriously affected aquatic life. In Ghana thousands of cubic meters of mine wastewater contaminated with cyanide and heavy metals spilled in the Asuman River. According to the South African company involved in the spill, Goldfields Ltd., the waste water system design failed because of heavy rain. In all of the above examples, the scientific knowledge of a particular chemical at a given time was limited or partial and not able to anticipate the full effects and long-term dynamics in a given ecological system.

Part of the problem in the unpredictability of the environmental consequences has to do with the limitations of scientific knowledge about these toxic chemicals and their dynamics in the ecological systems. Heavy metals and other toxic chemicals provide good examples to illustrate this point. Mercury has been known and used for centuries in the extraction of precious metals such as gold and silver and in the industrial production of batteries. Chlorine and sodium hydroxide also require the use of an amalgam of mercury. Yet it is only recently that some of the side effects of this metal on living organisms have been scientifically studied and understood as in the formation of methylmercury in water and how it is deposited and stored in the bodies of fish and humans. Similarly, lead has been known and used for a long time. It has been used in water ducts, pipes, cooking utensils, ammunition, building materials, paint, batteries, and gasoline. But how lead moves through environment, the chemical forms it takes from one compound to another ,and the way it disturbs the metabolism of living organisms has only been understood in the last few decades.

Another example of the partial nature of our knowledge of toxic chemicals has to do with PCB's. There are about 210 different kinds of PCB's. If one takes into account the fact that PCB's were used since 1929 and given the number of different uses to which they were put, it becomes extremely difficult to predict and anticipate all the different reactions these products will have with different living organisms. Information about degradation in the environment and bio-

13 See "Annobon: Once a Paradise, Now Africa's Dumping Site for Toxic and Radioactive Wastes." Monalige's Quarterly Newsletter, #3, July, 2000.

14 See the State of the Environment Report on Zambia.

accumulation in organisms is difficult to obtain. Different kinds of PCB's accumulate at different rates in the fat tissues of organisms. What's more, under conditions of high temperatures PCB's may form TCDD commonly known as dioxin, or if heated in the presence of a source of oxygen it can form some amount of dibenzofuran, which is structurally similar to dioxin.

In the case of radioactivity there are at least three factors that determine its dangerous effects. The first deals with the number of disintegrations per second; the second has to do with the length of time or half-life in which radiation stays active; and the third concerns the type of radiation involved, being either alpha, beta, or gamma. One also has to consider how a radioactive substance is incorporated in a living organism and how the latter relates to its environment. Complexity challenges predictability. Clearly, fast moving radiation can cause damage to tissues of organisms by ionization, excitation, and breaking bonds in the tissues' atomic or molecular structure. This can lead to harmful somatic and genetic effects.

In the case of both radioactivity and toxic chemicals the notion of reductionist knowledge suggests that we are unable to create a model of reality because of its complexity. Sometimes our senses are unable to immediately assess the danger of environmental pollutants, as with harmful gasses that are odorless and colorless. Radioactivity's effects are difficult to detect until it's too late. The same is true of toxic chemicals with a long period of latency in that certain cancers show up (or are detectable) decades after exposure. Because many harmful environmental toxins often go undetected by our senses, even when there is a real danger, we may be totally unaware, and when our bodies do register the negative effects that information may take years to reach our consciousness. These limitations to human knowledge suggest the need to be cautious, humble, and open to alternative views.

Certainly one of the reasons for these unanticipated impacts is the finite and reductionist nature of scientific knowledge. But even when knowledge is available it's not always used to anticipate or prevent negative impacts. In West Harlem, for example, though the effects of diesel exhaust were already scientifically documented, it did not keep the city from purchasing diesel buses and housing them in the community. This demonstrates how reductionism, as a concentration on a single outcome, has infiltrated social thinking. In business, for example, thought is narrowly focused on production or profit. They do not use holistic thinking to consider the richer, more encompassing function of a social and ecological well-being. In this sense, as Horkheimer (1972) argued, scientific knowledge has gone from the control and destruction of nature to that of human beings as well.

Conflict and Complementarity

This lack of holistic thinking, discussed earlier by Bohm (2000) and Oelschlager (1991), has also resulted in the conflicting character of the scientific knowledge. Bohm argues that fragmentary analytical thinking is the cause of much of the societal disharmony we experience. Oelschlager, and Abram (1996) as well, talk about how intuitive and bodily knowledge is in conflict with the objective mechanistic nature of scientific knowledge. Conflict also arises, according to Lewontin (1992), because of an underlying class conflict, whereby scientific knowledge serves the interests of the dominant classes.

Conflicts may come from genuine misunderstandings or they may be result of conflicting objectives. But regardless of the reason behind the conflict it would be dangerous to assume that if there was tremendous honest and shared interest there would be no conflict. We must keep in mind that knowledge is shaped by many factors, including genuine epistemology limitations of the models we use to understand reality, and the fact that our insertion in a given class in society orients our perception of what is true and what is false and ultimately determines the tools we use for analysis.

It's not only that human knowledge of nature may not be complete enough to anticipate all of the future consequences of a particular chemical or process on the environment; in many cases a particular knowledge will conflict with other knowledge. The conflicting nature of knowledge, in the cases assembled here, showed up in many ways. One of the ways was that residents were given conflicting information. In the case of Midway Village, residents were told that there was no contamination remaining on the site. It was later revealed that the soil on the site contained polynuclear aromatic hydrocarbons. While county health officials were telling residents to avoid contact with the soil and bathe their children frequently, federal scientists with the U.S. Agency for Toxic Substances and Disease Registry dismissed a survey that showed a high number of chromosome aberrations in 32 of 34 local children and DNA irregularities in 19 of 24 adults.

Two studies of the relationship between radiation exposure of men and effects on their children illustrate the way in which science can contradict itself. An Idaho study of 233 children with cancer concluded that children whose fathers were exposed to low-level radiation do not have a higher risk of developing childhood cancer. But according to local activists, a British study found that children with leukemia were six times more likely to have a father who was exposed to radiation.

In Hunter's Point, scientists from ARC Ecology who found extremely high concentrations of vinyl chloride in the soil (55,000 times higher than expected) suggested that it may have spilled into the ground. However, Navy scientists challenged their results. In regards to material contaminated with nuclear radiation, Navy personnel may have been aware of the danger involved, yet their containment strategies seemed to show that they had a limited assessment. Though they have been examining the same site, the results of Navy scientists and those of Monterey Institute scientists are in conflict. Such conflicting views between scientists are common. A few decades ago Professor Hamilton of UC Berkeley argued that the materials contaminated by radiation being handled at Hunter's Point were safe while Professor Warren of UCLA was convinced that the long-term effects of the radioactivity might be harmful.

There are several other examples of conflicting information as well. In Anniston, Alabama, officials told residents to find shelter and lock doors and windows, suggesting minimal danger; on the other hand, the same officials ordered the Department of Health to immediately test all children. And in Richmond, Chevron officials quoted studies about the community that indicated industrial facilities in the area are not a significant source of dioxin. Communities for a Better Environment dispute Chevron's claim on the grounds that they have identified numerous locations in Richmond that are polluted by dioxins. Similarly in Midway Village residents sensed that their health problems were related to the contamination from the site. But what they sensed was dismissed by the court on the grounds that it was in contradiction with scientific findings. In the case of a cyanide and heavy metal spill in the Asuman River there was contradictory information as well. While the senior environmental coordinator agreed that there was cyanide spillage, the managing director of the company denied any presence of cyanide and attributed the damage to excess chlorine. Villagers on the other hand, through their perceptual knowledge at the sight of the damage concluded there must have been a cyanide spillage.

However, in some cases scientific and traditional knowledge compliment one another. In Anniston, Alabama, residents, based on their experience, knew that something was wrong. Two of local resident Cassandra Roberts' children died of leukemia. On the basis of this traditional or bodily knowledge, community members sought scientific information and found that the community, though small, had numerous cases of kidney damage, liver disease, and cancer. This scientific survey reinforced their sense that there were health hazards in their environment. They went on to find out how much PCBs was on their property and in their bodies.

A similar situation took place in West Harlem where residents complained about the foul odors coming from the sewage plant which had started its operations two years earlier. Residents also complained about respiratory problems. These complaints, based on body-based or experiential knowledge, prompted local authorities to commission a scientific study. The study affirmed the experience of the residents when it found that emissions from the plant far exceeded allowed levels for pollutants.

In Midway Village, when residents experienced skin rashes, bloodshot eyes, vomiting and difficulty breathing, they also sought out scientific confirmation. They organized health surveys and collected health histories from members of the community. In Camden, residents' experience of respiratory problems led to research about the health and the environment in the community. And Hunter's Point residents, suspicious that a fire that burned for several months in the landfill close to their homes may have released toxic chemicals into the atmosphere, called for a public health assessment that confirmed their suspicions.

In Holfontein, South Africa, odors and respiratory difficulties prompted concerns of air pollution. In response to these concerns scientists began collecting data, and the Department of the Environment and Tourism reviewed technical documents. In Tanzania, in the Bukombe area, and in the Serengeti district, local people were alarmed by the pollution of land, water, and air as the result of uncontrolled gold mine activity. Detailed surveys conducted by a local university confirmed the presence of heavy metal concentrations in water, sediment, and the air.

These examples support the notion that knowledge, because of its partial and limited character, can lead to both conflict and complementarity at the same time. As such it will not be possible to iron out disagreement in all cases of environmental injustices.

Withholding

Perhaps because it is known that disclosing information related to pollution may lead to legal action that could force the polluting party to pay damages or redress the negative impact, technical knowledge is often withheld from the communities most affected. In South Africa, laws prohibit the release of information about pollution to the public. Results of tests of soil samples performed by the EPA and an independent company at Midway Village were withheld from residents on the grounds that the EPA was checking the quality of the results. And in Shiprock, New Mexico, the elders, who are the decision-makers for the community, were not informed of the potential hazards of uranium. The Vanadium Corporation of America and Kerr-McGee, the principal owners of the mines, neglected to inform their workers about the dangerous effects of uranium. As a result of this lack of information, people unknowingly built their houses with uranium tailings.

The same pattern of withholding information can be seen in other communities as well. In Hunter's Point, the Navy knew that the landfill contained toxic substances and yet when the fire at the landfill burned for three weeks, local residents were not notified that they were at risk. During the discussions of the transfer of this property to the city, very little information was disclosed to the city about the extent of toxic risk to the local community. Environmental contractors hired to assess these risks at the Hunter's Point Naval shipyard did not have access to the records they needed to evaluate the situation. In some cases the Navy was restricted from notifying health regulators about the nuclear contamination of some of the buildings on the site and asserted they did not have records pertaining to what was dumped in that site. In Richmond, chemicals released into the air by an explosion at the General Chemical Plant were not reported either by the company or by the regulators. It was the environmental rights organization, Communities for a Better Environment, who reported the presence of some of these harmful chemicals. In Mossville and Clacasieu Parish, Louisiana, the name of the harmful product vinyl chloride monomer (VCM) was changed to just vinyl as a way of withholding the information about the potential health threats from VCM.

Another example of withholding information is in the Anniston case where community members were told there was "a little" PCB on their property and were urged to sell. When residents asked the amount of PCB's they were unable to get that information. When the community met with Monsanto, information was still not given about the effects of PCB's on human organisms. It was a local community organization, The Southern Organizing Committee, who finally brought in a scientist and a lawyer to explain the potential effects of PCB's. Monsanto withheld information and tried to buy people's property without full disclosure of contamination so they could pay less on the buyout options.

Most cases of toxic waste dumping take place in part because knowledge of the nature of the substance is withheld from local community organizations and from government officials. This happened in South Africa with respect to the importation of cupric arsenate from Finland in 1996. When it was discovered that the traded product was dangerous the ship was sent back.

In addition to the conscious withholding of information there are also cases where people are kept deliberately uneducated and untrained. In Zambia for example, there is a lack of disposal and treatment technology for the obsolete pesticides accumulated in the country. And in Ethiopia local people were told that if they did not buy pesticides the locusts would come and destroy their crops even when the arrival of locusts was not anticipated. Also, when information is available it is often not in the language of the local community nor is it communicated in a way that they can understand and utilize. Because of this misinformation, chemicals are often not used according to directions to the detriment of local people and environment. There are also cases of straightforward corruption as in Equatorial Guinea where bribes were given to government officials in order to facilitate the dumping of toxic and nuclear waste on the island of Annabon.

Effectiveness and Strategies

Even though the necessary scientific knowledge was often withheld, misused or conflicted, in other cases it proved helpful to affected communities. In Anniston, the residents sued Monsanto who opted for an out of court settlement of $42.8 million. In West Harlem, the community created an organization that brought a lawsuit against the City of New York for using a treatment plant that polluted their neighborhood and caused respiratory illnesses in the local population. The community retained a lawyer and a science expert as consultants to obtain the legal and technical information they needed for their lawsuit. The parties reached a settlement, and Metropolitan Transportation Authorities was cited for situating a disproportionately large number of diesel busses in a densely populated minority neighborhood and increasing the health risks of diesel exhaust in the community. As a result of the court case and the effective use of technical and social knowledge, the governor mandated that all new Metropolitan Transportation Authority depots be compressed natural gas depots and that the company buy 300 new compressed natural gas buses in the 2000-2004 purchase plan. Scientific knowledge and testimony were crucial to the positive outcome of this case.

Unfortunately, not all lawsuits and uses of experts were successful in redressing instances of environmental racism. In Shiprock, New Mexico, the Navajo Nation lost several court battles at both state and federal levels. However, a local political organization worked with the U.S. Congress to introduce a bill to compensate the victims of radiation. After an initial defeat the bill was passed. Navajo uranium workers and uranium workers from other tribes are now eligible for compensation including comprehensive medical care and public education on the detrimental effects of uranium exposure for the community members.

In the majority of these cases, the use of local and environmental organizations —WE ACT, the Office of Navajo Uranium Workers, South Camden Citizens in Action, Communities for a Better Environment, GreenAction, and the Southern Organizing Committee—were an important elements in dealing with issues of toxic waste and environmental injustice. This was especially true in the U.S. and in a more limited way in Africa. In South Africa, Earthlife was instrumental in challenging several cases of environmental pollution and helped establish of a commission of inquiry into the case of cupric arsenate imports. Greenpeace and Basel Action Network pressured the South African government to take a stand against the importing of toxic waste.

As can be seen the legal system played an important role in many of these cases. Racial discrimination laws were often used in the U.S. as the basis on which to seek remedies in cases of environmental injustice. In Africa, however, the lack of legislation or the presence of loopholes within existing legislation has been most significant. For example, Basel Convention used the notion of "reprocessing" as a way around legislation regulating the importation of toxic substances for disposal. According to the South African government, toxic waste was imported from Australia for "recycling" with residues to be returned to Australia. However, it is not clear that the residues were ever sent back nor what the effect of "reprocessing" was on the health of the African workers dealing with these substances that included lead, arsenic, and other toxic chemicals.

Discussion, Conclusion, and Policy Recommendations

In terms of discussion, a number of questions can be raised about the above observations and findings. First, to what extent are these cases representative? After all, both the U.S. and Africa are quite large to be represented by such a small number of cases. On the other hand, most studies done about minorities and environmental conditions suggest that minority communities are more likely to be located close to environmental toxic waste. In this sense the communities we examined could be representative of minority communities in that they are African American, Native American, or Latino. In Africa, one of the reasons ecological abuse happens is racism. For most Westerners, Africans have an inferior status, and thus their ecological harm is not assessed in the same way as the harm done to Westerners. Second, if these cases were to represent only special conditions, to what extent do these results apply to other cases of environmental injustices? Precisely because these cases are disparate and geographically diverse they are more general since similar observations are found in very different and distant places. In this sense the results can be broadly applied as initial points of departure for strategies or policies dealing with the use of knowledge in cases of environmental injustice. And finally, many of these cases are unresolved and ongoing. Strategies that have been successful in the past may not continue to work in the future, but lessons from these cases may be useful in thinking about how to approach future problems. In many areas of social research the best way to predict a future may still be the use of lessons from the past.

Based on the cases discussed in this paper several factors helped to make the use of knowledge for environmental justice more effective. First, community members expressed their health concerns and experiences. It is this expression of body-based knowledge that in most cases of environmental injustice initiates action. Community leaders took to the streets or took some kind of action. Commissions of experts were set up to study the problem. Legal action was taken against the perpetrators. Consultants were used to monitor the situation and ensure that the community was fully informed. Community organizations worked on the issue raising awareness and gathering support. Studies were conducted and community members educated about the issues. Political and legal processes are used in conjunction with both scientific and traditional community-based knowledge to seek resolution and redress.

Because reality is too complex to ever be entirely captured a partiality of knowledge is inevitable. It is impossible to anticipate all outcomes and therefore to absolutely control either nature or society. Knowledge's inherently partial character means that its periodic failure is inevitable. Even if knowledge could contend with reality's infinite multiplicity it still may not be able to address reality's ever evolving nature. Additionally, conflict between different kinds of knowledge or contradictions within the same system of knowledge can create further uncertainty.

In regards to policy, in order for knowledge to be helpful in cases of environmental injustice a number of things need to happen. First, there has to be encouragement and strong support, including financial support, for the use of available knowledge by organizations, local and non-local, that can work for the protection of the local environment and its people. Second, training, education, and awareness programs must be provided to affected community members. Studies need to be implemented to look into the health of both the people and the environment. Analysis and monitoring of the environmental pollution are essential. Knowledge experts—lawyers and scientists—who are not beholding to corporate interests must be used to counteract the high potential for conflict of interest. Legislation needs to be enacted to regulate the use of toxic substances and ban the import of dangerous chemicals into vulnerable communities. In order to be effective, such legislation must allow for a means of enforcement. And finally, the technical education of community members is essential. There has to be encouragement and financing for the development of techniques and technology in the handling, storage, and treatment of the waste already present in the local community.

In environmental justice while it may be the case that disproportionate exposure of people of color to excessive amounts of toxins is perhaps due to either malicious or racist behavior of the decision-makers, what is in fact happening may be something more profound. On the one hand there is a stratified and undemocratic society with extreme economic inequalities which affects people's perceptions and interests in environmental issues. On the other hand one is dealing with deep human limitations to grasp complex physical and social reality in a way that would be reflective of the totality of the social and the physical existence. The problem of environmental justice, therefore, will remain intractable because of these social and epistemological limitations and cannot be tackled or dealt with except by implementing more democratic and participatory processes that would bring together a multiplicity of perspectives to decision-making.

Though lacking in foresight and at times conflicting with itself, human knowledge, scientific or other, can be used effectively in environmental justice cases if used democratically. Therefore, the decision of the government of Ghana not to allow the importation of "toxic monkeys" is not due to a lack of correct or "sound" knowledge, but rather that decision represents and suggests a model of democratic participation which would bring the perspective of those most affected into the decision-making process.

References

Abram, D. (1996). *The Spell of the Sensuous*. New York: Vintage Books.

Africa Recovery. (2001). Pesticide 'Time-Bomb' Ticking in Africa. New York: United Nations, *15*(1-2), 42.

Althusser, L. (1969). *For Marx*. New York: Ben Brusters New Left Books.

Amoruso, C. (1997). WEACT for Environmental Justice. *Third Force, 5*(15),19-23.

Ashfield, B. (1993), December 8). Something Smells Like Environmental Racism. *Modern Times*. No page number available.

Baird, C. (1995). *Environmental Chemistry*. New York: W.H. Freeman and Company.

Bay City News Service. (1993, December). *Coalition Wants $60 Million from Chevron*. San Francisco, California.

Beiles N. (2000). What Monsanto Knew. *The Nation*, 270(21),18-22.

Berger, M. (n.d.). *In the News: Bus Depots and Racism*. Retrieved April 19, 2002, from http://www.gothamgazette.com

Bergin, T. G., & Fisch, M. H. (1961). *The New Science of Giambattista Vico*. New York: Cornell University Press.

Bernson, V. (1997). *Proceedings of the Conference on Environmental Justice and Global Ethics: The Role of Science and Values in Environmental Decision Making*. Melbourne, Australia: University of Melbourne.

Bohm, D. (2000). *Science, Order and Creativity*. New York: Routledge.

Bullard, R. D. (2001, November 27). *Chemical Assault on an African American Community: Community Group Wins $42.8 Million Settlement. The People vs. Montsanto: An interview with Cassandra Roberts*. Clark Atlanta University, Environmental Justice Resource Center. Retrieved from http://www.ejrc.cau.edu/cassandraroberts.html

Capra, F. (1996). *The Web of Life: A New Scientific Understanding of Living Systems*. New York: Anchor Books.

Carnie, T. (n.d.) South Africa Bucket Brigade Joins Battle for Clean Air. *The Mercury*. Durban, South Africa. (See also *Global Community Monitor* entry.)

Chisupa, K. (2002). Toxic Waste Dumping in Africa. *Voices from Africa*. Number 6: Sustainable Development Part 2. New York: United Nations

Non-Governmental Liaison Service. Retrieved from http://www.un-ngls.org/orf/documents/publications.en/voices.africa/number6/vfa6.04.htm

Communities for a Better Environment. (1998, November). *Fact Sheet: Bayview/Hunters Point*. Oakland and Huntington Beach, California.

Communities for a Better Environment. (1998). *Why Do We Oppose the Expansion of Potrero Power Plant?* Oakland and Huntington Beach, California.

Communities for a Better Environment. (1999, July). *Bay Area Dioxin Sources.* Oakland and Huntington Beach, California.

Communities for a Better Environment. (1999, April). *Chevron Fire, Richmond March 25, 1999 Richmond/San Pablo Bucket Brigade Summary Report.* Oakland and Huntington Beach, California.

Communities for a Better Environment. (2000, August). *Dioxins and Refineries: Analysis in the Bay Area, August 2000.* Oakland and Huntington Beach, California.

Communities for a Better Environment. (2001, May). *General Chemical May 2001 Bucket Result Summary.* Oakland and Huntington Beach, California.

Community Window on the Hunters Point Shipyard. *The Hunters Point Shipyard Cleanup: An Overview.* San Francisco, California. Retrieved 2003 from http://www.communitywindowontheshipyard.org/cleanupguide/index.htm#factsheets

Davis, L. (2001, May 9). Fallout. *San Francisco Weekly.* Retrieved from http://www.sfweekly.com/2001-05-09/news/fallout/

Dougan, K. (2000, February). *PCBs in Anniston's Soul, Air.* Retrieved from http://www.annistonstar.com.

Ellis, B. (2002). *Pesticide Dumping in Africa.* CSF Colorado. (No page number available.)

Foucault, M. (1972). *The Archaeology of Knowledge.* London: Tavistock.

Foucault, M. (1970). *The Order of Things.* London: Tavistock.

Francis, M. B. (1994). *Toxic Substances in the Environment.* New York: John Wiley and Sons.

Global Community Monitor. GCM Assists in Launch of New Bucket Brigade in Zululand: Richards Bay. Retrieved May 23, 2009 from http://www.gcmonitor.org/article.php?id=222

Greenpeace. (2000, February). *Environmentalists Call on South Africa to Reject Imports of Hazardous Waste.* Washington, D.C..

Greenpeace. (2000, February). *PVC: The Poison Plastic.* Washington, D.C..

Grunwald, M. (2002, January 1). Monsanto Hid Decades of Pollution; PCBs Drenched Ala. Town, but No One was Ever Told. *The Washington Post.* Retrieved from http://www.ewg.org/node/14319

Horkheimer, M., & Adorno, T. (1972). *Dialectic of Enlightenment.* New York: Herber and Herber.

Hughes, E. (2002, February). *Hunters Point Shipyard Parcel E Sampling and Analysis.* Morris Plains, NJ: Tetra Tech EC Inc.

Inner City Press. (2000). *Inner City Press Environmental Justice Reporter 2000 Archives.* New York City.

Laudencia, J. (2001). South Africa Journal. *Apen Voices,* 6 (1), 23-28.

Lewontin, R. C. (1992). *Biology as Ideology: The Doctrine of DNA.* New York: Perennial Press.

London, L. (1995, March). The Health Hazards of Organophosphate use in South Africa. *Pesticides News, 27,* 6-7.

London, L. (2006, September). South African Waste Study Highlights Need for Prevention. *Pesticides News, 73,* 14-15.

Lyotard, J. F. (1984). *The Postmodern Condition.* Manchester, UK: Manchester University Press.

Massey, S.E. (2001). *North River Sewage Treatment Plant.* New York City: West Harlem Environmental Action.

Masten, S. (1999, August 11). Residents Plan to Seek Tests for Dioxin. *West County Times,* No page number available.

Masten, S. (2000, December 7). Activists Want Blood Tested for Toxins. *West County Times,* No page number available.

Maturana, H. R., & Varela, F. J. (1987). *The Tree of Knowledge.* Boston: New Science Library.

McMillan, M. (2000). Midway Village Housing Project: A Struggle for Environmental Justice. *Environmental Justice Case Studies from University of Michigan Students.* Ann Arbor: University of Michigan. Retrieved from http://www.umich.edu/~snre492/cases.html

Merchant, C. (1991). *The Death of Nature: Women, Ecology and the Scientific Revolution.* San Francisco: Harper & Row Publishers.

Merchant, C. (1999). *Ecology*. (1st ed.). Key Concepts in Critical Theory Series. New York: Humanities Press.

Monalige. (2000, July). Annobon: Once a Paradise, Now, Africa's Dumping Site for Toxic and Radioactive Wastes. *Monalige's Quarterly Newsletter,* 41(3). Retrieved from http://www.equatorialguinea-monalige.com/monalige.htm

Morris, W. (1998, July 31). Activists Seek Review of Richmond Facility. *West County Times,* No page number available.

Morris, W. (1994, June). Chevron Will Give Neighbors $850,000. *West County Times,* No page number available.

Oelschlaeger, M. (1993). *The Idea of Wilderness: From Prehistory to the Age of Ecology.* New Haven, CT: Yale University Press.

Pence, A. (2001, August 25). Ridding Midway Village of Tainted Soil—Again. *San Francisco Chronicle.* Retrieved from http://www.sfgate.com/cgi-bin/article.cgi?f=/c/a/2001/08/25/MNL121153.DTL&hw=Midway+village&sn=002&sc=736

Permanent People's Tribunal on Industrial Hazards and Human Rights. (1996). *Charter on Industrial Hazards and Human Rights.* Retrieved from http://www.pan-uk.org/Internat/indhaz/Charter.pdf

Pesticides News. (1996, December). *Organophosphate Insecticides Fact Sheet.* London: Pesticides Action Network, *34*, 20-21.

Pesticides News. (1998, June). *DDT Fact Sheet.* London: Pesticides Action Network, *40*, 18-20.

Pimentel, B. (1999, August 12). Refinery Neighbors Want Their Blood Tested for Dioxin. *San Francisco Chronicle.* Retrieved from http://www.sfgate.com/cgi-bin/article.cgi?f=/c/a/1999/08/12/MN86938.DTL&hw=dioxin+richmond+pimentel&sn=001&sc=1000

Poaletta, M. (1993, January). Somali Waste Imports From Europe and Civil War. *TED Case Studies*, #64. Retrieved from http://www1.american.edu/ted/class/all.htm

Prigogine, I. (1997). *The End of Certainty: Time, Chaos, and the New Laws of Nature.* New York: Free Press.

Richman, T.M. (2002, October). New York State Tackles Environmental Justice. Retrieved from http://www.underberg-kessler.com/press.

San Francisco Fire Department. (2001). *Hunters Point Fire Department Run Index for 2001.* San Francisco.

Selinger, B. (1998). *Chemistry in the Marketplace.* New York: Harcourt Brace.

Soule, J. D., & Piper, J. K. (1991). *Farming in Nature's Image: An Ecological Approach to Agriculture.* Washington, DC: Island Press.

U.S. Department of Energy, Office of Environmental Management. (1997). *Baseline Environmental Management Report 1996: Shiprock, NM site.* Washington, D.C.: U.S. Government Printing Office.

U.S. Department of Health and Human Services, Agency for Toxic Substances and Disease Registry. (1999, November 19). *Health Consultation and Exposure Investigation Report: Calcasieu Estuary, Lake Charles, Calcasieu Parish, Louisiana.* Retrieved from http://www.atsdr.cdc.gov/HAC/pha/calcas/cal_toc.html

U.S. Department of Health and Human Services, Agency for Toxic Substances and Disease Registry. (2001, March 2). *Health Consultation: Parcel E Landfill Fire at Hunters Point Shipyard.* Retrieved from http://www.atsdr.cdc.gov/HAC/pha/hunterspoint/hun_toc.html.

U.S. Environmental Protection Agency. (2001). *US EPA Activity in Mossville, LA and Greater Calcasieu Parish, 1998-2001.* Washington, D.C.: U.S. Government Printing Office.

U.S. Navy, Naval Facilities Engineering Command, Southwest Division. (2001, July-September). *Hunters Point Shipyard Environmental Cleanup Newsletter.* Washington, D.C.: U.S. Government Printing Office.

West County Toxics Coalition. *History of the West County Toxics Coalition.* Richmond, California. Retrieved from http://www.westcountytoxicscoalition.org/

Winokur, S., and Berthelsen, C. (2001, July 29). Power Plant Fight Intensifies: Potrero Hill Residents Battle Mirant. *San Francisco Chronicle.* Retrieved from http://www.sfgate.com/cgi-bin/article.cgi?f=/c/a/2001/07/29/BU224397.DTL&hw=power+plant+fight+winokur&sn=001&sc=1000

Woellert, L. (2001, November 19). Dumping on the Poor? Cement Plant that Stirred Up a Low Income Area May be Shut. *Business Week, 3758,* 120.

Zimbabwe Institute of Permaculture Research. (1997, September). Zimbabwe Hazards: Too Close to Home. *Pesticides News, 37,* 3.

6

KNOWLEDGE MAKING AS INTERVENTION: THE ACADEMY AND SOCIAL CHANGE

Angana P. Chatterji, Ph.D. and Richard Shapiro, Ph.D. *

No matter how terrifying a given system may be there always remain the possibilities of resistance, disobedience, and oppositional groupings (Foucault, 1993:162).

The world is a broken place mired in death, starvation, violence, and injustice. Water is not a basic resource available to millions. Dominant and irresponsible development denies vast numbers a subsistence livelihood while globalization floods the present, decimating cultures and ecosystems. Poverty and terror haunt everyday lives. Kashmir, Kabul, New York, West Bank, Jaffna, Teheran, Java, Baghdad, Gujarat, Tirana, Jerusalem, Managua, Buenos Aires, Belgrade, Johannesburg, Kinshasa, Lahore, Moscow, Tibet, Mecca, and countless other places are causalities of 20th Century irresponsibility. In the putrefying decay of expanding civilization, the American professorate and intelligentsia by and large continue to function without urgency in the face of these realities. For those enraged, our voices are barely audible in challenging the all too comfortable assumptions that what we as public intellectuals do is enough, that our actions are just, that what we think is true, that how we intervene is ethical.

Academic practice has powerful legacies of relevant engagement. The Academy in the United States and elsewhere has been instrumental to processes

* Angana P. Chatterji is Associate Professor of Social and Cultural Anthropology at the California Institute of Integral Studies, San Francisco. Since 1984, she has been working with postcolonial social movements particularly in India, public lands reform, gender equity, sustainable development, and participatory and secular democracy.

Richard Shapiro is the Director of the Social and Cultural Anthropology program at the California Institute of Integral Studies. Since 1985, Richard has been involved in shaping emancipatory education in the Bay Area, and his areas of scholarship include philosophical anthropology, gender, sexuality, multicultural pedagogy, feminism, postmodern and critical social thought, and social movement in the U.S.

of ethical knowledge production, and has made significant contributions to social change.[1] The Academy has also been a primary site that continues to sanction unjust and undemocratic processes of knowledge production that legitimate radical inequities based on race, ethnicity, class, gender, sexuality, age, ability, nationality, religion, and ecology. The Academy in the United States overwhelmingly prepares narrow specialists and technically trained experts who respond to the demands of tenure and disciplinary interest. It is important to add that even while academics who are prolific scholar-activists continue to work in solidarity with social movements, they are often required to journey on parallel paths – one of scholarly activism and another of disciplinary scholarship. The opportunity to rethink academic practice in ways that integrate thought and action still do not proliferate.

The Academy largely functions on the assumption that the accumulation of neutral, impartial, and objective information makes social and technical progress possible. Knowledge is understood as either of value in itself or is made valuable through its application to social and technical problems. Knowledge is foregrounded as the central concern of researchers and scholars. Everyday practices that organize knowledge production are linked to funding agencies, disciplinary discourse, and patriarchal cultural traditions. These forces shape narcissistic, technocratic, and instrumental understandings of knowledge, separate from power dynamics, language games, embedded cultural assumptions, and inherited historical legacies (Bhabha, 1994; Foucault, 1994).

Critical knowledge may seek to expose these forces as problematic, dangerous, or oppressive, but this is largely done as an academic practice oriented toward critiques of knowledge (Giroux, 2000; Hall, 1998; Hall, 1996; McRobbie, 2000). Critical approaches to knowledge often reproduce the very dimensions of the normalized practices of knowledge production it critiques. It too is focused on the question of knowledge or truth and defines critical activity as intellectual intervention in relation to disciplinary knowledge

---

1 In recent times in the social sciences and humanities, the work of Bina Agarwal, M. J. Akbar, Kwame Anthony Appiah, Hannah Arendt, Talal Asad, Homi Bhabha, Simone De Beauvoir, Bhola Chatterji, Noam Chomsky, Ward Churchill, Angela Davis, Jacques Derrida, Arturo Escobar, Frantz Fanon, Walter Fernandes, Michael Foucault, Paulo Freire, Eduardo Galeano, M. K. Gandhi, Paul Gilroy, Emma Goldman, Stephan Jay Gould, Ranajit Guha, Ifran Habib, Stuart Hall, Suheir Hammad, Donna Harraway, Pervez Hoodbhoy, bell hooks, Fredric Jameson, M. L. King, Rajni Kothari, Smitu Kothari, Herbert Marcuse, Albert Memi, Chandra Talpade Mohanty, Mark Poffenberger, Paul Rabinow, Salman Rushdie, Edward Said, Sumit Sarkar, Jean-Paul Sartre, Vandana Shiva, Gayatri Spivak, Romila Thapar, Alice Walker, Simone Weil, Cornel West, and so many others have set formidable precedence to linking political practice to academic scholarship.

(Foucault, 1980). Such practice remains distant from community concerns or social movements in the definition of what should be "studied" and how knowledge agendas are to be set, and thus fails to ask how the Academy may increase its relevance to concerns of social justice, ecological sustainability, equity, livelihood, and peace.

In stating this we sincerely acknowledge that the Academy is a diverse and, of necessity, a contradictory space. We would like to also acknowledge the multifarious emancipatory traditions within the Academy and the distinctions and differences within such traditions in the sciences, social sciences, arts, and humanities (Cohen, 2001; Spivak, 1999). Our plea is not for the assimilation of such differences, but rather that we continually reframe the profession and the space (Academy) attentive to a world in despair.

How can the Academy in the United States be concerned with growing an intelligentsia that asserts a will toward justice? How might difference operate as an active force toward knowledge making? How do we sustain and advocate the labor of freedom? Michel Foucault, speaking to the injustices of the penal system, stressed that the discipline of philosophy would be altered if the penal system were to break down through insurrection (Foucault, 1977). One could contend similarly that if structural global injustices were to be acknowledged seriously within international institutional contexts, the Academy would be forced to radically rethink discipline, research, scholarship, curricula, teaching, and methods of knowledge production and their effects (Asad, 1973; Bhabha, 1994). If issues of social justice and ecological sustainability were central to academic practice, the very nature of knowledge would be radically transformed.

Knowledge and truth are products of power relations. To foreground processes of knowledge production that link thought to sites of action would radically transform the Academy. Such transformation faces numerous obstacles in that it challenges sanctified truths on which the Academy is based and through which it understands itself. To make knowledge subservient to sustaining life requires a reversal of the will to truth with deep roots in Western culture (Bhabha, 1994; Said, 1993). The primacy of knowledge dominates academic practice in mainstream and critical practitioners. Finding, discovering, and producing the truth, as well as demystifying, challenging, recreating, and deconstructing the truth, all reproduce a will to know that maintains the Academy as privileged, irrelevant, and technocratic (Foucault, 1978; Foucault, 1980; McRobbie, 2000).

Marginalized communities remain distant or potential objects, spoken of and spoken about. When spoken with, it is in their role as holders of data, awaiting interpretation by higher level discourse that is the exclusive property of "properly" trained experts (Gupta and Ferguson, 1997). Their voices are the raw materials we refine into knowledge through our labor. To shift to alliance with such communities in defining research, scholarship, curricula, teaching, and extra-curricular culture would be to create a public intelligentsia in service of social change toward justice, freedom, sustainability, diverse cultural expression and vibrant public interaction. Crisis, responsibility, suffering, accountability, and ethics as they pertain to thinking and acting in a complex, multicultural, and postcolonial world brutalized by global and institutionalized racism, neocolonization, injustice, and prolific in its resistance would be the substance of academic life, replacing the knowledge agendas sponsored by corporate, government, military complexes maintained by the privilege and alienation of the privatized subjects inhabiting the Academy. In an Academy allied in the struggle to the disenfranchised where thinking is linked to sustaining life, it is not simply the marginal who are served. The isolation, alienation, and privatization that in part define upward mobility in the U.S. would be undermined, unleashing new energies and liberating intellectuals in the process.

Such shifts in the Academy would require knowledge production as a complex process of social intervention (Giroux, 2000; McRobbie, 2000). Such interventions would act with communities toward sustainable knowledge. Sustainable knowledge is understood as that which results from particular processes of knowledge production. Such processes require alliance with communities in defining what needs to be known and how knowledge is produced. Sustainable knowledge results from multiple intersections: between academic communities and communities outside, between thought and action, between disciplines of knowledge, between diverse social constituencies, and between social justice and ecological practice. Knowledge resulting from such processes acts as an intervention in the social world. As such it is partial, contingent, provisional and problematic. Sustainable knowledge is not an object or thing. "It" does not exist to be found and applied. Sustainable knowledge, as intervention, acts, and produces effects toward certain forms of sustainability that will themselves be partial. As such, continued processes of intervention toward sustainability define "sustainable knowledge." Sustainable knowledge is that real phantasm that evaporates the moment it is reified. Sustainable knowledge moves toward the creation of sustainable worlds, to be understood as ongoing practices, never fully realized, always already necessary commitments in realms of partial (im)possibility (Chatterji 2001a; Shapiro, 2002).

I was born in postcolonial India, raised as a secular woman, educated mostly in Calcutta and Delhi.[2] Since 1984, I have been working with postcolonial social movements in India toward enabling participatory democracy for social and ecological justice. Since 1993, I have been working both in India and the United States as a university teacher and activist. Since 1997, I have been teaching in the Social and Cultural Anthropology Program at the California Institute of Integral Studies. This Anthropology Program offers a critical, activist approach to education that prioritizes issues of social and ecological justice in the context of a multicultural, postcolonial, and globalizing world.[3] Committed to emancipatory traditions within the Academy, the Program deeply engages the intersections of thought and action, critical social analysis, emancipatory research, strategic thinking, and alliance building.[4]

My academic practice in the Program is very much informed by, and accountable to, my commitments to social change in India, South Asia, and the United States. The courses Richard Shapiro and I teach and the curriculum utilized in our program use research, social thought, history, and social movements to problematize thought and practice, development, postcoloniality, globalization, North-South relations, global and environmental racism, and structural and institutional inequities.[5] Such deconstructive frameworks enable the labor of resistance that prioritizes sustainable knowledge production.[6] It

---

2 This paper is self-referential in that it speaks to my (Angana's) work and associations to allow the reader to look critically at the problematics and possibilities of knowledge making. I have worked in urban north India, and in north, west, and eastern rural India with policy and advocacy issues. While Richard has also been working in India since 1997, in this paper we draw in particular on my work. The analysis is written in collaboration with Richard.

3 Postcolonialism is defined as the diverse field of thinking, resistance, and action within the North and the South, defined through a critical relationship to colonized history. It does not refer to the "end" of colonization. It delineates the relations of power defined within the context of the North and the South, South and the South, and the East and the West, since colonialism began. Postcolonialism is a contested space that operates within specific histories and contexts (Payne, 1997; Bhabha, 1994; Spivak, 1994).

4 For further details, see http://Anthropology.ciis.edu. Also see course offerings in Appendix I.

5 Courses taught by Angana include: Women, Culture, Social Change; Crosscultural Issues in Social and Environmental Justice; Applied Advocacy Research: Postcolonial and Feminist Practices; Engendering and Reframing Development; Colonization: Remembering Silenced Histories; History and Imagination of 20th Century Revolutions; War and Peace: Alliance and Confrontation; and Postcoloniality in South Asia: Confronting Religion, Nationalism and Politics. Richard's courses include: Critical Social Thought; Critical History of the Human Sciences, Self and Society: Building Alliances Across Differences, Reading and Writing Culture; Nietzsche/Foucault/An Archaeology of Western Culture; Advanced Seminar in Social Thought: Marx and Freud; and Emerging Issues in the Humanities.

6 For an elaboration of deconstructive process see: Derrida, 1967; Derrida, 1968; Shapiro, 2002.

helps students situate anthropology as a discipline in the service of such work and facilitates capacity building. It foregrounds the participatory construction of sustainable knowledge. As we struggle to engage the world meaningfully, our academic practice reflects the political commitments we carry. These commitments also make necessary that we continually and critically assess the relevance of our own labor and claims. Teaching is a responsibility that makes us accountable to students and them to us. A desire for certain emancipatory effects leads us to generate the curriculum we use. The classroom becomes a site of intimate intersection between the lives of the students and those various and stratified stakeholders that define our communities elsewhere. It allows subaltern voices and positions to be persistently present in the shaping of Academic priorities.

Since 1990, I have been working with movements for public forest lands reform in West Bengal and Orissa, with policy and advocacy research.[7] Such association has deeply influenced the curriculum I teach in development, environmental justice, history, colonization, and research. Alliances at the village, district,[8] and state levels have been integral to my work, in determining the relevance and focus of all research that I have facilitated. These alliances are provisional and enduring, fraught with the subtext of unjust histories.

In this paper, a cursory elaboration of these movements provides a context for our reflections on the production of sustainable knowledge and the role of the Academy within this process.[9] In so far as we work in a graduate program for postcolonial anthropology that prioritizes social and ecological justice, continual examination of the relationship between our lives in the Academy and elsewhere is integral to our own capacity building. Such reflection seeks to enhance our effectiveness as activists, scholars, and citizens.

Public Lands Reform: Dissent for Democracy and Livelihood

Public forest lands refer to all nationalized forest lands whose jurisdiction falls within the purview of the state. Lands managed by state agencies such as

7 Orissa and West Bengal are states in eastern India. Refers to Angana's work.

8 Administrative Boundaries in India — Districts are administrative boundaries and the district administration oversees legal, jurisdictional, land, and rural development matters. The forest divisions are forest boundaries; the forest departments, at the divisional levels, oversee forest jurisdiction and administrative, legal, and financial matters related to the specific forest division. The forest division usually falls within the administrative boundaries of the district it is located in.

9 Refers to Angana's work, even while Richard's work with multicultural alliance building in the United States is integral to empowering such reflection.

the forest or revenue departments are identified as public forest lands. Public lands reform refers to social and political processes, initiated by community groups and supported by activists, intellectuals, and state and donor agencies that seek to reform rights, access, allocations, entitlements, inequities, and agreements related to public lands in favor of marginalized communities that live in conjunction with such lands (Chatterji, 1998). In response to entrenched injustices, political processes are underway throughout India that link ecological restoration with social equity. They address inequities premised on history, caste, culture, religion, ecology, class, and gender. These processes are rooted in social movements that have impacted all levels of Indian society from marginalized communities in rural areas to policymakers in national government. The precarious, problematic, and enduring alliances across vast cultural strata make India an exciting example of social change in a hierarchical and multicultural society. While the need for sustainable development is crucial in urban environments because of their intensive resource consumption, one of the primary areas of sustainable change has been among rural communities that live in contiguity to forest areas. This is evidenced in movements for public forest lands reform (Chatterji, 1998).

Forest lands in India are predominantly nationalized and under the legal and managerial jurisdiction of state agencies, such as the forest or revenue departments. The primary stakeholders of forest lands are the communities that depend on the forests for subsistence, state agencies, development organizations, and the industrial sector. Since the 18th Century, India's forests have been savagely degraded through commercial exploitation during colonization and post-independence felling to support the infrastructure for national growth (Poffenberger and McGean, 1995). The colonial and postcolonial state's custodianship and policing of forests has vitiated human-nature interactions. In 1950, 48 percent of the total land area was under healthy forest cover. Subsequently, in the late 20th Century only 19.4 percent of the country's total land area was under some forest cover, and eight percent of it was healthy (Poffenberger, 1995; Mukhopadhyay, 1994). By the 1950s, increasing numbers of people became dependent on the few remaining forests. These communities no longer had any rights over forest lands, only "privileges". Unilaterally, with a few honorable exceptions, women were the most adversely affected by forest degradation (Sarin, 1999). Poor rural women in India constitute the lowest sociocultural and economic "caste". Rural women perform housework, agricultural work, and non-formal forest-based and other industrial work (Chatterji, 2001b). Their work days are invariably 1.5 times longer then men's workdays (Tinker, 1994).

There were sal forests before. The sal did not prove as economically beneficial so they [foresters] thought, "Let's cut them and plant others which will be more useful." They felled the sal and planted cashews. This [planting of cashews] was not known to us. It was useless. To them it was valuable. Then came eucalyptus. This grows fast in five years. It fetches a lot more money. With the old sal, the herbs and creepers that grew at the bottom of them also went. Other food trees also went.... The oal tree, only the oal tree gives flowers. This is a lot gone (Bishu Baski, Santal Adivasi (Tribal) Community Elder, Arabari, Chatterji, 1996:119).

What was left was no longer ours, the land was taken from us, it was gone. How were we free? (Harihar Singh. Naik Community Elder, Arabari, in Chatterji, 1996:64).

In response to the crisis, various strategies for public lands reform and ecological restoration emerged in independent India, some exclusively among community groups, others that involved community groups and state agencies in collaboration. Community, Participatory and Joint Forest Management systems emerged out of the failure of colonial and social forestry and the Indian government's forest policies in general. The term Community Forest Management (CFM) refers to local community initiatives and organization toward regenerating, protecting, and managing public and other forest lands. The state forest departments are generally unsupportive of such initiatives and prefer to adopt a state-community co-management framework instead. Participatory Forest Management (PFM) is widely used when describing forest management systems that are collaborative in nature involving local community groups, state forest departments, and other agencies. Joint Forest Management (JFM) is the preferred forest department option of formalized agreements between local community and the state relating to protecting and managing public forest lands (Chatterji, 1998).

These forest management systems were meant to include and empower people. In post-independent India, initiatives for a transition to PFM and JFM systems emerged during the 1970s-1990s, preceded by thousands of communities forming CFM groups since the 1940s to protect their degrading forests, primarily in eastern India's tribal forest tracts (Poffenberger, 1995). In 1988 and 1989 respectively, the Governments of Orissa and West Bengal passed a number of resolutions clarifying the terms of inclusion of local community groups in forest management, and recognizing the village as the formal unit of management. The National Forest Policy of 1988 legitimated the prior claims of forest dependent communities to these public resources. The Government of India passed a resolution in 1990 encouraging community-state collaboration in forest management. In response to the 1990 circular, 24 states have issued formal JFM directives in the last decade. It is estimated that 44,000-70,000 villages are currently engaged in organized forest protection. The Government of India revised the guidelines in February 2000, more attentive to the complex conditions under which JFM operates (Saigal, 1999; Saigal, 2001; Government of India, 2000).[10]

Stabilizing India's natural forests and watersheds is seen as a significant step in sustaining a rural environment that can support a still expanding population. The fundamental premise of JFM and CFM is sustainable forest management through people's participation and a reinstatement of their subsistence rights over forests. Operationalizing such rights would engender the empowerment of the millions of people that live under survival conditions. Their empowerment would in turn make possible a devolution of authority over forest lands from state agencies to community groups. The state would begin to play a supportive role in management. Community groups would take responsibility for sustainable use and conservation using decentralized mechanisms for local self-governance, drawing on local knowledge of their environment (Poffenberger, 1995).

Political and operational constraints have slowed the transfer of rights to user communities. Community protection and natural regeneration have been remarkably effective in halting further degradation and restoring productivity to these environments, now estimated to cover around 35 million hectares (Government of India, 2000). While financial support from government and development agencies for JFM increased exponentially during the 1990s, numerous issues remain unaddressed. Such issues include critical JFM policy weaknesses and the need for procedural, tenurial, and legal changes. There is a felt absence of effective mechanisms to operationalize field learning and forums for dialogue between primary government planners, state forest departments, and the diversity of development agencies entering the arena at the state and national level (Chatterji, 2001b). Sustainable knowledge has not sufficiently impacted national policy. Such recognition and legitimation is necessary for sustainable knowledge to endure.

---

10 Sushil Saigal, Winrock International, Personal Communication (1999 and 2001); N.C. Saxena, Planning Commission, Personal Communication (2001). Also see Government of India, Guidelines for Strengthening of Joint Forest Management Program, Ministry of Environment and Forests, No. 22-8/2000-JFM (FPD) (New Delhi: Government of India, 2000).

At present, the National Ministry of Environment and Forests has limited capacity to guide the transition in public forest management systems. To shift the enduring injustices that characterize development interventions and civil society, forest reform processes and programs require major political and legal reframe from the state custodial and industrial management models operational for almost 150 years. There is tremendous resistance among critics of JFM in India in favor of new initiatives that are required to maintain the larger national effort to reform public forest lands management (Poffenberger and Chatterji, 2000). Rather than endorse the formal inequitable agreements between the state and community groups, JFM stakeholders are stressing the need for the transfer of authority over forest lands to local community groups. They are opposing agreements related to benefit sharing that allocate a greater percentage of profits and resources to the state forest department. They are also organizing against the unsustainable management practices such as annual felling employed by the forest department. Community groups engaged in CFM initiatives are concerned about the lack of state endorsement and infrastructural investment into watershed and microcredit development, and availability of processing and marketing facilities for non timber forest products. The growing grassroots mandate for a complete reform of the jurisdictional and managerial policies related to public forest lands is an extremely significant development.

Statewide political shifts increasingly endorse greater democratization of control over forest lands through communitarian governance in the form of Panchayat rule (Saxena, 2000b).[11] The conviction behind such reform increasingly prescribes a revolutionary reorganization of rights and responsibilities between states and marginalized communities. Shifting the very fabric of agreements between the state and community for forest management, ongoing social and political processes seek to alter allocations and entitlements related to all nationalized forests. They advocate abrogation of state control over public forest lands, tenurial and custodian rights for marginalized communities, and the initiation of community management frameworks. Grassroots political will is committed to enabling community control at the micro level in ways that foreground local self-governance. Such shifts, if furthered, would revolutionize the allocation of power over land. To support these shifts, forest department

11 In independent India, the Panchayat system of government, or Panchayati Raj (rule), refers to the three tier structure of local governing bodies from village to district level; gram (village), samati (block — a collective administrative unit constituted of a group of villages), and zilla (district — an administrative unit constituting of a group of blocks). The passage of the 72 and 73 Constitutional Amendments in 1992 enabled Panchayati rule, thus enforcing a national mandate for greater democratization and decentralization (World Bank, 2000).

initiated forums like the divisional working groups need to be dissolved, and community participation in forest department controlled forums must be replaced by the department's participation in community convened platforms. Such departure would necessitate that forest management objectives be made compatible with the 1988 Forest Policy and the 1996 legislation for extending the Panchayati Raj system to adivasi (tribal) areas.[12] The role and function of the forest department needs to be reassessed and its revenue generation practices relocated. Currently, the state determines and defines the structure of institutional arrangements between itself and community groups as they operate on public forest lands, and it does so through mechanisms of decision-making that are not participatory or equitable or sustainable.

Such processes for radical social reform are key to the production and maintenance of sustainable knowledge. The survival of sustainable knowledge requires shifts in power relations that enshrine sustainable practices in conscience and policy. For sustainable practices to endure demands legitimation of these practices in multiple sites. Alliance with academic practice is one site that empowers and makes legitimate sustainable knowledge. Engaging in processes that produce sustainable knowledge at local levels is crucial, but is insufficient for social change. Maintaining and legitimating such knowledge/practice requires alliances that wield political impact. To alter state and international policy to support sustainability requires legitimation of disqualified knowledge by foregrounding their effects.[13] Sustained and intimate involvement of the Academy is thus of great strategic importance to empowering marginalized communities. Political change requires alliance among multiple constituencies. The Academy is one body whose resources are needed in this endeavor.

In a postcolonial state where public lands represent resources critical to the survival of marginalized people, these reforms foreground issues of livelihood in the context of ecological sustainability for 300 million people living in close relationship to the forests (Chatterji, 2001a). Struggles over public lands reflect the larger violations imposed on the disenfranchised by the state via dominant development processes. In India, development remains unattainable for 350 million of its poorest citizens. The absence of social and political reform

---

12 Adivasi: Sanskrit for original dweller. A term often used by "tribal" and indigenous communities in India to refer to themselves.

13 Disqualified knowledge, later spoken of as subaltern knowledge, refers to knowledge that lives on the margins and is systematically de-legitimized. It refers to knowledge that fails to achieve the statues of official "truth". For an elaboration of disqualified knowledge, see Michel Foucault, Language, Counter-Memory, Practice (New York: Cornell University Press, 1977).v

that addresses entrenched inequities of gender, caste, and religion endanger any possibility of equitable development. Gandhi's vision of sustainable development has been undermined through large-scale industrialization, urbanization, and modernization (Saxena, 2000a). Since 1951, five year economic plans have been adopted to propel India's development in industry and agriculture, and to remedy the political dissension, debt, and infrastructural disarray that plagued the newly independent country (Indian Social Institute, 1988). Development actions have succeeded in exponentially increasing India's industrial, military, and agricultural production, national income, and middle class. Yet in 2003, almost 56 years after independence, development has failed to alleviate poverty and related socioeconomic oppressions within the most disenfranchised caste, class, and adivasi communities. The scale and implications of this poverty and the magnitude of the bondage it reinforces is experienced by most nations of the Global South, forcing its citizens to live in a constant state of war. These conditions are languaged as impoverishment, in circumstances where people's most basic human rights are violated.

International bodies such as the International Monetary Fund and the World Bank, national development ministries and departments in Southern countries, corporations, and oligarchies finance development that lacks political integrity (Danaher, 1994; Hoogvelt, 1997). These systems have institutionalized development ideologies through action plans that promote the irresponsible globalization of cultures, economies and ecologies (Patnaik, 1997). Their interventions continue to devastate the earth, enhancing social dislocation and alienation, and furthering the dominance of technological rationality. Such rationality involves the quantification of life based predominantly on market productivity rather than social capability (Chatterji, 2001a; Sen, 1995). The international community has at best been concerned with adequate representation, not self-determination, of marginalized communities within development. Neither European nor North American nations have taken accountability for the political and economic crimes they have committed through colonization and neocolonization. Such considerations do not factor into organizing reparations to the disenfranchised in the once colonized countries of the Global South. Rather development institutions continue to assert processes that systematically de-legitimize traditional livelihoods by impoverishing the natural resource base upon which the lives of subsistence communities depend (Escobar, 1995). Aggressive deforestation continues to haunt rural communities globally. In Sri Lanka 23 percent of its land remains forested, in India it's eight percent, in Pakistan it's 4.5 percent, and in Bangladesh it is six percent (Poffenberger, 2000).

The failure of dominant development and its promised freedoms bear testimony to a deep unconcern for social and ecological justice. It also bears grievous testimony to the apparati of knowledges, practices, and processes that endow and legitimize maldevelopment. It reflects on the state of the world, society, polity, and the Academy.

Impacts of Ethical Dissent on Knowledge Production

> *Participation is a very imperfect thing, it cannot....be measured by any others....then those who participate, and those who participate are often not [accounted for] in the process.* (Anonymous, Community Activist, Bhubaneswar, Orissa. Chatterji, 1998:117)
>
> *Perhaps what is not working is that our voices are not unified, not strong enough so they can be heard by the state. Perhaps what is working is that our voices contradict each other, our differences emerge and highlight a road to more a democratic social process.* (Samarendu Satpaty, Peoples Institute for Participatory Action Research, Chatterji, 1998:155)

Defending self-determination in local economies and confronting the invasion of global and corporate capitalism challenges inherited oppressions at local levels, simultaneous to affirming local knowledges as crucial to sustainable knowledge production. Such commitments seek to operationalize frameworks for sustainability that link economic and ecological well being. Such practice endows sustainability as central to the assessment of the health of society, where well being must be calculated in relation to the empowerment of the most marginalized. Commitments to sustainable development, knowledge, the Academy, and social movements are manifested through collaborative processes of research and advocacy that make various stakeholders accountable to each other. Commitment to a shared process that is diverse in its priorities is both problematic and necessary. Conflict and contestation do not lead to a questioning of commitment, but rather to clarification of our different approaches and priorities. It is perhaps the engagement of differences that permits relationships to endure.

Participation, one's own and that of others, in the process of knowledge production is inherently flawed. It varies with entitlement and access. It is impacted by the process of its solicitation, and it is framed by the level at which it was being solicited (Chatterji, 2000). Participation must be profoundly linked to empowerment, while understanding both as always partial and incomplete. This work has afforded me[14] a discursive understanding of the organization of

---

14 Refers to Angana's work.

social movements related to public lands reform. It has rendered problematic development alternatives and interventions within the social particularities of class, caste, gender, power and government in rural Orissa. It has highlighted, in acute detail, the inequities of class and gender that reverberate through social movements and disable change. It has made visible women's struggle within state and development agencies, as well as within the claustrophobic patriarchal structures that organize caste villages, to define their empowered participation in forest management. It has demonstrated the distinctions between caste and adivasi realities vis-à-vis the production of gendered spaces. In such overdetermined contexts, how do we foster relations that make necessary explanations of action at every juncture? If we are not continually reflecting on the effects of knowledge production as intervention, can we ever claim such knowledge to be sustainable?

In the classroom, practicing sustainable knowledge requires methods and processes attentive to the context of history and culture, people and place, and power and equity. Viewing the relationship between the ecology and people as integral to practicing and learning effective procedures for sustaining natural resources allows us to look for varieties of applicable methods that empower and encourage communities to protect the environment. In situating knowledge within relevant local and global, genealogical, interdisciplinary, cross-cultural, anthropological, environmental, historical, and postcolonial frameworks, teaching and learning become acts of alliance building.[15] The politics and integrity of commitments that inform education is what makes sustainable knowledge possible in the classroom. Such practice questions the essentializing of truth, identity, thinking, and action that often organizes the production of knowledge. Such practice neither infers a lack of conflict, contradiction or dissonance, nor does it assume consensus. It refers to strategic relationships that advocate justice. It is precisely such practice that produces forms of sustainable knowledge as ongoing intervention (Chatterji, 2000). Such questions and struggles of relevance extend to social movements. They inform the relationship between the Academy and other worlds.

Ongoing and self-reflective processes of knowledge production shift the focus from traditional interventionist research as an instrument for "objective"

15Alliance building refers to processes that empower collaborative social action. Such collaboration does not infer the lack of conflict, contradiction, or dissonance; neither does it assume consensus. It refers to strategic relationships that dismantle inequities and operate at multiple levels.

knowledge production.[16] In the last 50 years such production has been challenged by human rights movements for social justice and self-determination across the globe. These movements have been deeply concerned with the use of knowledge for establishing authority and legitimizing unequal structures and institutions. These struggles contend that non-consensual intervention in the lives of others, whether academic, advocacy, and/or action oriented, is an act of political domination. Such intervention, these movements assert, is particularly oppressive where social relations between those intervening and those who become the focus of intervention are drastically inequitable. A critical objective of my[17] research has centered around dismantling the fictions related to the construction of knowledge for the sake of knowledge. It is useful to question the impact of knowledge construction and its effects as it circulates in a lived world. To engage the manufacturing of emancipatory knowledge requires that we ask: Who participates in its construction? Who defines the ends and means of knowledge production? Where are we as participants situated? Attentiveness to such knowledge/power dynamics is crucial to sustainable knowledge production as an ongoing practice (Chatterji, 2000; Shapiro, 2002).

Within the Global South, the practice of action research as a process of generating sustainable knowledge was shaped in the 1960s-1970s. Framing the relevance of research as a tool for social change, participatory and participatory action research methods were generated as instruments of social action.[18] These frameworks were influenced by neo-Marxist, feminist,

---

16 See Homi Bhabha, The Location of Culture (London: Routledge, 1994); Gayatri Spivak, Can the Subaltern Speak? In P. Williams and L. Chrisman (Eds.), Colonial Discourse and Post-colonial Theory: A Reader. (New York: Columbia University Press, 1994); Edward Said, Culture and Imperialism (New York: Vintage Books, 1993); Talal Asad (Ed.), Anthropology and the Colonial Encounter (New York: Humanities Press, 1973); Ann Stoller, Race and the Education of Desire (Durham: Duke University Press, 1995); Akhil Gupta and James Ferguson, Culture, Power, Place: Explorations in Critical Anthropology (Durham: Duke University Press, 1998).

17 Refers to Angana's work.

18 Participatory research is primarily concerned with collaborative knowledge making. Participatory action research is concerned with inquiry that is enacted through participatory processes and seeks to facilitate action. Participatory research or participatory action research is not located within a particular disciplinary frame. It utilizes a variety of qualitative, quantitative, and organic tools as appropriate. Fals-Borda, Fernandes, Freire, and Tandon are some of the key proponents of participatory (action) research in the South. See Paulo Freire, Orlando Fals-Borda, Muhammad Anisur Rahman, Walter Fernandes and Rajesh Tandon. Fernandes and Tandon are two of the major proponents of participatory action research in India. During the years of 1989-1991, I (Angana) was privileged to work with Walter Fernandes. Also, see the work of the International Council for Adult Education and Budd Hall in Toronto. Also, see Denzin and Lincoln, 2000; Gupta and Ferguson, 1998 and 1999; and Marcus and Fischer, 1986.

and human rights activism in postcolonial Bangladesh, India, and Sri Lanka in Asia, and by liberation theology in Colombia and other areas in Latin America. Research and knowledge production were discoursed as practices and as processes of empowerment where participants are agents rather than subjects. Knowledge, co-produced and shaped through collective agency, was legitimized. The objective of such knowledge was to facilitate social restructuring and re-framing of power relations to redistribute resources (Chatterji, 2000).

It is important to mention that some of the major critiques of participatory research and action emerge from the spaces in which they are practiced. Participation is often solicited without capacity building to enable it. Transition from autocratic inquiry to collaborative practice is sporadic. When attempted, unequal social relations reflecting class/caste privilege, differences in education, language, gender socialization, and capability disrupt it. Democratization of knowledge demands a subordination of the researcher to processes of social change. Collective knowledge production demands questions related to the process of research. What epistemological and political determinants govern the production of knowledge and enable and constrain the engendering of relevant knowledge? How do processes of inquiry privilege enable and silence specific forms of knowledge and representation? How are political and social shifts reorganizing research as intervention? Attentiveness to dynamics of inclusion and exclusion as necessary and constraining elements of a legacy of domination are central to processes of sustainable knowledge making (Chatterji, 2002a).

Postcolonial movements in India and elsewhere have used research to legitimize disqualified and subaltern knowledges that explicitly resist inequity. The last decade has produced extensive research from Orissa, for example, that is action oriented and locally situated. Local community members, non-governmental organizations, academics, institutions, and allies have initiated research processes as a mechanism of reform. Some of these inquiries interrogate public lands reform in Orissa and foreground recommendations for policy and social action.[19] Producing knowledge through such generative methods offers insights into social processes. Postcolonial research prompts contested narratives that make certain voices, factors, and players relevant and visible. The priorities of such production shift continually, and in their mobility they navigate practices that respond to change (Spivak, 1994).

19 For Orissa research, see publications authored by Agragwamee, Peoples Institute for Participatory Action Research; Neera Singh, Regional Council for Development Cooperation; Madhu Sarin; S.K. Sarangi; Sudhir Patnaik; Ashok Babu; N.C. Saxena; Nandini Sundar; Kundan Kumar Singh; and Mark Poffenberger.

Knowledge production within a postcolonial framework emphasizes critical intellectual activity within a context of social action. Within the research processes this paper refers to such practice shifted the focus of inquiry from interpreting and representing knowledge to the emergent participation of various and subaltern stakeholders within knowledge making. Such research resides within a complex diagnostic of power/knowledge relations, emphasizing knowledge making as relational and vulnerable. It undermines the obsession with "truth" at work in knowledge construction. Such knowledge provides spaces where truth is negotiated and operationalized (Derrida, 1968; Foucault, 1980; Gupta and Ferguson, 1998). It problematizes universalistic and relativist approaches to knowing and being. Such shifts permit research to live as an emancipatory practice, rooted in a relation of acknowledgement of its colonial past and challenged by its subaltern practitioners. It fosters a relentless, genealogical critique of society. It seeks to empower marginal voices. Such priorities must inform thinking as a practice in the Academy and influence curricula and research agendas. To do so requires shifts in the politics, practices, and desires that enframe knowledge production within the Academy (Stoller, 1995). Foregrounding such practice within the Academy destabilizes the notion of a self in search of knowledge for enlightenment. Instead, it locates the self within society and empowers commitments to a rigorous and ethical future.

An Academy for Justice?

Postcolonial justice is fictive in so many ways. If the lives of the most disenfranchised have improved in the last century it is only as an afterthought of development and the nation state. Postcoloniality struggles with the death of memory where its promises to the poor are least honored. Their actions for survival and self-determination are policed to benefit the advantaged. In such a context, when I[20] broach the subject of human rights to those suffering from its most severe violation, I am faced with silence. Human rights has failed to language itself in ways that resonate with the concerns of the marginalized.

On December 16, 2000, Abhilas Jhodia, Raghu Jhodia, and Damodar Jhodia, three adivasi community members, aged 25, 18 and 43 years respectively, were killed in a police firing in Kashipur, Orissa, protesting the violation of constitutional provisions barring the sale or lease of tribal lands to non-tribals or to private companies without their consent. Their protest was against a consortium of industries mining bauxite. Their deaths

20 Refers to Angana's work.

give testimony to the savage nature of globalization where multinational corporations and state governments unite to perpetrate genocide and ecocide. Their lives, lived in resistance to this onslaught, sought cultural survival that maintained diverse ecosystems necessary to livelihood. To respond to this aggression named free trade, local community groups mobilized in dissent to these corporations demanding constitutionally guaranteed protections of tribal peoples and their lands.

A conversation I[21] had with Kali Babu, a community elder in Arabari, West Bengal in 1996 leads me to reflect on the role of resistance (Chatterji, 1996). Non-violent civil disobedience has been an integral practice in public lands reform. The practice of resistance seeks a radical shift from inherited conditions where the structural predicament of inequity endures. A key element of resistance has been the emphasis that alleviation of poverty must be distinct from the dissolution of culture (Escobar, 1995). External structural interventions that attempt to mitigate poverty encourage a decomposition of local cultures. The rationality of progress and the infrastructure of globalized capitalism require the quantification of culture into its productive and profit capability. Such quantification undermines local efforts. Diversity and sustainability are detrimental to such homogenization. Community leaders and non-governmental organizations in Orissa are outraged at the misrepresentations of their cultures and lifestyles assembled to augment irresponsible development. Dominant development is neither sustainable nor organic. It rewrites the premise of development from local enfranchisement to cultural, economic, and ecological mutations that sustain inequity and produce uniformity.

Local research agendas intent on the production of sustainable knowledge are attentive to such disregard. These agendas focus on addressing injustices through critical and affirmative relations to local culture and knowledge. Such agendas allow for a prioritization of necessary interventions and detect aspects of local social conditions that must change to support self-determination (Escobar, 1995). In addition, internalized colonization, caste, and gender relations have yet to be explicitly engaged. Such engagement is critical to renovating the infrastructure toward equitable self-governance.

It has been a privilege for me[22] to be a part of these processes. I have learned accountability in labor. I have witnessed anger and resistance as magnificent and humble, fraught with tension and contradiction. The ethics

21 Refers to Angana's work.

22 Refers to Angana's work.

that define these ongoing associations have produced work and relationships that nurture places of profound meaning. Such collaboration finds courage to acknowledge the impossibility and absolute necessity of this labor.

The task of intervention is continually problematic as I inhabit the contradictions and estrangement of bi-nationality. It is a chosen diaspora that seeks continual, if impossible, return. In this context, how might I, as a woman from postcolonial India, engage the political horror of "First" world inequities in the context of "Third""world resistance? How might concerns of "Third" world subsistence live within the "First" world Academy through critical intellectual activity and social action? How might particular forms of knowledge constructed through collective practice in both places question their relevance?

Dominant processes of academic knowledge production are organized to support inquiring subjects scrutinizing knowable objects. Methods for knowledge construction generally assume a world that is knowable through properly prepared subjects. The individual is endowed with reason, capacities for reflection, empathy, intuition, and consciousness that makes the objective world able to be apprehended. The subject is generally understood to be able to access truth as an individual (Foucault, 1977; Foucault, 1980). The world is knowable in so far as it is objectifiable. The social, cultural, political, historical, linguistic, and economic processes that constitute the world as objects accessible to properly prepared subjects remains largely unproblematized in human science research. Ethics are reduced to consent, safeguards for risks, kind interaction, and "honest" representation. The ethics of organizing knowledge in terms of object-subject relations and the problematics of the effects of both the process and content of knowledge is insufficiently thought in the culture of academia (Giroux; 2000; Hall, 1996; Heidegger, 1988; McRobbie, 2000). How to create inclusive, interactive, regularly assessed processes of knowledge construction deserves fuller attention. The agendas that define worthwhile research and the funding of such research constrain and marginalize emancipatory knowledge production.

The voices and silences we encounter during research resound with histories of domination and the rigid ordering of difference. Endemic to the very process of intervention is the danger of reproducing the interests of those who are dominant or misrepresenting the interests of those who are marginalized. Sustainable knowledge production seeks to shift power relations by inclusion of multiple constituencies in the process of knowledge making and the product provisionally defined as knowledge. The inevitability of privileging certain voices and reproducing existing social hierarchies demands continual attention to the power dynamics that shape knowledge. The inquiry is made necessary because of the very inequities of class, gender, race, and caste that largely privilege us.

How can we as academics participate in political practice through which research agendas are generated? How can we practice research with communities with whom we have established relationships? How can we cooperate in the establishment of research agendas, seek reciprocally beneficial forms of knowledge, and create funding mechanisms that support such research? To engage in such practice explodes the universe of inquiring subjects and knowable objects, creating complex social networks in which relevant, contested, and partial knowledge results. How do we seek methods that facilitate ways of knowing reflecting rigorous engagement with context? Context specific knowledge inhabits the realm of the true and confronts the conditions of its existence in assessing its claims. The process of liberatory knowledge making involves negotiating the interrelationships in and between the multiplicity of stakeholders, contexts, meanings, and realities that organize social life and facilitate social change.

The legitimacy of relevant and therefore sustainable knowledge hinges on the consequences that result. Emancipatory knowledge as advocacy addresses problematics and enters into contested representations. It confronts the truths that sanction existing power relations and our own embeddedness.[23] Such knowledge is dangerous and uncomfortable. Sustainable knowledge making is an ongoing practice. It can only be attempted in collaboration with diverse stakeholders. Alliance between the Academy and outside stakeholders produces transformations in both spaces. Such alliance informs social practice and influences academic curriculum. Social sites and the classroom must intersect to enable a rethinking of the terms, methods, and utility of knowledge production. Sustainable knowledge is that which supports movements toward sustainable worlds, which responds to the world in a manner is at once engaged and critical, affirmative of possibilities that inhere in a given situation and deconstructive in relation to the effects of such knowledge. Sustainable knowledge questions the very ground that defines our social being as we strive to dismantle the conditions that produce us as "voiced" and others as "voiceless."

23 Ideas on power, resistance, and method delineated here are very much influenced by the work of Michel Foucault. See Michel Foucault, 1977, 1978, 1980, 1993, and 1994 in the reference section of this article for his formidable conceptual frameworks that language the facticity of power that is produced within the diversity of human relations and social practices.

References

Asad, T. (Ed.). (1973). *Anthropology and the Colonial Encounter*. New York: Humanities Press.

Bhabha, H. K. (1994). *The Location of Culture*. London: Routledge.

Chatterji, A. P. (1996). *Community Forest Management in Arabari: Understanding Sociocultural and Subsistence Issues*. New Delhi: Society for Promotion of Wastelands Development.

Chatterji, A. P. (1998). *Toward an Ecology of Hope: Community and Joint Forest Management in Orissa*. Sweden: Scandisconsult Natura AB; and Berkeley: Asia Forest Network.

Chatterji, A. P. (2000). Decolonizing Anthropology: Knowledge Making Toward Social Change. Paper presented at the Society for Applied Anthropology. San Francisco. March 2000.

Chatterji, A, P. (2001a, September). Postcolonial Research as Relevant Practice. *TAMARA: Journal of Critical Postmodern Organization Science, 1*(3), 1-13.

Chatterji, A. P. (2001b). A Critique of Forest Governance in Eastern India. *International Journal for Economic Development, 3*(2).

Cohen, T. (2001). *Jacques Derrida and the Humanities. A Critical Reader*. New York: Cambridge University Press.

Danaher, K. (Ed.). (1994). *50 Years Is Enough: The Case Against the World Bank and the International Monetary Fund*. Boston: South End Press.

Denzin, N. K., and Lincoln, Y. S. (Eds.). (2000). *Handbook of Qualitative Research*. (2nd ed.). California: Sage Publications.

Derrida, J. (1967). *De La Grammatologie*. (*Of Grammatology*. Translation Gayatri Chakravorty Spivak.) Baltimore: Johns Hopkins Press.

Derrida, J. (1968). Différance. In *Margins of Philosophy*. Translation Alan Bass. Chicago: Chicago University Press.

Escobar, A. (1995). *Encountering Development: The Making and Unmaking of the Third World*. Princeton: Princeton University Press.

Fals-Borda, O. and Rahman, M. A. (1991). *Action and Knowledge: Breaking the Monopoly with Participatory Action Research*. Walnut Creek: Sage Publications.

Fernandes, W. and Tandon, R. (1981). *Participatory Research and Evaluation: Experiments in Research as a Process of Liberation.* New Delhi: Indian Social Institute.

Foucault, M. (1977). *Language, Counter-Memory, Practice.* New York: Cornell University Press.

Foucault, M. (1978). *The History of Sexuality. Volume I: An Introduction.* New York: Pantheon Books.

Foucault, M. (1980). *Power/Knowledge.* New York: Pantheon Press.

Foucault, M. (1993). Space, Power and Knowledge. In S. During (Ed.), *The Cultural Studies Reader.* New York: Routledge.

Foucault, M. (1994). The Order of Things. In J. D. Faubion (Ed.) and P. Rabinow (Series Editor), *Aesthetics, Method and Epistemology. Essential Works of Michel Foucault. 1954-1984.* Volume 2. New York: The New York Press.

Freire, P. (1970). *Pedagogy of the Oppressed.* New York: Seabury Press.

Giroux, H. (2000). Public Pedagogy as Cultural Politics: Stuart Hall and the 'Crisis' of Culture. In P. Gilroy, L. Grossberg, and A. McRobbie (Eds.). *Without Guarantees: In Honour of Stuart Hall.* London: Verso.

Government of India. (2000, February 21). *Guidelines for Strengthening of Joint Forest Management Program. Ministry of Environment and Forests.* No 22-8/2000-JFM (FPD). New Delhi: Government of India.

Gupta, A. and Ferguson. J. (Eds.). (1997). *Anthropological Locations: Boundaries and Grounds of a Field Science.* Berkeley: University of California Press.

Gupta, A. and Ferguson, J. (1998). *Culture, Power, Place: Explorations in Critical Anthropology.* Durham: Duke University Press.

Hall, S. (1996). The Formation of a Diasporic Intellectual: An Interview with Stuart Hall by Kuan-Hsing Chen. In D. Morley and K. H. Chen. (Eds.), *Stuart Hall: Critical Dialogues in Cultural Studies.* London: Routledge.

Hall, S. (1998). Aspiration and Attitude – Reflections on Black Britain in the Nineties. *New Formations 33*(Spring), 38-47.

Heidegger, M. (1988). *The Basic Problems of Phenomenology.* Bloomington: Indiana University Press.

Hoogvelt, A. (1997). *Globalization and the Postcolonial World. The New Political Economy of Development*. Baltimore: Johns Hopkins University Press.

Indian Social Institute. (1988). *The Five Year Plan System*. New Delhi: Indian Social Institute.

McRobbie, A. (2000). The Universities and the 'Hurly Burly'. In P. Gilroy, L. Grossberg, and A. McRobbie (Eds.), *Without Guarantees. In Honour of Stuart Hall*. London: Verso.

Marcus, G. E, and Fischer, M. J. (1986). *Anthropology as Cultural Critique*. Chicago and London: The University of Chicago Press.

Mukhopadhyay, J.K. (Ed.). (1994). *Statistical Outline of India. 1994-95*. Bombay: Tata Services Limited. Department of Economics and Statistics.

Patnaik, P. (1997). *Whatever Happened to Imperialism?* New Delhi: Tulika.

Payne, M. (Ed.). (1997). *A Dictionary of Cultural and Critical Theory*. Oxford: Blackwell Publishers.

Poffenberger, M. (2000). (Ed.). *Communities and Forest Management in South Asia*. Gland, Switzerland: The World Conservation Union-IUCN.

Poffenberger, M. (1995). *Public Lands Reform: India's Experiences with Joint Forest Management*. Berkeley: Asia Forest Network.

Poffenberger, M. and Chatterji, A. (2000). *Joint Forest Management Support Project: Linking State and National Concerns*. Berkeley: Project Proposal. Asia Forest Network.

Poffenberger, M. and McGean, B. (Eds.). (1995). *Village Voices, Forest Choices*. Delhi: Oxford University Press.

Said, E. (1993). *Culture and Imperialism*. New York: Vintage Books.

Saigal, S. (1999). Personal Communication.

Saigal, S. (2001). Personal Communication.

Sarin, M. (1999). *Policy Goals and JFM Practice: An Analysis of Institutional Arrangements and Outcomes*. New Delhi: World Wildlife Federation and the International Institute for Environment and Development.

Saxena, N.C. (2000a, October 7). How Have the Poor Done? Mid-Term Review of the Ninth Plan. *Economic and Political Weekly, XXXV*(41). New Delhi.

Saxena, N.C. (2000b). *Decentralization and Panchayati Raj Institutions*. Unpublished manuscript.

Saxena, N.C. (2001). Personal Communication.

Sen, A. (1995). Gender Inequality and Theories of Justice. In M. Nussbaum and J. Glover (Eds.), *Women, Culture and Development. A Study of Human Capabilities*. Oxford: Clarendon Press.

Shapiro, R. (2002). *Self, Community and Pleasure: Michel Foucault and Contemporary Sexual Politics*. Unpublished manuscript.

Society for Promotion of Wastelands Development. (1998). *Joint Forest Management Update 1998*. New Delhi: Society for Promotion of Wastelands Development.

Spivak, G. (1994). Can the Subaltern Speak? In P. Williams and L. Chrisman (Eds.), *Colonial Discourse and Postcolonial Theory: A Reader*. New York: Columbia University Press.

Spivak, G. (1999). *A Critique of Postcolonial Reason: Toward A History of the Vanishing Present*. Massachusetts: Harvard University Press.

Stoller, A. (1995). *Race and the Education of Desire*. Durham: Duke University Press.

Tinker, I. (Ed.). (1990). *Persistent Inequalities: Women and World Development*. New York: Oxford University Press.

World Bank. (2000). *Entering the 21st Century. World Development Report 1999/2000*. New York: Oxford University Press.

7

CLIMATE AND ENVIRONMENTAL JUSTICE

Dale Jamieson, Ph.D.*

The basic strategy of substituting research for meaningful action is politically effective for a number of reasons. First, Americans love science, and it is hard to resist the idea that when faced with difficult public policy questions, the more science the better. But science does not only answer questions, it also produces new questions. Research may reduce some uncertainties, but it also generates new ones. The more science that is produced, the more handholds and footholds there are for those who are skeptical of mainstream views. No amount of scientific research will refute those who see the International Panel on Climate Change (IPCC) as the scientific expression of a "one-world" conspiracy aimed at putting an end to American freedom and prosperity.

Introduction

In the 20th Century humans had a profound impact on the fundamental systems that govern life on earth, especially by altering the carbon and nitrogen cycles and the composition of the atmosphere. Human action is now responsible for fixing more nitrogen in the terrestrial biosphere than all natural processes combined (Vitousek, et al., 1997). The viability and existence of many forms of life are now threatened because as much as half of Earth's primary biological productivity is appropriated for human purposes (Daily, 1995). The stratospheric ozone layer, which protects the biosphere from deadly ultraviolet radiation, has substantially thinned because of the manufacturing and use of chlorofluorocarbons. The most dramatic

---

• Dale Jamieson, Ph.D. is the Director of Environmental Studies at New York University, Professor of Environmental Studies and Philosophy, and Affiliated Professor of Law. Formerly he was a Henry R. Luce Professor at Carleton College. His most recent book is *Morality's Progress: Essays on Humans, Other Animals, and the Rest of Nature* (Oxford, 2002), He would like to thank Bunyan Bryant and Beth Raps for their comments on an earlier version of this paper.

manifestation of human impact on the planet is the climate change that is now underway. All life on Earth lives in wary relation to the climate regime that has prevailed since the end of the last ice age, some 15,000 years ago. Exactly how climate change will impact life on Earth remains unclear. However, former President Clinton may well have been correct when he said in his State of the Union address on January 27, 2000 that climate change "is the greatest challenge of the new century."

Any investigation of the relationship between climate change and environmental justice should begin with a vivid understanding of the current international order. Climate change is another shock to a world already fractured by nationalism, fanaticism, and inequality. While many dimensions of the current international order are relevant, I want to highlight the following:

- Between 1700 and 1952, India's share of world gross domestic product (GDP) declined from 22.6% to 3.8%. (Davis, 2001)
- Between 1820 and 1952, China's share of world GDP declined from 32.4% to 5.2%.(Davis, 2001)
- Even on the most conservative assumptions, between 1820 and 1970 global inequality doubled. (Dollar and Kraay, 2002)
- In 1960 the 20% of the world's people who live in the richest countries had 30 times the income of the poorest 20% — by 1995 this had risen to 82 times as much income. (UNDP, 1998)
- The wealth of the 15 richest people in the world exceeds the total GDP of sub-Saharan Africa. (UNDP, 1998)
- The assets of the 84 richest individuals in the world are greater than the current GDP of China. (UNDP, 1998).
- The 225 richest people in the world have combined wealth that is equal to the annual income of the poorest 47% of the world's population. (UNDP, 1998)
- More than one billion people live on less than $1 per day; nearly three billion live on less than $2 per day. (World Bank, 2001)

These facts remind us that the people of the world do not enter the era of anthropogenic global environmental change from a common baseline. There are great disparities in people's standards of living, their resources for coping with change, and their power to assert claims. While these facts should be obvious, they are often neglected or ignored. Discussions of climate change tend to focus almost exclusively on scientific or economic considerations, yet an adequate understanding of this issue must appreciate the role of justice.

Ethics and Climate

Anthropogenic climate change may be new, but climate variability and extremes are not. Ancient texts such as the Bible are full of stories about droughts, floods, and other extreme events devastating humans and nature. The Genesis story of the Great Flood, in which God spared Noah, his family, and two of every animal, is one which is particularly rich in allusion.

Still, some may be skeptical about the juxtaposition of "climate" and "ethics". Ethical questions involve human agency, and "normal" climate seems to be a brute natural fact. One might as well speak of ethics and volcanos.

Moreover, when considerations about climate have entered social scientific or humanistic discourse, it has often been in crude, naïve, or distasteful ways. In the first half of the 20th Century the climatic determinism of the eugenicist, Ellsworth Huntington, was extremely influential in the United States. The rejection of this view led to the denial of climate as an important force in human affairs. Subsequent American social science largely treated climate as a minor constraint, easily overcome by technology.

This began to change in the early 1970s when climate anomalies occurred in much of the world. Particularly striking was the El Nino-related Sahel drought and famine which brought images of human suffering into the homes of the affluent and well-fed. In recent years, climate has begun to be theorized in a more sophisticated way, not in the form of climatic determinism, but as a potent force, implicated in complex webs of human suffering and environmental degradation.

Consider some specific cases. From 1876 to 1878 an El Nino produced serious drought in large sections of India, leading to a famine which claimed 6-10 million victims between 1876 and 1879. Prior to this famine India was a large-scale exporter of wheat to Great Britain. Once the famine began, these exports increased dramatically. From 1875 to 1876 exports more than doubled, and then almost doubled again from 1876-77. While Indians were dying of hunger, food was moving away from famine-stricken areas. While this may seem paradoxical, it reflects the logic of market allocation. The drought triggered a series of events that ruptured the existing system of food entitlements. Unable or unwilling to learn from their mistakes, the British colonial administration reprised the policies that they had instituted 30 years before in Ireland when famine killed one-sixth of the population and drove another sixth into diaspora. The colonial authorities were generally hostile to famine relief, content to let the market allocate grain. Because the drought-stricken regions were in economic collapse, the consumer demand expressed in the market came from England, not India, so the grain moved to where people could pay for it (Davis, 2001)

More recently, the 1992 El Nino caused serious drought in southern Africa, leading to crop shortfalls and pushing 80 million people into the early stages of famine. Under pressure from the International Monetary Fund (IMF) to reduce a budget deficit and inflation, the Zimbabwean government exported most of its six month food reserve. As the famine progressed the government had to go back to the market and buy maize at three times the price for which they had sold it (Betsell et al., 1997).

In 1998 Central America was hit by Hurricane Mitch, one of the deadliest storms to affect Central America in the last 200 years. Honduras, the poorest country in the region, suffered the worst impacts. Nearly 20,000 people were killed or went permanently missing, one-third of the population was hurt or lost property, and between 70-90 percent of the nation's infrastructure was destroyed. Massive deforestation, soil degradation, and chaotic urbanization had created the conditions for devastating floods and mudslides. A society in which more than half the population lived below the poverty line and nearly one-third did not have access to basic healthcare was extremely vulnerable to disturbance. Twenty-five years earlier a much weaker hurricane, Fifi, had caused similar damage in Honduras. In its wake reports were written about the need for poverty reduction and changes in land-use patterns, but very little reform was actually implemented. Unsurprisingly, when the next large hurricane struck Honduras, the results were the same (Glantz and Jamieson, 2000).

In each of these cases extreme climatic events figured prominently in causal chains that led to enormous human suffering. While the exact onset of these events was unpredictable, in each case they were an expected part of normal climate variability. What made them so devastating was the poverty and vulnerability of the victims, and the failure to act on the part of those who could have mitigated their effects. Indeed, when the authorities did act—for example, the British colonial authorities and the IMF—they made things worse.

What these cases illustrate is that natural occurrences, such as extreme climatic events, confront us with ethical issues because the impacts of these occurrences depend on social, economic, and political conditions which are functions of human agency. To put the point aphoristically, ethics is related to climate because of the following simple equation: Natural hazards + human action (or inaction) = natural disasters.

If what I have said is correct, then even if humans were not changing climate, extreme events that are part of natural variability would still confront us with important questions of social justice. The fact that humans are changing climate makes the neglect of climate ethics even less excusable.

The Rise of Climate Change

For many people in the United States, climate change first appeared on the horizon on June 23, 1988, a sweltering day in Washington, D.C. in the middle of a severe national drought when climate modeler James Hansen testified to the U.S. Senate Committee on Energy and Natural Resources that it was 99 percent probable that global warming had begun. Hansen's testimony was frontpage news in the *New York Times* and was extensively covered in other media as well.

Climate change had been a major topic of concern in the scientific world since at least the first World Climate Conference in 1979. Throughout the 1980s various high-level international meetings took place to discuss the issue. In 1985 an international group of scientists meeting in Villach, Austria under the auspices of the World Meteorological Organization, the United Nations Environment Programme (UNEP), and the International Council of Scientific Unions concluded that "in the first half of the next century a rise of global mean temperature would occur which is greater than in man's history." They recommended that "scientists and policymakers …begin active collaboration to explore the effectiveness of alternative policies and adjustments" (Agrawala, 1998:608). During the same year Mustafa Tolba, the Egyptian-born Director of UNEP who had spearheaded the negotiations leading to the Ozone Protocol, called for an international climate convention and wrote to U.S. Secretary of State George Schultz, urging U.S. action on this issue. The United States government replied to Tolba's letter by proposing the establishment of an intergovernmental mechanism to carry out internationally coordinated scientific assessments of the magnitude, impact, and potential timing of climate change. By the time the issue hit the frontpage of the *New York Times,* a great deal of international activity was already underway.

The American proposal led to the establishment late in 1988 of the Intergovernmental Panel on Climate Change (IPCC). In 1989 the UN General Assembly adopted a resolution proposed by Malta which essentially authorized the negotiation of a climate change convention. The International Negotiating Committee (INC) was established in 1990, and the Framework

Convention on Climate Change (FCCC) was opened for signature at the Rio Earth Summit in 1992.

The signatories to the Convention, numbering more than 160 countries, committed themselves to the goal of achieving "stabilization of greenhouse gas concentrations in the atmosphere at a level that would prevent dangerous anthropogenic interference with the climate system." As a first step, the developed countries agreed to voluntarily stabilize greenhouse gas (GHG) emissions at 1990 levels by the year 2000. It soon became clear that while some European countries might succeed in keeping this commitment, the United States, Australia, New Zealand, Japan, Canada and Norway clearly would not. In 1995 the parties to the FCCC adopted the Berlin Mandate: they pledged that by the end of 1997 they would reach an agreement establishing binding "quantified, limitation, and reduction objectives" for the industrialized countries and no new obligations would be imposed on other countries during the compliance period. From December 1-10, 1997 the parties met in Kyoto, Japan in order to negotiate the agreement.

In the run-up to Kyoto there was serious conflict between the developed and developing countries, as well as within both groups. The United States wanted an agreement that required stabilization at 1990 levels between 2008 and 2012 while the European Union pressed for 15 percent reductions by 2010. Australian Foreign Minister Alexander Downer stated that "...the only target that Australia could agree to at Kyoto would be one that allowed reasonable growth in our greenhouse emissions" (Australian Conservation Foundation, 1998). The Alliance of Small Island States (AOSIS), whose very existence is threatened by sea level rise, proposed stronger measures than anyone would accept. India and China were mainly concerned to avoid undertaking new commitments, but some Latin American countries, such as Chile and Argentina, signaled a willingness to do more.

Less than five months before the Kyoto meeting the United States Senate unanimously passed the "Byrd Resolution," directing the President not to sign any agreement that required the United States to limit or reduce GHG emissions unless the same agreement also "mandates new specific scheduled commitments to limit or reduce greenhouse gas emissions for Developing Country Parties within the same compliance period." The Clinton Administration, which had agreed to the Berlin Mandate, also supported the Byrd Resolution declaring it would strengthen the American hand at Kyoto. When President Clinton announced the American negotiating position on October 22, 1997, he stated

"...the United States will not assume binding obligations unless key developing nations meaningfully participate in this effort."

The Kyoto meeting was a "make or break" moment in the development of an international climate regime. Had the parties to the convention not been able to reach an agreement in Kyoto it is likely that the global effort to limit GHG emissions would have fallen apart. But after pulling some "all nighters," the delegates to the conference managed to hammer out an agreement.

Four provisions are central to the Kyoto Protocol. First, the developed countries agreed to differentiated, binding targets that would reduce their GHG emissions to about five percent below 1990 levels sometime between 2008 and 2012. Second, performance in meeting these targets would be assessed on the basis of "sinks" (e.g., tree-planting) as well as "sources," and virtually all GHGs, not only carbon dioxide, would be taken into account. Third, emissions trading among developed countries and between developed countries and developing countries would be permitted. Finally, the Protocol reaffirmed that developing countries would not be subject to binding emissions limitations during the compliance period of this Protocol.

Because the Kyoto negotiators wanted an agreement at all costs, some of the most contentious issues were left for future resolution. The Protocol did not specify sanctions for nations that do not keep their commitments. Nor does it address the extent of emissions trading and exactly how it would be implemented. Enormous uncertainties about how emissions can be monitored and how changes in sinks can be measured were left unresolved. A subsequent meeting in Buenos Aires in November,1998 identified the most important issues that would have to be resolved in order to implement the Protocol. Things began to go wrong in The Hague in November, 2000 when negotiators met to try to resolve these issues. A lame-duck American administration and its allies including Japan, Russia, Canada, Australia, and New Zealand (collectively known as JUSCAN), failed to reach agreement with the European Union over how much emissions reduction credit could be claimed on the basis of sinks and emissions trading. Rather than admitting defeat, the meeting was suspended until July 2001. In the interim, in March 2001, the George W. Bush administration caught the world by surprise when it renounced the Protocol. Ironically this improved the negotiating position of America's JUSCAN partners since in order to come into force the Protocol needed to be ratified by at least 55 countries emitting 55 percent of the world's 1990 greenhouse gas emissions, and the U.S. share of 1990 emissions was 36 percent. Thus it became imperative to keep the rest of JUSCAN in the Protocol if there was any hope of it coming into effect. In addition, some hoped that by offering concessions, the U.S. could be persuaded to climb down from its extreme position and rejoin the negotiation. The result was that in July, 2001 in Bonn, the European Union (EU) acceded to most of the demands that the Americans had made earlier in The Hague. The Protocol was further weakened in Marrakech in November, 2001 when negotiators gave in to Russia's demand that its transferable credits for sinks be doubled.

Essentially what has happened is that the loopholes that were embedded in the text of the Kyoto Protocol, rather than being eliminated, have been quantified and transformed into central features of an emissions control regime. In order to convey the flavor of these loopholes I will mention only the example of Russian "hot air." As a result of the post-communist economic collapse, Russian GHG emissions have sharply declined since 1990. What has happened, in effect, is Russia has been allowed to sell the rights to emissions that would not have occurred to countries that will in fact emit these GHGs. The result is that more GHG emissions will occur than would have been the case under a regime that simply established mandatory emissions limits. Russia benefits economically, countries with high levels of GHG emissions are allowed to carry on business more or less as usual, and global climate change continues unabated.

In 2002 when the article was written it was too early to tell exactly what would be the effect of the Kyoto Protocol, but it is clear that it has been radically transformed by the Bonn and Marrakech agreements. Once it was envisioned that the Protocol would reduce developed country GHG emissions by about five percent over the next decade; now it is expected it will allow about a nine percent increase in emissions (Babiker, et al., 2002). There appears to be very little difference between this path and a "business as usual" scenario.

Whatever optimism remains centers on the idea that any agreement is a step forward, and once a price is associated with carbon emissions industry will begin to move towards conservation and renewables. This was always the core idea behind the Kyoto Protocol. Even without the Bonn and Marrakech revisions, the immediate emissions reduction effect of the Kyoto Protocol would have been quite small. In 2010 the difference between a world of perfect conformity to the Kyoto Protocol and a world with no such agreement is 1.5 parts per million (ppm) of carbon dioxide, the difference between an atmospheric concentration of 382 ppm and 383.5 ppm (Bolin, 1998). To put the point in perspective, in the 1990s we experienced a .25°C warming from the 1961-90 baseline; perfect conformity to the Kyoto Protocol would have reduced the expected warming in 2050 from 1.4°C to 1.395°C (Parry, et al., 1998).

On the positive scenario, the FCCC process is like the ozone regime. The initial highly publicized agreements at Vienna and Montreal were not sufficient for repairing the ozone layer or even for preventing further depletion. The really strong agreements to phase out CFCs happened later in London and Copenhagen with much less publicity. From this perspective what is important is bringing the countries of the world into an emissions control regime by getting them to agree to take some initial steps and then to revisit the agreement as the science develops and the consequences of warming are felt. Moreover, mandatory limits, even if they are weak at present, send signals to the markets that the era of fossil fuels is over. New investment will move away from fossil fuels towards renewables, bringing about technical innovation and lower prices.

Science, Power, and Climate Change

It is clear that American resistance has been the most important obstacle to developing a meaningful global response to climate change. Various arguments have been put forward on behalf of American obstructionism including: 1) climate change would be a net benefit (at least for the U.S.); 2) mitigating its effects would be too expensive; and 3) the Kyoto Protocol is unfair to America. The motives of those who favor action have also been attacked. However, the strategy that has been most effective centers on calling the science into question. In some cases this has simply involved reiterating in a louder voice the scientific uncertainties that have already been identified in the mainstream literature or in the IPCC reports. In other instances it has meant telling improbable stories about the possible effects of changing the composition of the atmosphere. Even if these skeptical arguments are not seen as convincing, they still have the effect of creating the impression that the science in this area is full of uncertainties and is highly contested. Thus, it might seem reasonable to defer action until the scientists get their act together.

While there is quite a lot to say about this strategy, the point I want to make here is that science, rather than ethics, has provided the *lingua franca* or the common language for discussions about climate change. Climate change reached the political agenda largely through the efforts of scientist-advocates, and it has been a science-driven issue from the beginning. From one perspective this is not surprising since climate information is highly technical and to a great extent quite unintuitive. What we experience in everyday life is weather and variability; climate and climate change can only be understood and assessed over long time scales and large geographical regions. The compelling evidence for climate change is largely based on simulations produced by climate models run on supercomputers, and observational evidence obtained from remote sensing, satellite observation, and statistical analysis. Thus, it should not be surprising that scientists effectively made the case for the reality and seriousness of climate change even before this issue had received much attention from environmental interest groups.

Yet in this issue, as in so many others, science has played a complex and even contradictory role. In the 1970s and into the 1980s the United States championed global environmental protection. During the same period it was the undisputed leader in climate-related research. Much of the early concern with climate change emanated from United States' government laboratories such as the National Center for Atmospheric Research, the Goddard Institute of Space Studies, and the Geophysical Fluid Dynamics Laboratory. In the 1970s and 1980s the United States undertook some of the first important assessments of the impacts of climate change and variability (e.g., Mormino, et al., 1975; NRC 1977, 1979, 1983; EPA , 1983, 1986). As we have seen, the United States was instrumental in proposing a science-based response to climate change leading to the establishment of the IPCC. Yet the U.S. government has given much less credibility to these reports than most other governments, and some influential figures in or near the U.S. government have accused American scientists who work with the IPCC of something close to fraud and deception (Lahsen, 1999).

In the 1980s the Reagan administration had managed to defer action on acid rain by establishing an extremely well-funded comprehensive research program to study the issue (Herrick and Jamieson, 1995). The first Bush administration followed the same approach with climate change in 1989 establishing the U.S. Global Change Research Program (USGCRP) as the first Presidential Initiative. The program was written into law with the passage of The Global Change Research Act of 1990. This legislation mandated that the USGCRP should provide "usable information on which to base policy decisions relating to global change" (P.L. 101-606: Sec. 104.b.1). However, the last thing the Bush administration wanted was policy advice from scientists, and they successfully channeled most of USGCRP's research in directions quite remote from policy. Throughout the 1990s the budget of the USGCRP continued to grow, but science and policy continued to develop on largely independent tracks. In 2001 the USGCRP spent more than $1.7 billion on research, of which less than $100 million was devoted to the human dimensions of global change.

The administration of George W. Bush signaled its intention to follow in the tradition of substituting research for policy. The climate change plan announced on February 14, 2002 funded the USGCRP at about the same level as the year before. This while many other discretionary programs were slated to be cut. In addition, the administration proposed a $150 million research program directed towards developing a hydrogen fuel cell powered automobile—something far enough off in the future to be unthreatening to the administration's friends in the oil industry. On the policy side, the administration proposed a voluntary plan that, if successful, would lead to a 12 percent growth in emissions over the next decade, virtually indistinguishable from a "business as usual" scenario. It is sobering to remember that when the first President Bush signed the FCCC in 1992, he committed the U.S. to voluntarily return to 1990 emissions by 2000. His son's plan by 2002 U.S. emissions would be 30 percent greater than in 1990.

While the George W. Bush administration has been supportive of climate change research it has also taken further steps to isolate research from policy. Apparently in response to complaints from ExxonMobil, the U.S. government led a campaign to remove U.S. citizen Robert Watson from the chairmanship of the IPCC. President Bush was openly dismissive of the *Climate Action Report 2002*, his own government's official communication to the UN required by the FCCC, because it endorsed the mainstream view that the unprecedented warming now underway is (at least to a great extent) caused by human action. More ominously, some of President Bush's right-wing allies have attempted to use the Data Quality Act, an Orwellian law passed by Congress as part of the FY 2001 Consolidated Appropriations Act (Pub. L. 106-554, codified at 44 U.S.C. § 3516, note), to suppress the expression of mainstream scientific views in government documents. The Center for Regulatory Effectiveness has petitioned the U.S. government to withdraw the first National Assessment on Climate Change on the ground that "it violates the objectivity…requirements of the Data Quality Act" (Herrick, 2002).

The basic strategy of substituting research for meaningful action is politically effective for a number of reasons. First, Americans love science, and it is hard to resist the idea that when faced with difficult public policy questions, the more science the better. But science does not only answer questions, it also produces new questions. Research may reduce some uncertainties, but it also generates new ones. The more science that is produced, the more handholds and footholds there are for those who are skeptical of mainstream views. No amount of scientific research will refute those who see the IPCC as the scientific expression of a "one-world" conspiracy aimed at putting an end to American freedom and prosperity. Moreover, being generous with funds for scientific research is one way of muffling or marginalizing these voices within the scientific community that have been the most effective advocates of climate change action.

Thus we find ourselves in the present situation. Despite the fact that there is near unanimity in the scientific community about the reality and seriousness of anthropogenic climate change, skepticism about the science is strongest in the country that produced much of the scientific information on which it is based. While other countries debate what should be done in response to climate change, high officials in the United States continue to express doubts in its reality. Although dressed in the language of science, the debate is not really epistemological: it is a way of evading the demands of justice.

Adaptation or Mitigation?

In recent years influential voices in the research community have been calling for a shift away from a concern with mitigation to a focus instead on adaptation (Rayner and Malone, 1997; Pielke Jr., 1998; Parry, 1998; Pielke Jr. and Sarewitz, 2000). Most countries are not well-adapted to the variability that is intrinsic to any climate regime, so greater attention to adaptation would clearly be beneficial.

However a policy of adaptation without mitigation runs serious practical and moral risks. The practical risk is that a GHG forcing may drive the climate system into some unanticipated, radically different state to which it is difficult to adapt. The moral risk is that a policy of adaptation will hit the developing countries hardest. This is because adaptation policies are typically national or subnational and require resources and knowledge. Since the developed countries have resources and knowledge, they may succeed in adapting to climate change. Since the developing countries also do not have the right kinds of resources and knowledge, they will suffer the worst effects of climate change.

Some would deny this, pointing to the long history of mutual accommodation between indigenous people and their environments. Putting aside the risk of romanticization, it is important to recognize that underdevelopment is not the same as lack of development. In some regions of the world people are less able to feed themselves and to manage their environments than they were in the distant past. In some cases contact with the Northern-dominated global economy has brought the risks of capitalism without the benefits. Traditional ways of coping have been lost or driven out, while modern approaches are not available. From this perspective underdevelopment should be thought of as something that has been produced by the global economy rather than as some point of origination from which development proceeds.

We could try to internationalize adaptation by creating a global fund which countries contribute to on the basis of their GHG emissions and make withdrawals from on the basis of the climate change impacts that they suffer. Indeed, something like this is supported by those in the research community who champion adaptation. Even more grandly we could envision, like former U.S. Vice President Al Gore (1992), a "Global Marshall Plan" aimed at "heal[ing] the global environment." But even if there was significant support for such a proposal, there is not much reason to be optimistic. Rich countries, especially the United States, have the political equivalent of attention deficit disorder. Grand promises are made and big money promised when a hurricane devastates Honduras, for example, this is all forgotten when the next humanitarian crisis erupts. A "Global Marshall Plan" would require a level of sustained non-crisis commitment that most Western societies seem incapable of maintaining. Indeed, if we had the moral and political resources to internationalize adaptation, then the attempt to control emissions would succeed, and we could effectively mitigate the effects of climate change.

Finally, the idea that adaptation is a neglected option is strange since it is a plain fact that to a great extent a global policy of adaptation to climate change will prevail. As the U.S. government's *Climate Action Report 2002* states, "[b] ecause of the momentum in the climate system and natural climate variability, adapting to a changing climate is inevitable" (U.S. Department of State, 2002). The adaptations may be clumsy, inefficient, or inadequate, but it is clear the people of the world and the rest of the biosphere will have to adapt to climate change, or they will perish. What is in question is not whether a strategy of adaptation will be followed, but whether there will be any serious global attempt to mitigate climate change.

Why Mitigation Matters

Mitigating climate change by reducing GHG emissions is important for a number of reasons. First, slowing down the rate of change allows humans and the rest of the biosphere time to adapt and reduces the threat of catastrophic surprises. Second, mitigation, if properly done, holds those who have done the most to produce climate change responsible to some extent for their actions. It is a form of moral education. As the earlier President Bush has said in other contexts, it is important for actions to have consequences.

Throughout the 19th and 20th Centuries the nations of Europe and North America became rich by developing powerful industrial economies driven by fossil fuels. Four out of five pounds of carbon dioxide currently in the atmosphere were emitted by these countries. Carbon dioxide has a residency time of 120 years in the atmosphere. Although in recent years emissions have been growing in the less-developed countries, the United States and China are the world's largest emitters. Each year since 1990 the actual increase in American carbon emissions has been greater than any country except China and greater than the total carbon emissions of Brazil. On a per capita basis, Americans are responsible for more than seven times the emissions of the Chinese and 18 times the emissions of the Indians. Moreover, many of the

American emissions are "luxury" emissions, a consequence of driving gas-guzzling SUVs, and living and working in large, over-heated and over-cooled homes and offices (Shue, 1993). Developing world emissions are typically the necessary by-products of the quest for minimally decent lives. The rich countries are the ones that have caused the problem, continue to emit more than their fair share per capita, and have the resources to develop and adopt alternative technologies. Moreover, they promised to stabilize their emissions at Rio in 1992, but failed to keep their promise. It now appears that even the Kyoto Protocol has been rigged to allow these countries to continue to increase their emissions.

For reasons that are amply documented in the IPCC reports, GHG emissions should be limited. If GHG emissions are limited, then the question arises as to how emissions permissions should be distributed. It is difficult at least initially to see why Americans or Australians should have the right to emit more GHGs than Indians or Rwandans. Indeed, it seems clear that there is an initial presumption of equality.

One contrary argument might be that the emissions of Americans and Australians should be "grandfathered." These countries currently emit more GHGs per capita than people in developing countries so they have the right to continue to do so. This argument seems to confuse temporal priority with moral entitlement. Suppose that I started grazing a large herd of cows on some land that we own together before you were able to afford any cows of your own. Now that you have a few cows you want to graze them on our land. But if you do, some of my cows will have to be taken off the land, and as a result I will be slightly less rich. Surely you would be right in saying that since we own the land in common you have a right to your fair share. The fact that you haven't been able to exercise that right does not mean that you forfeited it.

Another argument for overturning the presumption of equality might appeal to economic efficiency. It is generally true that developed countries use energy more efficiently than developing countries. For that matter, the EU and Japan use energy much more efficiently than the U.S. These facts do not in themselves justify an initial allocation of emissions permissions to high-efficiency users. Rather they challenge us to develop a system that will satisfy the demands of justice and also produce efficient outcomes. Several such schemes have been suggested.

Elsewhere, I have sketched a scheme in which we would establish a downward sloping annual ceiling of world GHG emissions (Jamieson, 2001). Next we would allocate these emissions permissions on a global per capita basis, indexed to national populations fixed at some particular year. Finally, we would establish an unrestricted market in emissions trading. There are serious political problems in establishing such a scheme, as well as institutional problems in monitoring behavior and enforcing agreements. There are also familiar questions of domestic justice about how nations would distribute the benefits and costs of this (or any other scheme) among their own people. However such a scheme is not open to some objections that have been made to emissions trading in other cases. Since GHGs are not "pollutants" and primarily have regional effects through their impact on the global climate system, the problem of pollution "hot spots" does not arise to the same extent. I contend that the system that I have sketched is at least in principle both fair and efficient.

Mitigation, as envisioned by the FCCC, is important because it embodies aspects of the "Polluter Pays" principle. By bearing some costs to reduce GHG emissions, those who have been most instrumental in causing the climate change now underway bear some of the burdens. An exclusive focus on adaptation is an instance of the "Polluted Pays" principle. Those who suffer from climate change bear the costs of coping with it.

At present the movement to address climate change as a problem of social justice appears seriously stalled, another victim of the war on terrorism. But while climate change as a problem may have dropped from public view, GHGs continue to concentrate in the atmosphere. The result will be that tens of millions of people will be affected by flooding and rising sea levels; water availability will be reduced in some already water-scarce areas; agriculture will be adversely affected in the tropics and subtropics; and many more people will be exposed to vector-borne diseases such as malaria (McCarthy et al, 2001). Most of those seriously affected will be in the developing world; most of them have not yet been born. Within both rich and poor countries it is the most disempowered and disadvantaged who will suffer most. The global middle class, whether in Malaysia or Michigan, will find a way to thrive. Nonhuman nature, without any representation at all in our systems of decision-making, will be affected most of all.

When it comes to responding to fundamental changes in the systems that control life on Earth, denial and distortion are not viable long-term strategies. Eventually, the climate change issue will reemerge, and a movement towards creating a law of the atmosphere will gain momentum. In the meantime, those of us who care about social justice should continue to remind the world that those who suffer from extreme climatic events are often the victims of greed, indifference, and mendacity. Human beings and their societies are to blame, not nature or fortune.

References

Australian Conservation Foundation. (1998).

Agrawala, S. (1998). Context and Early Origins of the Intergovernmental Panel on Climate Change. *Climate Change, 39*(4), 605-620.

Babiker, M. H., Jacoby, H. D., and Reilly, J. M. (2002). *The Evolution of a Climate Regime* (No. 82). Cambridge, MA: MIT Joint Program on the Science and Policy of Global Change.

Betsell, M. M., Glantz, M. H., and Crandall, K. (1997, December). Preparing for El Nino - What Role for Forecasts? *Environment, 39*(10), 6-13.

Bolin, B. (1998, January 16). The Kyoto Negotiations on Climate Change - A Science Perspective. *Science, 279*(5349), 330-331.

Daily, G. C. (1995, July 21). Restoring Value to the World's Degraded Lands. *Science, 269*(5222), 350-354.

Davis, M. (2001). *Late Victorian Holocausts : El Nino Famines and the Making of the Third World.* London: Verso Press.

Dollar, D., and Kraay, A. (2002, January/February). Spreading the Wealth. Foreign Affairs, 81(1), 120-133.

Environmental Protection Agency. (1983). *Can We Delay Greenhouse Warming?: The Effectiveness and Feasibility of Options to Slow a Build-up of Carbon-dioxide in the Atmosphere*. Washington, D.C.: Environmental Protection Agency.

Environmental Protection Agency. (1986). *Effects of Changes in Stratospheric Ozone and Global Climate*. Washington, D.C.: United Nations Environment Programme.

FY 2001 Consolidated Appropriations Act. (2001, December 15). Pub. L. 106-554.

Glantz, M. H., and Jamieson, D. (2000). Societal Responses to Hurricane Mitch and Intra- Versus Intergenerational Equity Issues: Whose Norms Should Apply. *Risk Analysis, 20*(6), 869-882.

Global Change Research Act of 1990. (1990, November 16). Pub. L. 101-606. Stat. 3096.3104.

Gore, A. (1992). *Earth in the Balance*. Boston: Houghton-Mifflin.

Herrick, C. (2002). Ogmius Exchange: Chuck Herrick Responds. *Ogmius*, (2), 3. Retrieved June 21, 2002 from http://sciencepolicy.colorado.edu/ogmius/archives/issue_2/ogmius.pdf. Herrick quotes from Center for Regulatory Effectiveness. (No date.) CRE Requests Withdrawl Of The National Assessment On Climate Change On Data Quality Act Grounds. Retrieved with no date from http://www.thecre.com/quality/20020211_climate-letter.html.

Herrick, C. N., and Jamieson, D. (1995). The Social Construction of Acid Rain: Some Implications for Science/Policy Assessment. *Global Environmental Change, 5*(2), 105-112.

Jamieson, D. (2001). Climate Change and Global Environmental Justice. In C. Miller and P. Edwards (Eds.), *Changing the Atmosphere: Expert Knowledge and Environmental Governance*. Cambridge: The MIT Press.

Lahsen, M. (1999). The Detection and Attribution of Conspiracies: The Controversy Over Chapter 8. In G. E. Marcus (Ed.), *Paranoia Within Reason: A Casebook on Conspiracy as Explanation*. Chicago: The University of Chicago Press.

Lavalle, M. and Coyle, M. (1992, September 21). Unequal Protection: The Racial Divide in Environmental Law. *The National Law Journal*, 15(3), 1-43.

McCarthy, J. J., et al. (2001). *Climate Change 2001: Impacts, Adaptation, and Vulnerability*. New York: Cambridge University Press.

Mormino, J., Sola, D., and Patten, C. (1975). *Climate Impact Assessment Program: Development and Accomplishments 1971-1975* (No. DOT-TST-76-41). Washington, D.C.: Department of Transportation.

National Research Council. (1977). *Energy and Climate*. Washington, D.C.: The National Energy and Climate Academy of Sciences.

National Research Council. (1979). *Carbon-dioxide and Climate*. Washington, D.C.: The National Academy of Sciences.

National Research Council. (1983). *Changing Climate: Report of the Carbon-dioxide Assessment Committee*. Washington, D.C.: The National Academy of Sciences.

Parry, M., Arnell, N., Hulme, M., Nicholls, R., and Livermore, M. (1998). Adapting to the Inevitable. *Nature, 395*, 741.

Pielke Jr., R. (1998). Rethinking the Role of Adaptation in Climate Change Policy. *Environmental Change, 8*(2), 159-170.

Pielke Jr., R., and Sarewitz, D. (2000). Breaking the Global-Warming Gridlock. *The Atlantic Monthly, 286,* 55-64.

Rayner, S., and Malone, E. L. (1997, 27 November). Zen and the Art of Climate Maintenance. *Nature, 390*(332-334).

Shue, H. (1993, January). Subsistence Emissions and Luxury Emissions. *Law and Policy, 15*(1), 35-59.

United Nations Development Program. (1998). *Human Development Report*. Oxford: Oxford University Press.

U.S. Department of State. (2002, May). *US Climate Action Report 2002*. Retrieved June 21, 2002 from http://www.epa.gov/oppeoeel/globalwarming/publications/car/ch6.pdf.

Vitousek, P. M., Mooney, H. A., Lubchenco, J., and Melillo, J. M. (1997). Human Domination of Earth's Ecosystems. *Science, 277*(5325), 494-499.

World Bank. (2001). *Global Economic Prospects and the Developing Countries 2001*. Washington, D.C.: The World Bank.

8
SUMMARY AND CONCLUSION

Bunyan Bryant, Ph.D.

Who decides the research agenda? Who profits from such an agenda? To what extent is the research agenda for the common good? Because certain sectors of society have access to knowledge more so than do other sectors, they use their position to increase their economic and political power. Why is it that we have only a few rich people in the world who control wealth that is greater than the Gross National Product (GNP) of most countries in the world? Why does there continue to be abject poverty throughout the world? Why is it that wherever there is extreme wealth, there is extreme poverty?

Attending the 2002 World's Summit on Sustainable Development in Johannesburg, South Africa, I found that the overwhelming majority of the Summit failed to focus on sustainable knowledge or the critical role that knowledge plays in development. The Summit did, however, focus on the unanticipated social and environmental consequences of knowledge development and its use. At the end of the Summit, I was able to find a discussion paper entitled "Towards a Convention on Knowledge, Draft 7" (Ho, no date) that spoke to the issue of knowledge and its use. But why was the issue of sustainable knowledge or sustainable epistemology not raised more forcefully within the context of the Summit itself? Why is it taking so long to move upstream to challenge certain epistemologies or the very way in which we know the world and the crisis it presents? The call for a convention on knowledge is long overdue, and we should move forward with organizing such a conference with all deliberate speed.

Studying how knowledge is created, distributed, and used by both the corporate and public sectors to maintain structural inequalities that contribute to world poverty should be a top priority for the United Nations, but not exclusively so. People across the world are faced with unanticipated results of what Mpanya calls the "partiality" of knowledge; they are also faced with conflicting and limited scientific information. They are faced with dangerous pollutants which are odorless and tasteless and undetectable to the human senses. They often find themselves in situations where information has been withheld to prevent them from their pursuit of justice. As development increases across the world, there seems to be a corresponding increase on the part of communities to protect themselves against certain knowledge and misguided technology that poison or destroy communities.

We should be concerned with research that cuts across time and space dimensions. Although the pollution of space, bounded in time, is a top concern to people of color and low-income groups, pollution impacts over time scales of hundreds of years must also be factored into the equation. How much ongoing environmental harm, unbounded in time and space, are we doing that goes beyond our ability to grasp? Time scales of long latency periods and phenomena beyond our grasp may not be scientific questions, but rather ethical and moral ones. Robert raises moral and ethical questions when he asks: 1) Is the chemical or material naturally found in nature?; 2) How persistent is the material?; 3) Does it bio-accumulate?; and 4) Is it possible to predict the tolerance level of the chemical or material? Anderson, too, is raising ethical issues by stating that we must build cities and production systems that mimic nature. And people who call for energy conservation and alternative energy technology and energy sources also may be raising ethical questions. Both Sharpe and Callewaert raise ethical issues within their chapters and call for Rawls' theory for social justice to provide clarity of purpose. Although not conclusive, the ethical questions and recommendations made by Robert and Anderson are ways of dealing with the impact of time scales and long latency periods and ungraspable phenomena unbounded in time and space. Both Robert and Anderson, as well as others, have set the framework for doing research in nature which will more likely put us on the right road to produce sustainable knowledge.

Mpanya (p. 158) states, "Environmental justice will remain intractable because of these social and epistemological limitations and cannot be dealt with except by implementing more democratic and participatory processes that will bring together a multiplicity of perspectives to decision-making." To continue our research of nature will also continue our business as usual leading to a deeper epistemological crisis. The ethical answers posed to questions above to study in nature will undoubtedly raise ethical issues of academic freedom where faculty members will feel restrictions on their freedom to research the universe.

Should academic freedom protect faculty members' abilities to do research regardless of the danger and potential danger of that research to the common good? Should academic freedom protect these faculty members to do research of nature, even though it might deepen the environmental or ecological or epistemological crisis? Should faculty members continue business as usual when that knowledge or the embodiment of that knowledge or its by-products will be disposed of as toxic waste materials in communities of color and low-income communities? Should we support research or technologies if their negative effects are unbounded by time? Should we continue to fund the research of faculty members who support oppressive military regimes or a whole host of social and environmental inequities as put forth in the chapter by Chatterji and Shapiro? Does a faculty member have the right to create knowledge without considering its short- and long-term impacts? This is not to say that these are devious scientists who are working overtime in their laboratories to create sinister outcomes. But the unconsidered long-term effects of their work can be of great peril to the poor and people in general. This takes us back to the age-old question: "Should we create knowledge for knowledge's sake, regardless of the consequences?"

Jamieson states that Americans in particular are science-fascinated and will call for more and better science particularly in the face of tough policy decisions. He goes on to state that science will answer questions and provide new questions, and opponents of science will find counter arguments for inaction believing, that such science will end American prosperity. Generous funding for research should not be used to disquiet scientists who are advocates for change. Throughout this book, we have raised a considerable number of epistemological and environmental injustice issues. Research for sustainable knowledge also needs to be done within an interdisciplinary context and be participatory in nature with the community integrally involved. Although interdisciplinary research is easily talked about, it is very difficult to do. It is very difficult to do because scientists are trained as individuals in a reductionist mode, not as team members willing to experiment with innovation in the pursuit of knowledge. The pursuit of knowledge should include indigenous knowledge that has been tried and tested for hundreds of years or knowledge that is more holistic. We saw in the chapter by Ranco that the Penobscots were attempting to get the EPA to be more holistic in its approach for safety and cultural reasons.

One creative act that universities can employ is to create a position of vice provost of sustainable knowledge and environmental justice. The person in this position would be responsible for stimulating a debate between the foxes and the hedgehogs. Universities must be brought in line with sustainability practices by funding research projects and classes that embrace interdisciplinary and holistic research, teaching, and learning in nature. We must question *how* we know and how that may lead to outcome events beyond our control. We must ask ourselves the question: should knowledge be accessible to all or should it be privately owned or controlled? We must also question whether knowledge should be ecologically accountable. And we must allocate resources to find solutions in indigenous communities as well as other communities. In the process we must respect indigenous knowledge and agree that such knowledge is not to be exploited or plagiarized for private gain. No one episteme community has cornered the market on knowledge. No one episteme community has all the answers to the problems facing the modern world since the chemicals and toxins are often beyond our senses of smell, taste, and sight. No one episteme community has the methodology to help us solve these toxic problems because of their persistent "non-biodegradableness" and long latency periods that extend in some cases across the generations.

We can perform our research in nature according to questions raised by Robert or by recommendations made by Anderson to build systems that mimic nature, but we still will not have done away with structural inequalities that threaten democracy and world disequilibrium. Sharpe in her chapter speaks to the issue of social determinants of health depending upon where one lives. If one lives in a society where there is a substantial discrepancy of income and wealth between rich and poor, then that person is less likely to be as healthy as a person who lives in a society where the discrepancy of income and wealth between rich and poor is small. They will probably live longer and will perhaps be better educated. Narrowing the boundaries of structural inequalities in the United States, I believe, will enhance environmental and health conditions for people regardless of their race or background. People in communities as reflected in the case studies by Callewaert and Mpanya will be better off generally and subjected to fewer environmental insults. Structural inequality applies to people in this country, but to the world at large. Chatterji and Shapiro believe that universities can play a role in narrowing the boundaries of structural inequality and the eradication of poverty and oppression. They advocate participatory research where the community is integrally involved in all phases of the research process. It is within this context of participatory research that they feel sustainable knowledge can be achieved.

If we build cities to mimic nature, then we will have gone a long way to reduce pollutants that differentially impact the poor and people of color, and we will also have gone a long way to reduce greenhouse gases which are responsible for global warming. To build cities to mimic nature, for instance, will require us to remove ourselves from dependence on the fossil fuel economy. As long as we depend upon the fossil fuel economy, we will be threatened by poisons and environmental degradation. We will continue to manipulate synthetic chemicals that cause cancer, endocrine disruption, sterility, and the disproportionate allocation of pollutants over time-space that will affect people of color and other high-risk populations and result in unforeseen circumstances. We should strive to cut our waste stream to zero, making landfills obsolete and polluted skies and water non-existent so people in communities such as Columbus, Ohio; Robbins, Illinois; Richman, California; West Anniston, Alabama; West Harlem, New York; Camden, New Jersey; Native American quasi-sovereign nations such as the Penobscots or Pueblo of Isleta; or communities beyond U.S. borders will no longer have to struggle to protect themselves against environmental harm.

Future leaders must educate the people of the importance of reducing global warming with all its catastrophic effects. Future leaders of the world must help us redefine progress to be based more upon personal growth and development, self-actualization, and quality of life rather than upon conspicuous accumulation. Further, leaders should measure progress by the growing number of people in the village square who participate in democratic decision making with the confidence that they can make a difference in their lives. Is this a tall order? I believe that it is, but in this country we have the talent, the creativity, and the brainpower to build the sustainable cities of the future. As the culture becomes more aware of the importance of sustainable knowledge, the resultant cultural impact will influence the way in which science is done. Tesh believes that epidemiologists will be freed from the shackles of the way risk assessment has been structured to engage in innovative research. People from all walks of life can play a role, particularly students and biologists, if their knowledge is in nature. In addition we must make sure that people can realize their highest potential within the context of a sustainable and productive environment. If we fail to heed the crisis of epistemology today, we will blunder into a future plagued with higher levels of crime and delinquency, unequalitarian values, unemployment, sub-standard housing, unhealthy and polluted environments, food shortages, and regional conflicts which may lead to global ones as people migrate across geo-political boundaries in response to global climatic conditions.

Although the ideas in this book are by no means conclusive, I hope it has triggered some substantive discussion on the issues presented in the preceding chapters. I hope we are able to move beyond debate to action in order to address the crisis that looms on the horizon. As leaders in our field, we must use our power and influence to set an example for the rest of the world. I have hope that we will rise to the occasion because we are smart and creative. As our culture changes and there is more right headedness among the masses, people are more apt to experiment with new and creative ideas. I conclude this book by offering my definition of environmental justice. This definition reads like a community of the future; it embraces all the significant parameters of what a decent and just community could be like. It is as follows:

> *Environmental Justice: Environmental Justice (EJ) refers to those cultural norms and values, rules, regulations, behaviors, policies, and decisions that support sustainable communities where people can interact with confidence that their environment is safe, nurturing, and productive. Environmental Justice is served when people can realize their highest potential without experiencing discrimination based on race, class, ethnicity or national origin. Environmental Justice is supported by decent paying and safe jobs, quality schools and recreation, decent housing and adequate health care, personal empowerment, and communities free of violence, drugs and poverty. These are communities where both cultural and biological diversity are respected and highly revered, and where distributive justice prevails.*

References

Ho, M. (No date). *Towards a Convention on Knowledge, Draft 7*. Institute of Science in Society.

APPENDIX
ENVIRONMENTAL CRISIS OR CRISIS OF EPISTEMOLOGY:
WORKING FOR SUSTAINABLE KNOWLEDGE

A Report by Grace Lee Boggs,* Participant Observer

I am writing a detailed report of this conference (1) because of its intrinsic significance and (2) because it gives me an opportunity to revisit two questions that I am often asked: What is Philosophy? Why aren't you a university professor?

Last June I received an invitation from Bunyan Bryant to present a paper to a spring 2002 SNRE Environmental Justice/Philosophy Conference which would focus on "the role of knowledge in society, who benefits from that knowledge and who benefits the most." I immediately replied in the affirmative because over the years Bunyan's conferences have been landmarks in my own political/philosophical journey. For example, at a Futuring Conference during MLK week in 1992, Bunyan challenged participants to create a vision for the 21st Century and gave us about an hour to do so.[1] Since then, I rarely make a speech or write an article without projecting a vision of an alternative that I hope will take my listeners or readers beyond "Protest Politics." Two years later, after participating in a huge Environmental Justice Symposium in D.C. (moderated by Bunyan and Gerry Poge) I helped convene Detroit's First Environmental Justice Gathering and found Detroiters Working for Environmental Justice (DWEJ).[2]

---

1 Bryant, B. Rehearsing the Future. *In Context: A Quarterly for Sustainable Development.* www.context.org/ICLIB/IC40/Bryant.htm.

2 See Boggs' autobiography *Living for Change*, pp. 245.-249 for my account of this Symposium.

---

* Grace Lee Boggs is a first-generation Chinese American who has been a speaker, writer and movement activist in the African American community for 55 years. Since 1953, she has lived on the East Side of Detroit and most of that time in the same house. She co-authored with her husband James Boggs. Concurrently as a volunteer, she is active with Health Detroit, Detroit Summer, Detroiters Working for Environmental Justice, and Detroit Growers Support Group.

Bunyan's conferences are such eye/mind-openers because (1) he is willing to confront the contradictions and challenges that are inevitable around Environmental Justice (EJ) issues; and (2) he structures his conferences to include small core groups which meet throughout the gathering, enabling participants to interact personally, share information from concurrent workshops, discuss thoughts and questions, and bring back a group summation and proposals to the final plenary. Sometimes they even provide a way for conferees to affect the course of the proceedings. At the 1994 Environmental Justice Symposium, for example, my core group reported back to the conveners that grassroots delegates were not happy with the way that government agency representatives were dominating discussions. As a result, at the plenary session the following morning, we staged a 1960s type demonstration which forced EPA administrator Carol Browner to tear up her speech and open the mike to community people to voice their concerns.

In June, I had agreed to present a paper for this conference (as yet unnamed), but as the February 2002 deadline for papers drew near, I felt that I didn't really have an adequate sense of the concrete struggles. So I suggested that I do some critiques instead.

The Conference opened on Thursday night, April 4. By this time it had a name "Environmental Crisis or Crisis of Epistemology" and three goals::

1) Provide opportunities to explore the connection between knowledge generation and the environmental justice crisis and/or solutions;
2) A plan of action for implementing an environmental justice curriculum at other universities;
3) A plan of action to encourage environmental policymakers to accept alternative forms of knowledge (such as community-based knowledge) and methods for environmental protection and health.

We were welcomed by SNRE Dean Rosina Bierbaum and enjoyed an opening exercise (which involved sharing our favorite person, movie, book, hobby with four and then eight people), received our folders with agendas, assignments to core groups, met briefly with our core groups to decide attendance at concurrent workshops, and adjourned until the next morning.

Figuring Out the Issues

My first real sense of the philosophical questions confronting the EJ movement at this juncture came during the second series of workshops at 11 a.m. on Friday, when I attended the "Sustainable Knowledge" workshop. The presenter was Angana Chatterji, a Pakastani professor in Social and Cultural Anthropology at the California Institute of Integral Studies which is located in San Francisco, has about 400 students, and is accredited to award M.A. and Ph.D. degrees.

Angana made a passionate appeal for the kind of knowledge that is generated by working with communities to address their issues and develop public policy to serve their needs. Accompanying her were five colleagues from the Institute: Professors Richard Shapiro (her husband) and Mutombo Mpanya (from the Congo), two students, and a community organizer from India who described how Institute people work with her community to help it generate its own knowledge. Regrettably, only about a dozen people, nearly half of whom were from the Institute, attended the workshop. So only a handful of conferees heard her presentation, and my impression (from the reports of other core groups to the final session) is that most people were not even aware of, let alone influenced, by the Institute's pioneering views on sustainable knowledge.

Fortunately the session was videotaped and I hope that it will be widely shared. (I would very much like to have a copy.) On Friday evening, Angana's colleague, Mutombo Mpanya, presented a somewhat puzzling critique of "universally valid truths" which complemented Angana's presentation; but, again, there were relatively few people present and the connection to Angana's workshop was not made in the discussion.

Critiquing Dale Jamieson's paper Friday afternoon further helped me to appreciate "the epistemic crisis" facing the EJ movement. To my amazement, the paper, entitled "Climate and Environmental Justice," did not deal with any philosophical questions even though Jamieson is a Professor of Philosophy and has edited a book of Essays on Environmental Philosophy. The only remotely philosophical statements that I found in the paper were: "Science rather than ethics has provided the lingua franca for discussion on climate change" and the final sentence "The first step is to hold responsible those who are now degrading the atmosphere." So, after his presentation, I made the following comments:

"Dale Jamieson's data-rich paper challenges me as a philosopher-activist to grapple with the question 'what kind of philosophy (i.e., what concept of what it means to be a human being and what theory of knowledge) do we need to empower ourselves and others to go beyond moralizing about the environmental crisis?'

"I believe that the first thing we need to do is to repudiate Scientific Rationalism, the individualistic, I-It, Subject-Object, 'correspondence theory of knowledge' that Descartes developed in the 17th Century. Cartesian thinking made possible the industrial revolution which led to the technological revolutions that now threaten the survival of ourselves and our biosphere. As Einstein put it a half century ago: 'The spliting of the atom has changed everything except the way we think and thus we drift towards catastrophe.'

"How do we change the way we think? What will another way of thinking look like? Who will create it?

"Over a hundred years ago the American pragmatists, Wm. James, John Dewey, and George Herbert Mead (on whom I wrote my dissertation) pointed a completely new direction for philosophy when they mounted the first American challenge to Cartesian rationalism, rejecting the elitist/spectator theory of knowledge of professional/academic philosophers, criticizing their obsession with universally valid Truths and their narrow concept of humans only as cognitive - **and** projecting instead a more social and activist method of knowledge created by and useful to real human beings whose lives consist not only of intellectual cognition but of suffering, loving, hoping, desiring, choosing. (See the section on Dewey in *The American Evasion of Philosophy* by Cornel West).

"In the course of the great social movements that have distinguished the last forty years of the 20th Century, the organic intellectuals of these movements have been creating the ingredients of this new social activist philosophy for our day and age. e.g. MLK's concept of Love as Agape ("the willingness to go to any length to restore community"); the Ecofeminists (see especially Starhawk's "Burning Times" in which she describes how the witchhunts of the 17th Century were organized by Establishment intellectuals to expropriate the intuitive ways of knowing of women); Native Americans like Tom Goldtooth ("your knowledge is inferior to ours because it is based only on humans while ours includes the trees and the animals); Liberation theologians like Matthew Fox and Tom Berry who are restoring the concept of the sacred; and Eastern activists and theoreticians like Vandana Shiva and Ashis Nandy who reject the either/or productivist, masculinist thrust of Western thinking. (See articles by Vandana Shiva, Val Plumwood and Rajni Kochari in Dale Jamieson's collection of *Essays in Environmental Philosophy.)*

"This new philosophy does not yet have a name, but it is providing the epistemological foundation for the emerging social movements of the new century which will center around transforming ourselves and reconstructing our communities. This transformation and reconstruction, so obviously and urgently needed in cities like Detroit and countries like Afghanistan, will require radical changes in education both at the university level (see Immanuel Wallerstein: *Unthinking Social Science: The Limits of 19th Century Paradigms* which calls for the deconstruction of university disciplines and departments) and at the public school level. (See my articles on Freedom Schooling and on "Education for Democracy; Not Incarceration." Boggscenter.org/)."

How Is Sustainable Knowledge Created?

By Saturday, after having attended Angana's workshop, listened to the papers of the academic presenters and the critiques by fellow academicians, and struggled with members of my core group, I had acquired a pretty good sense of the current epistemic tensions or tendencies in the Environmental Justice movement and why it is so important to address the Epistemic Crisis in relationship to the Crisis in Ecology. On the one hand, there are the academics who pride themselves on being advocates for Environmental Justice and see themselves as serving the needs of the grassroots communities who suffer most from Environmental Injustice but whose philosophy/epistemology remains that of the elite spectator in relationship to grassroots communities. They use the input of grassroots informants to acquire the information to write their Ph.D. dissertations, scholarly articles and books, which are then discussed in academic circles, advancing their own careers and the agenda of the university. But in and through this process they objectify and downgrade the knowledge of community people while privileging the "universally valid truths" produced by and embodied in their own work as academics.

By contrast, the ongoing work of the California Institute and the Boggs Center to Nurture Community Leadership is based on the conviction that sustainable knowledge can only come from the long-time commitment of intellectuals who work with real communities in real places to generate the ideas and the public policies that they need to create sustainable communities. This is because we begin from the philosophical position that grassroots community people struggling for Environmental Justice and for sustainable communities are the knowing subjects. We consciously refuse to objectify them because, as Freire put it, "People cannot enter the struggle as objects and emerge as subjects."

One of the many profound insights that came out of my core group on the question of sustainable knowledge was that in a world polluted by toxic and radioactive waste we need a different sense of time.

Late Saturday afternoon at the "Free University" session I showed the Adamah video which is a living example of how sustainable knowledge is actually being created in Detroit.

Adamah, meaning "of the earth," is a vision for a self-reliant sustainable community in one of the most devastated sections of Detroit beginning one block from my east side home where I have lived for 40 years. The Adamah vision, based on urban agriculture as starting point and metaphor, was created by architectural students in a studio at the University of Detroit Mercy School of Architecture conducted by architectural theorist Kyong Park. But its inspiration was the community gardening that the residents themselves have actually been doing on vacant lots for years - not only to provide food but to impart a different sense of time and process to young people growing up in the city.[3] In turn, the Adamah vision is now being used to encourage community groups to think more imaginatively about rebuilding their own communities.

In introducing the video I explained how what took place at the World Trade Center building in five seconds has been happening in slow motion in Detroit over the last fifty years, giving birth to the many struggles and programs that have contributed to the creation of Adamah, e.g. Jimmy Boggs' speech on Rebuilding Detroit which came out of the Casino Gambling struggle, Detroit Summer, Gardening Angels, Detroit Agricultural Network, Catherine Ferguson Academy, Artists and Children Creating Community Together (AC3T).

I doubt that viewing the Adamah video changed anyone's mind. But I hope it gave them a glimpse of another, more social activist and sustainable way of generating knowledge than getting your Ph.D. I would be very interested in what people said about this session in their evaluations

Who Are "We the People"?

At the final plenary session, in response to my question, I discovered that none of the conferees had ever seen the video of the First People of Color Environmental Leadership Summit at which the 17 Principles of Environmental Justice, which are the cornerstone of the Environmental Justice movement, were created.

I believe that these principles provide the basic tenets for the new U.S. Constitution that we need to struggle to create in the 21st Century. They take us beyond Representative Democracy to Participatory Democracy and beyond Distributive Justice to Participatory and Restorative Justice.

That is why it is so important that we remind ourselves and each other that "the people" who created these principles were African Americans, Latinos, Native Americans and Asian Americans, 300 People of Color who out of their experiences of environmental racism are challenging themselves and

3 See "Ways Out, Kritische Utopisten," Interview with Kyong Park, Grace Lee Boggs, Paul Weertz and Maxine Elam, filmed by Boris Gerrets and Ronald van Tienhoven, Naked Eye Video, December 2001. Also www.boggscenter.org/.

everyone in this country to think about Self-Government, Democracy and our relationships to one another and to our biosphere in a new way.

***

Bunyan brought the conference to a close at 1 p.m. Sunday by presenting Sarah Swanson with a plant for her heroic work in organizing the conference. He then read this poem that he had stayed up all night to create.

Scientific Knowledge as Oppression

Oh beautiful, oh precious skies no more,
The price we pay for being poor,
We have been beaten down by theories,
By long complicated stories,
By officials who question our memories.
And by scientists enhancing self-serving careers,
Rather than exploring fundamental change and new frontiers,
And from college professors who fail to acknowledge,
The power of our worthwhile knowledge,
Failing to take what we say at heart,
Because they feel we are less than smart.

Scientific priest talking in tongue,
Refusing to tell us what is wrong,
Claiming Superfund siting of no intent,
When we know what was meant,

Demanding of proof of our answer,
In spite of our sores, rashes, and cancer,
Talking in tongue and in pride,
We feel they have something to hide,
You have us believe that it's class—not race,
You had better get out of my face.

We have been belittled and patronized,
But we stood our ground without compromise,
We have been put off, lied to, put on hold,
Only to be told that we were too bold,
You view us as hysterical crazies wanting to shout,
And you would rather see us less suspicious and less in doubt.
Divergent emotions trying to cope,
Science fails to give us hope,

We are scared and anxiety ridden,
Of future trends of sickness forbidden,
To the doctor we say— we need your help sir,
This crisis is burning hot in our belly with bleeding ulcer.

Government scientists have us believe,
That recommended parts per billion achieved,
is safe for us to heed,
Pollution not money trickles down, down, down,
Poisoning red, black and brown,
The struggle in Kettleman City, East Los Angeles,
South Side Chicago, and Cancer Alley too,
Are good examples of what to do.
We may not be educated but we are smart,
We will pester you until you clean up or depart.
We refuse to be the canary bird of destruction,
And we will resist to the death the poisoning of people of nonwhite complexion.

References

Boggs, G. L. (1998). *Living For Change: An Autobiography*. Minneapolis: University of Minnesota Press.

Bryant, B. (1995, Spring). Rehearsing the Future. *In Context: A Quarterly for Sustainable Development, 40*, 39.

Index

B

C

D

E

F

H

I

J

M

N

O

P

S

T

U

V

W

Y

Z